AUDUBON GUIDE
to the National Wildlife Refuges

Southwest

AUDUBON GUIDE
to the National Wildlife Refuges

Southwest

Arizona · Nevada · New Mexico · Texas

By Daniel Gibson

Foreword by Theodore Roosevelt IV

Series Editor, David Emblidge

A Balliett & Fitzgerald Book
St. Martin's Griffin, New York

Cartography: © Balliett & Fitzgerald, Inc. produced by Mapping Specialists Ltd.
Illustrations: Mary Sundstrom
Cover design: Michael Storrings and Sue Canavan
Interior design: Bill Cooke and Sue Canavan

Balliett & Fitzgerald Inc. Staff
Sue Canavan, Design Director
Maria Fernandez, Production Editor
Alexis Lipsitz, Executive Series Editor
Rachel Deutsch, Associate Photo Editor
Kristen Couse, Associate Editor
Paul Paddock, Carol Petino Assistant Editors
Howard Klein, Editorial Intern
Scott Prentzas, Copy Editor

Balliett & Fitzgerald Inc. would like to thank the following people for their assis-
tance in creating this series:
At National Audubon Society:
    Katherine Santone, former Director of Publishing, for sponsoring this project
    Claire Tully, Senior Vice President, Marketing
    Evan Hirsche, Director, National Wildlife Refuges Campaign
At U.S. Fish & Wildlife Service:
    Richard Coleman, Chief, Division of Refuges, U.S. Fish & Wildlife Service
    Janet Tennyson, Outreach Coordinator
    Craig Rieben, Chief of Broadcasting & Audio Visual, U.S. Fish & Wildlife
        Service, for photo research assistance
    Pat Carrol, Chief Surveyor, U.S. Fish & Wildlife Service, for map information
    Regional External Affairs officers, at the seven U.S. Fish & Wildlife Service
        Regional Headquarters
    Elizabeth Jackson, Photographic Information Specialist, National
        Conservation Training Center, for photo research
At St. Martin's Griffin:
    Greg Cohn, who pulled it all together on his end, as well as Michael
        Storrings and Kristen Macnamara
At David Emblidge—Book Producer:
    Marcy Ross, Assistant Editor
Thanks also to Theodore Roosevelt IV and John Flicker.

ISBN 0-312-20777-8
First St. Martin's Griffin Edition: March 2000

10 9 8 7 6 5 4 3 2 1

CONTENTS

ARIZONA

NEVADA

NEW MEXICO

TEXAS

Appendix

Foreword

America is singularly blessed in the amount and quality of land that the federal government holds in trust for its citizens. No other country can begin to match the variety of lands in our national wildlife refuges, parks and forests. From the Arctic Refuge on the North Slope of Alaska to the National Key Deer Refuge in Florida, the diversity of land in the National Wildlife Refuge (NWR) System is staggering.

Yet of all our public lands, the National Wildlife Refuge System is the least well known and does not have an established voting constituency like that of the Parks System. In part this is because of its "wildlife first" mission, which addresses the needs of wildlife species before those of people. That notwithstanding, wildlife refuges also offer remarkable opportunities for people to experience and learn about wildlife—and to have fun doing so!

The Refuge System was launched in 1903 when President Theodore Roosevelt discovered that snowy egrets and other birds were being hunted to the brink of extinction for plumes to decorate ladies' hats. He asked a colleague if there were any laws preventing the president from making a federal bird reservation out of an island in Florida's Indian River. Learning there was not, Roosevelt responded, "Very well, then I so declare it." Thus Pelican Island became the nation's first plot of land to be set aside for the protection of wildlife. Roosevelt went on to create another 50 refuges, and today there are more than 500 refuges encompassing almost 93 million acres, managed by the U.S. Fish & Wildlife Service.

The Refuge System provides critical habitat for literally thousands of mammals, birds, amphibians and reptiles, and countless varieties of plants and flowers. More than 55 refuges have been created specifically to save endangered species. Approximately 20 percent of all threatened and endangered species in the United States rely on these vital places for their survival. As a protector of our country's natural diversity, the System is unparalleled.

Setting NWR boundaries is determined, as often as possible, by the needs of species that depend on the protected lands. Conservation biology, the science that studies ecosystems as a whole, teaches us that wildlife areas must be linked by habitat "corridors" or run the risk of becoming biological islands. The resulting inability of species to transfer their genes over a wide area leaves them vulnerable to disease and natural disasters. For example, the Florida panther that lives in Big Cypress Swamp suffers from a skin fungus, a consequence, scientists believe, of inbreeding. Today's refuge managers are acutely aware of this precarious situation afflicting many species and have made protection of the System's biodiversity an important goal.

Clearly, the job of the refuge manager is not an easy one. Chronic underfunding of the System by the federal government has resulted in refuges operating with less money per employee and per acre than any other federal land-management agency. Recent efforts by some in Congress to address this shortfall have begun to show results, but the System's continued vulnerability to special interests has resulted in attempts to open refuges to oil drilling, road building in refuge wilderness areas, and military exercises.

The managers of the System have played a crucial role in responding to the limited resources available. They have created a network of volunteers who contribute tens of thousands of hours to help offset the lack of direct financing for the Refuge System. Groups like refuge "friends" and Audubon Refuge Keepers have answered the call for local citizen involvement on many refuges across the country.

I hope Americans like yourself who visit our national wildlife refuges will come away convinced of their importance, not only to wildlife but also to people. I further hope you will make your views known to Congress, becoming the voice and voting constituency the Refuge System so desperately needs.

—*Theodore Roosevelt IV*

Preface

Thank you for adding the *Audubon Guide to the National Wildlife Refuge System* to your travel library. I hope you will find this nine-volume series an indispensable guide to finding your way around the refuge system, as well as a valuable educational tool for learning more about the vital role wildlife refuges play in protecting our country's natural heritage.

It was nearly 100 years ago that Frank Chapman, an influential ornithologist, naturalist, publisher and noted Audubon member, approached President Theodore Roosevelt (as recounted by Theodore Roosevelt IV in his foreword), eventually helping to persuade him to set aside more than 50 valuable parcels of land for the protection of wildlife.

Because of limited funding available to support these new wildlife sanctuaries, Audubon stepped up and paid for wardens who diligently looked after them. And so began a century of collaboration between Audubon and the National Wildlife Refuge System. Today, Audubon chapter members can be found across the country assisting refuges with a range of projects, from viewing tower construction to bird banding.

Most recently, National Audubon renewed its commitment to the Refuge System by launching a nationwide campaign to build support for refuges locally and nationally. Audubon's Wildlife Refuge Campaign is promoting the Refuge System through on-the-ground programs such as Audubon Refuge Keepers (ARK), which builds local support groups for refuges, and Earth Stewards, a collaboration with the U.S. Fish and Wildlife Service and the National Fish and Wildlife Foundation, which uses refuges and other important bird habitats as outdoor classrooms. In addition, we are countering legislative threats to refuges in Washington, D.C., while supporting increased federal funding for this, the least funded of all federal land systems.

By teaching more people about the important role refuges play in conserving our nation's diversity of species—be they birds, mammals, amphibians, reptiles, or plants—we have an opportunity to protect for future generations our only federal lands system set aside first and foremost for wildlife conservation.

As a nation, we are at a critical juncture—do we continue to sacrifice wetlands, forests, deserts, and coastal habitat for short-term profit, or do we accept that the survival of our species is closely linked to the survival of others? The National Wildlife Refuge System is a cornerstone of America's conservation efforts. If we are to leave a lasting legacy and, indeed, ensure our future, then we must build on President Theodore Roosevelt's greatest legacy. I invite you to join us!

—*John Flicker, President, National Audubon Society*

Introduction
to the National Wildlife Refuge System

He spent entire days on horseback, traversing the landscape of domed and crumbling hills, steep forested coulees, with undulating tables of prairie above. The soft wraparound light of sunset displayed every strange contour of the Badlands and lit the colors in each desiccated layer of rock—yellow, ochre, beige, gold.

Theodore Roosevelt was an easterner. As some well-heeled easterners were wont to do, he traveled west in 1883 to play cowboy, and for the next eight years he returned as often as possible. He bought a cattle ranch, carried a rifle and a six-gun, rode a horse. North Dakota was still Dakota Territory then, but the Plains bison were about gone, down to a scattering of wild herds.

The nation faced a new and uneasy awareness of limits during Roosevelt's North Dakota years. Between 1776 and 1850, the American population had increased from 1.5 million to more than 23 million. National borders were fixed and rail and telegraph lines linked the coasts, but Manifest Destiny had a price. The ongoing plunder of wildlife threatened species such as the brown pelican and the great egret; the near-total extermination of 60 million bison loomed as a lesson many wished to avoid repeating.

Despite the damage done, the powerful landscapes of the New World had shaped the outlooks of many new Americans. From Colonial-era botanist John Bartram to 19th-century artists George Catlin and John James Audubon, naturalists and individuals of conscience explored the question of what constituted a proper human response to nature. Two figures especially, Henry David Thoreau and John Muir, created the language and ideas that would confront enduring Old World notions of nature as an oppositional, malevolent force to be harnessed and exploited. The creation in 1872 of Yellowstone as the world's first national park indicated that some Americans, including a few political leaders, were listening to what Thoreau, Muir, and these others had to say.

Roosevelt, along with his friend George Bird Grinnell, drew upon these and other writings, as well as their own richly varied experiences with nature, to take the unprecedented step of making protection of nature a social and political cause. Of his time in the Badlands, Roosevelt remarked "the romance of my life began here," and "I never would have been president if it had not been for my experiences in North Dakota." As a hunter, angler, and naturalist, Roosevelt grasped the importance of nature for human life. Though he had studied natural history as an undergraduate at Harvard, believing it would be his life's work, Roosevelt owned a passion for reform and had the will—perhaps a need—to be effective. Rather than pursuing a career as a naturalist, he went into politics. His friend George

Barren-ground caribou

Arctic Ocean

Alaska

Bering
Sea

Pacific Ocean

Washington

Oregon

Idaho

Montana

North
Dakota

South
Dakota

Wyoming

Nebraska

Nevada

Utah

Colorado

Kansas

California

Oklahoma

Pacific
Ocean

Arizona

New
Mexico

Texas

Midway

Hawaii

Pacific Ocean

New England Region
Middle Atlantic Region
Southeast Region
Northern Midwest Region
South Central Region
Southwest Region
Rocky Mountains Region
Alaska and Pacific Northwest Region
California and Hawaii Region

Migratory Flyway

G r e a t   L a k e s

Minnesota

Michigan

Wisconsin

New Hampshire
Vermont
Massachusetts

Maine

New York

Iowa

Pennsylvania

Rhode Island
Connecticut
New Jersey
Delaware
Maryland

Illinois

Indiana

Ohio

West Virginia

Virginia

Missouri

Kentucky

North Carolina

Tennessee

South Carolina

Arkansas

Mississippi

Alabama

Georgia

Atlantic Ocean

Louisiana

Florida

Puerto Rico

Gulf of Mexico

Bird Grinnell, publisher of the widely read magazine *Forest and Stream,* championed all manner of environmental protection and in 1886 founded the Audubon Society to combat the slaughter of birds for the millinery trade. Fifteen years later, TR would find himself with an even greater opportunity. In1901, when he inherited the presidency following the assassination of William McKinley, Roosevelt declared conservation a matter of federal policy.

Roosevelt backed up his words with an almost dizzying series of conservation victories. He established in 1903 a federal bird reservation on Pelican Island, Florida, as a haven for egrets, herons, and other birds sought by plume hunters. In eight years, Roosevelt authorized 150 million acres in the lower 48 states and another 85 million in Alaska to be set aside from logging under the Forest Reserve Act of 1891, compared to a total of 45 million under the three prior presidents. To these protected lands he added five national parks and 17 national monuments. The NWR system, though, is arguably TR's greatest legacy. Often using executive order to circumvent Congress, Roosevelt established 51 wildlife refuges.

The earliest federal wildlife refuges functioned as sanctuaries and little else. Visitors were rare and recreation was prohibited. Between 1905 and 1912 the first refuges for big-game species were established—Wichita Mountains in Oklahoma,

the National Bison Range in Montana, and National Elk Refuge in Jackson, Wyoming. In 1924, the first refuge to include native fish was created; a corridor some 200 miles long, the Upper Mississippi National Wildlife and Fish Refuge spanned the states of Minnesota, Wisconsin, Illinois, and Iowa.

Still, the 1920s were dark years for America's wildlife. The effects of unregulated hunting, along with poor enforcement of existing laws, had decimated once-abundant species. Extinction was feared for the wood duck. Wild turkey

Atlantic puffins, Petit Manan NWR, Maine

had become scarce outside a few southern states. Pronghorn antelope, which today number perhaps a million across the West, were estimated at 25,000 or fewer. The trumpeter swan, canvasback duck, even the prolific and adaptable white-tailed deer, were scarce or extirpated across much of their historic ranges.

The Depression and Dust-bowl years, combined with the leadership of President Franklin Delano Roosevelt, gave American conservation—and the refuge system in particular—a hefty forward push. As wetlands vanished and fertile prairie soils blew away, FDR's Civilian Conservation Corps (CCC) dispatched thousands of unemployed young men to camps that stretched from Georgia to California. On the sites of many present-day refuges, they built dikes and other

Saguaro cactus and ocotillo along Charlie Bell 4WD trail, Cabeza Prieta NWR, Arizona

water-control structures, planted shelterbelts and grasses. Comprised largely of men from urban areas, the experience of nature was no doubt a powerful rediscovery of place and history for the CCC generation. The value of public lands as a haven for people, along with wildlife, was on the rise.

In 1934, Jay Norwood "Ding" Darling was instrumental in developing the federal "Duck Stamp," a kind of war bond for wetlands; hunters were required to purchase it, and anyone else who wished to support the cause of habitat acquisition could, too. Coupled with the Resettlement Act of 1935, in which the federal government bought out or condemned private land deemed unsuitable for agriculture, several million acres of homesteaded or settled lands reverted to federal ownership to become parks, national grasslands, and wildlife refuges. The Chief of the U.S. Biological Survey's Wildlife Refuge Program, J. Clark Salyer, set out on a cross-country mission to identify prime wetlands. Salyer's work added 600,000 acres to the refuge system, including Red Rock Lakes in Montana, home to a small surviving flock of trumpeter swans.

The environmental ruin of the Dust bowl also set in motion an era of government initiatives to engineer solutions to such natural events as floods, drought, and the watering of crops. Under FDR, huge regional entities such as the Tennessee Valley Authority grew, and the nation's mightiest rivers—the Columbia, Colorado, and later, the Missouri—were harnessed by dams. In the wake of these and other federal works projects, a new concept called "mitigation" appeared: If a proposed dam or highway caused the destruction of a certain number of acres of wetlands or other habitat, some amount of land nearby would be ceded to conservation in return. A good many of today's refuges were the progeny of mitigation. The federal government, like the society it represents, was on its way to becoming complex enough that the objectives of one arm could be at odds with those of another.

Citizen activism, so integral to the rise of the Audubon Society and other groups, was a driving force in the refuge system as well. Residents of rural Georgia applied relentless pressure on legislators to protect the Okefenokee Swamp. Many other refuges—San Francisco Bay, Sanibel Island, Minnesota Valley, New Jersey's Great Swamp—came about through the efforts of people with a vision of conservation close to home.

More than any other federal conservation program, refuge lands became places where a wide variety of management techniques could be tested and refined. Generally, the National Park system followed the "hands off" approach of Muir and Thoreau while the U.S. Forest Service and Bureau of Land Management, in theory, emphasized a utilitarian, "sustainable yield" value; in practice, powerful economic interests backed by often ruthless politics left watersheds, forests, and grasslands badly degraded, with far-reaching consequences for fish and wildlife. The refuge system was not immune to private enterprise—between 1939 and 1945, refuge lands were declared fair game for oil drilling, natural-gas exploration, and even for bombing practice by the U.S. Air Force—but the negative impacts have seldom reached the levels of other federal areas.

Visitor use at refuges tripled in the 1950s, rose steadily through the 1960s, and by the 1970s nearly tripled again. The 1962 Refuge Recreation Act established guidelines for recreational use where activities such as hiking, photography, boating, and camping did not interfere with conservation. With visitors came opportunities to educate, and now nature trails and auto tours, in addition to beauty, offered messages about habitats and management techniques. Public awareness of wilderness, "a place where man is only a visitor," in the words of long-time advocate Robert Marshall of the U.S. Forest Service, gained increasing social and political attention. In 1964, Congress passed the Wilderness Act, establishing guidelines for designating a host of federally owned lands as off-limits to motorized vehicles, road building, and resource exploitation. A large number of refuge lands qualified—the sun-blasted desert of Arizona's Havasu refuge, the glorious tannin-stained waters and cypress forests of Georgia's Okefenokee Swamp, and the almost incomprehensible large 8-million-acre Arctic NWR in Alaska, home to vast herds of caribou, wolf packs, and bladelike mountain peaks, the largest contiguous piece of wilderness in the refuge system.

Sachuest Point NWR, Rhode Island

Nonetheless, this was also a time of horrendous air and water degradation, with the nation at its industrial zenith and agriculture cranked up to the level of "agribusiness." A wake-up call arrived in the form of vanishing bald eagles, peregrine falcons, and osprey. The insecticide DDT, developed in 1939 and used in World War II to eradicate disease-spreading insects, had been used throughout the nation ever since, with consequences unforeseen until the 1960s. Sprayed over wetlands, streams, and crop fields, DDT had entered watersheds and from there the food chain itself. It accumulated in the bodies of fish and other aquatic life, and birds consuming fish took DDT into their systems, one effect was a calcium deficiency, resulting in eggs so fragile that female birds crushed them during incubation.

Powerful government and industry leaders launched a vicious, all-out attack on the work of a marine scientist named Rachel Carson, whose book *Silent Spring,* published in 1962, warned of the global dangers associated with DDT and other biocides. For this she was labeled "not a real scientist" and "a hysterical woman." With eloquence and courage, though, Carson stood her ground. If wild species atop the food chain could be devastated, human life could be threatened, too. Americans were stunned,

Partially submerged alligator, Anahuac NWR, Texas

and demanded an immediate ban on DDT. Almost overnight, the "web of life" went from chalkboard hypothesis to reality.

Protecting imperiled species became a matter of national policy in 1973 when President Nixon signed into law the Endangered Species Act (ESA), setting guidelines by which the U.S. Fish & Wildlife Service would "list" plant and animal species as *threatened* or *endangered* and would develop a program for their recovery. Some 56 refuges, such as Ash Meadows in Nevada and Florida's Crystal River, home of the manatee, were established specifically for the protection of endangered species. Iowa's tiny Driftless Prairie refuge exists to protect the rare, beautifully colored pleistocene land snail and a wildflower, the northern monkshood. Sometimes unwieldy, forever politicized, the ESA stands as a monumental achievement. Its successes include the American alligator, bald eagle, and gray wolf. The whooping crane would almost surely be extinct today without the twin supports of ESA and the refuge system. The black-footed ferret, among the rarest mammals on earth, is today being reintroduced on a few western refuges. In 1998, nearly one-fourth of all threatened and endangered species populations find sanctuary on refuge lands.

More legislation followed. The passage of the Alaska National Interest Lands Conservation Act in 1980 added more than 50 million acres to the refuge system in Alaska.

The 1980s and '90s have brought no end of conservation challenges, faced by an increasingly diverse association of organizations and strategies. Partnerships now link the refuge system with nonprofit groups, from Ducks Unlimited and The Nature Conservancy to international efforts such as Partners in Flight, a program to monitor the decline of, and to secure habitat for, neotropical songbirds. These cooperative efforts have resulted in habitat acquisition and restoration, research, and many new refuges. Partnerships with private landowners who voluntarily offer marginally useful lands for restoration—with a sponsoring conservation

group cost-sharing the project—have revived many thousands of acres of grasslands, wetlands, and riparian corridors.

Citizen activism is alive and well as we enter the new millennium. Protecting and promoting the growth of the NWR system is a primary campaign of the National Audubon Society, which, by the year 2000, will have grown to a membership of around 550,000. NAS itself also manages about 100 sanctuaries and nature centers across the country, with a range of opportunities for environmental education. The National Wildlife Refuge

Coyote on the winter range

Association, a volunteer network, keeps members informed of refuge events, environmental issues, and legislative developments and helps to maintain a refuge volunteer workforce. In 1998, a remarkable 20 percent of all labor performed on the nation's refuges was carried out by volunteers, a contribution worth an estimated $14 million.

A national wildlife refuge today has many facets. Nature is ascendant and thriving, often to a shocking degree when compared with adjacent lands. Each site has its own story: a prehistory, a recent past, a present—a story of place, involving people, nature, and stewardship, sometimes displayed in Visitor Center or Headquarters exhibits, always written into the landscape. Invariably a refuge belongs to a community as well, involving area residents who visit, volunteers who log hundreds of hours, and a refuge staff who are knowledgeable and typically friendly, even outgoing, especially if the refuge is far-flung. In this respect most every refuge is a portal to local culture, be it Native American, cows and crops, or big city. There may be no better example of democracy in action than a national wildlife refuge. The worm-dunker fishes while a mountain biker pedals past. In spring, birders scan marshes and grasslands that in the fall will be walked by hunters. Compromise is the guiding principle.

What is the future of the NWR system? In Prairie City, Iowa, the Neal Smith NWR represents a significant departure from the time-honored model. Established in 1991, the site had almost nothing to "preserve." It was old farmland with scattered remnants of tallgrass prairie and degraded oak savanna. What is happening at Neal Smith, in ecological terms, has never been attempted on such a scale: the reconstruction, essentially from scratch, of a self-sustaining 8,000-acre native biome, complete with bison and elk, greater prairie chickens, and a palette of wildflowers and grasses that astonish and delight.

What is happening in human terms is equally profound. Teams of area residents, called "seed seekers," explore cemeteries, roadside ditches, and long-ignored patches of ground. Here and there they find seeds of memory, grasses and wildflowers from the ancient prairie, and harvest them; the seeds are catalogued and planted on the refuge. The expanding prairie at Neal Smith is at once new and very old. It is reshaping thousands of Iowans' sense of place, connecting them to what was, eliciting wonder for what could be. And the lessons here transcend biology. In discovering rare plants, species found only in the immediate area, people discover an identity beyond job titles and net worth. The often grueling labor of cutting brush, pulling nonnative plants, and tilling ground evokes the determined optimism of Theodore and Franklin Roosevelt and of the CCC.

As the nation runs out of wild places worthy of preservation, might large-scale restoration of damaged or abandoned lands become the next era of American conservation? There are ample social and economic justifications. The ecological justifications are endless, for, as the history of conservation and ecology has revealed, nature and humanity cannot go their separate ways. The possibilities, if not endless, remain rich for the years ahead.

—John Grassy

How to use this book

Local conditions and regulations on national wildlife refuges vary considerably. We provide detailed, site-specific information useful for a good refuge visit, and we note the broad consistencies throughout the NWR system (facility set-up and management, what visitors may or may not do, etc.). Contact the refuge before arriving or stop by the Visitor Center when you get there. F&W wildlife refuge managers are ready to provide friendly, savvy advice about species and habitats, plus auto, hiking, biking, or water routes that are open and passable, and public programs (such as guided walks) you may want to join.

AUDUBON GUIDES TO THE NATIONAL WILDLIFE REFUGES

This is one of nine regional volumes in a series covering the entire NWR system. **Visitable refuges**—over 300 of them—constitute about three-fifths of the NWR system. **Nonvisitable refuges** may be small (without visitor facilities), fragile (set up to protect an endangered species or threatened habitat), or new and undeveloped.

Among visitable refuges, some are more important and better developed than others. In creating this series, we have categorized refuges as A, B, or C level, with the A-level refuges getting the most attention. You will easily recognize the difference. C-level refuges, for instance, do not carry a map.

Rankings can be debated; we know that. We considered visitation statistics, accessibility, programming, facilities, and the richness of the refuges' habitats and animal life. Some refuges ranked as C-level now may develop further over time.

Many bigger NWRs have either "satellites" (with their own refuge names) separate "units" within the primary refuge or other, less significant NWRs nearby. All of these, at times, were deemed worthy of a brief mention.

ORGANIZATION OF THE BOOK

■ **REGIONAL OVERVIEW** This regional introduction is intended to give readers the big picture, touching on broad patterns in landscape formation, interconnections among plant communities, and diversity of animals. We situate NWRs in the natural world of the larger bio-region to which they belong, showing why these federally protected properties stand out as wild places worth preserving amid encroaching civilization.

We also note some wildlife management issues that will surely color the debate around campfires and

ABOUT THE U.S. FISH & WILDLIFE SERVICE Under the Department of the Interior, the U.S. Fish & Wildlife Service is the principal federal agency responsible for conserving and protecting wildlife and plants and their habitats for the benefit of the American people. The Service manages the 93-million-acre NWR system, comprised of more than 500 national wildlife refuges, thousands of small wetlands, and other special management areas. It also operates 66 national fish hatcheries, 64 U.S. Fish & Wildlife Management Assistance offices, and 78 ecological services field stations. The agency enforces federal wildlife laws, administers the Endangered Species Act, manages migratory bird populations, restores nationally significant fisheries, conserves and restores wildlife habitats such as wetlands, and helps foreign governments with their conservation efforts. It also oversees the federal-aid program that distributes hundreds of millions of dollars in excise taxes on fishing and hunting equipment to state wildlife agencies.

congressional conference tables in years ahead, while paying recognition to the NWR supporters and managers who helped make the present refuge system a reality.

■ **THE REFUGES** The refuge section of the book is organized alphabetically by state and then, within each state, by refuge name.

There are some clusters, groups, or complexes of neighboring refuges administered by one primary refuge. Some refuge complexes are alphabetized here by the name of their primary refuge, with the other refuges in the group following immediately thereafter.

■ **APPENDIX**
Nonvisitable National Wildlife Refuges: NWR properties that meet the needs of wildlife but are off-limits to all but field biologists.
Federal Recreation Fees: An overview of fees and fee passes.
Volunteer Activities: How you can lend a hand to help your local refuge or get involved in supporting the entire NWR system.

U.S. Fish & Wildlife General Information: The seven regional head-quarters of the U.S. Fish & Wildlife Service through which the National Wildlife Refuge System is administered.

National Audubon Society Wildlife Sanctuaries: A listing of the 24 National Audubon Society wildlife sanctuaries, dispersed across the U.S., which are open to the public.

Bibliography & Resources: Natural-history titles both on the region generally and its NWRs, along with a few books of inspiration about exploring the natural world.

Glossary: A listing of specialized terms (not defined in the text) tailored to this region.

Index
National Audubon Society Mission Statement

PRESENTATION OF INFORMATION: A-LEVEL REFUGE

■ **INTRODUCTION** This section attempts to evoke the essence of the place, The writer sketches the sounds or sights you might experience on the refuge, such as sandhill cranes taking off, en masse, from the marsh, filling the air with the roar of thousands of beating wings. That's a defining event for a particular refuge and a great reason to go out and see it.

■ **MAP** Some refuges are just a few acres; several, like the Alaskan behemoths, are bigger than several eastern states. The scale of the maps in this series can vary. We recommend that you also ask refuges for their detailed local maps.

■ **HISTORY** This outlines how the property came into the NWR system and what its uses were in the past.

■ **GETTING THERE** General location; seasons and hours of operation; fees, if any (see federal recreation fees in Appendix); address, telephone. Smaller or remote refuges may have their headquarters off-site. We identify highways as follows: TX14 = Texas state highway # 14; US 23 = a federal highway; I-85 = Interstate 85.

Note: Many NWRs have their own web pages at the F&W web site, http://www.fws.gov/. Some can be contacted by fax or e-mail, and if we do not provide that information here, you may find it at the F&W web site.

■ **TOURING** The **Visitor Center**, if there is one, is the place to start your tour. Some have wildlife exhibits, videos, and bookstores; others may be only a kiosk. Let someone know your itinerary before heading out on a long trail or into the backcountry, and then go explore.

Most refuges have roads open to the public; many offer a wildlife **auto tour,** with wildlife information signs posted en route or a brochure or audiocassette to guide you. Your car serves as a bird blind if you park and remain quiet. Some refuge roads require 4-wheel-drive or a high-chassis vehicle. Some roads are closed seasonally to protect habitats during nesting seasons or after heavy rain or snow.

Touring also covers **walking and hiking** (see more trail details under ACTIVITIES) and **biking.** Many refuge roads are rough; mountain or hybrid bikes are more appropriate than road bikes. When water is navigable, we note what kinds of **boats** may be used and where there are boat launches.

■ **WHAT TO SEE**
Landscape and climate: This section covers geology, topography, and climate: primal forces and raw materials that shaped the habitats that lured species to the refuge. It also includes weather information for visitors.

Plant life: This is a sampling of noteworthy plants on the refuge, usually sorted by habitat, using standard botanical nomenclature. Green plants bordering watery places are in "Riparian Zones"; dwarfed trees, shrubs, and flowers on windswept mountaintops are in the "Alpine Forest"; and so forth.

Wildflowers abound, and you may want to see them in bloom. We give advice about timing your visit, but ask the refuge for more. If botany and habitat relationships are new to you, you can soon learn to read the landscape as a set of interrelated communities. Take a guided nature walk to begin.

(Note: In two volumes, "Plants" is called "Habitats and Plant Communities.")

Animal life: The national map on pages 4 and 5 shows the major North American "flyways." Many NWRs cluster in watery territory underneath the birds' aerial superhighways. There are many birds in this book, worth seeing simply for their beauty. But ponder, too, what birds eat (fish, insects, aquatic plants), or how one species (the mouse) attracts another (the fox), and so on up the food chain, and you'll soon understand the rich interdependence on display in many refuges.

Animals use camouflage and stealth for protection; many are nocturnal. You may want to come out early or late to increase your chances of spotting them. Refuge managers can offer advice on sighting or tracking animals.

Grizzly bears, venomous snakes, alligators, and crocodiles can indeed be dangerous. Newcomers to these animals' habitats should speak with refuge staff about precautions before proceeding.

■ **ACTIVITIES** Some refuges function not only as wildlife preserves but also as recreation parks. Visit a beach, take a bike ride, and camp overnight, or devote your time to serious wildlife observation.

Camping and swimming: If not permissible on the refuge, there may be federal or state campgrounds nearby; we mention some of them. Planning an NWR camping trip should start with a call to refuge headquarters.

Wildlife observation: This subsection touches on strategies for finding species most people want to see. Crowds do not mix well with certain species; you

A NOTE ON HUNTING AND FISHING Opinions on hunting and fishing on federally owned wildlife preserves range from "Let's have none of it" to "We need it as part of the refuge management plan." The F&W Service follows the latter approach, with about 290 hunting programs and 260 fishing programs. If you have strong opinions on this topic, talk with refuge managers to gain some insight into F&W's rationale. You can also write to your representative or your senators in Washington.

For most refuges, we summarize the highlights of the hunting and fishing options. You must first have required state and local licenses for hunting or fishing. Then you must check with refuge headquarters about special restrictions that may apply on the refuge; refuge bag limits, for example, or duration of season may be different from regulations elsewhere in the same state.

Hunting and fishing options change from year to year on many refuges, based on the size of the herd or of the flock of migrating birds. These changes may reflect local weather (a hard winter trims the herd) or disease, or factors in distant habitats where animals summer or winter. We suggest what the options usually are on a given refuge (e.g., some birds, some mammals, fish, but not all etc..). It's the responsibility of those who wish to hunt and fish to confirm current information with refuge headquarters and to abide by current rules.

COMMON SENSE, WORTH REPEATING

Leave no trace Every visitor deserves a chance to see the refuge in its pristine state. We all share the responsibility to minimize our impact on the landscape. "Take only pictures and leave only footprints," and even there you'll want to avoid trampling plant life by staying on established trails. Pack out whatever you pack in. Ask refuge managers for guidance on low-impact hiking and camping.

Respect private property Many refuges consist of noncontiguous parcels of land, with private properties abutting refuge lands. Respect all Private Property and No Trespassing signs, especially in areas where native peoples live within refuge territory and hunt or fish on their own land.

Water Protect the water supply. Don't wash dishes or dispose of human waste within 200 ft. of any water. Treat all water for drinking with iodine tablets, backpacker's water filter, or boiling. Clear water you think is OK may be contaminated upstream by wildlife you cannot see.

may need to go away from established observation platforms to have success. Learn a bit about an animal's habits, where it hunts or sleeps, what time of day it moves about. Adjust your expectations to match the creature's behavior, and your chances of success will improve.

Photography: This section outlines good places or times to see certain species. If you have a zoom lens, use it. Sit still, be quiet, and hide yourself. Don't approach the wildlife; let it approach you. Never feed animals or pick growing plants.

Hikes and walks: Here we list specific outings, with mileages and trailhead locations. Smooth trails and boardwalks, suitable for people with disabilities, are noted. On bigger refuges, there may be many trails. Ask for a local map. If you go bushwacking, first make sure this is permissible. Always carry a map and compass.

Seasonal events: National Wildlife Refuge Week, in October, is widely celebrated, with guided walks, lectures, demonstrations, and activities of special interest to children. Call your local refuge for particulars. At other times of the year there are fishing derbies, festivals celebrating the return of migrating birds, and other events linked to the natural world. Increasingly, refuges post event schedules on their web pages.

Publications: Many NWR brochures are free, such as bird and wildflower checklists. Some refuges have pamphlets and books for sale, describing local habitats and species.

Note: The categories of information above appear in A and B refuges in this book; on C-level refuges, options are fewer, and some of these headings may not appear.

—David Emblidge

Southwest
A Regional Overview

The American Southwest is bigger than life in every way. This sprawling landscape of deserts, mountains, and canyonlands is home to some of the nation's largest states. Each landform is remarkable in its own way: America has no hotter, drier desert, no grander canyons, no bigger barrier islands.

It is by and large a harsh landscape; yet within this sometimes inhospitable place, life pulses, rivers push through, flowers turn their faces to the sun. Indeed, in the Southwest, the native wildlife is as diverse and exotic as that found anywhere in North America. From prehistoric times on, the Southwest has been a haven for the feathered, finned, and four-footed; rare plants and animals found nowhere else on earth thrive here.

The terrain is similarly diverse. Snow-capped summits rise out of sun-scorched deserts. The broad Gulf of Mexico limns the Texas coast from the Mexican border to Louisiana for 367 miles. If you count every twist and turn, however, this convoluted coastline of bays, coves, inlets, barrier islands, and peninsulas spans 3,359 miles. Here, high ground is only 10 feet above sea level. The rolling grasslands of the Great Plains unfold from the eastern flanks of New Mexico onto the flat, windless earth of the Texas midsection.

THE ANCIENT PAST

The bleakness of the deserts and the ruggedness of the mountains did not deter ancient peoples, who were drawn to the region's natural riches. Hunter-gatherer tribes occupied the Southwest more than 10,000 years ago, as the glaciers of the last Ice Age withdrew northward. These tribes were followed by more advanced civilizations, including the Anasazi, Hohokum, and Mogollon of Arizona and New Mexico and the Caddo of east Texas. Descendants of the Anasazi, the Pueblo people, still reside in north-central New Mexico, while the Paiutes and Shoshone made their home in Nevada in the wake of the Anasazi occupation. Around 1100, various Apache and other nomadic tribes entered the region. In Texas, at this time, coastal peoples were active, too—including the Coahuiltecan and the Karankawa.

The Spanish were the first Europeans to make forays into what is now the American Southwest. In 1519, Spanish explorer Alonso Álvarez de Pineda spent 40 days in the Rio Grande delta—now home to two national wildlife refuges—which he named *Rio de las Palmas* (River of Palms). The shipwrecked Cabeza de Vaca explored the region on foot as he wandered across Texas, New Mexico, and northern Mexico between 1528 and 1536, while Francisco de Coronado blazed a trail through Arizona, New Mexico, and Kansas in from 1539 to 1540. New Mexico's

Storm clouds gather over Buenos Aires NWR.

first capital, San Juan de Gabriel, was established in 1598 in north-central New Mexico. Centuries later, in the 1700s and 1800s, Anglo trappers, traders, cattlemen, farmers, and cavalry also discovered the Southwest, as the frontier moved west.

Although the national wildlife refuges primarily protect plant and animal life, many southwestern refuges also contain reminders of the people who settled here, from ancient times to the near past. All who lived here were informed by the land and climate; each civilization in turn has left its own, indelible impressions.

GEOLOGY

The American Southwest has a wildly complex geology. Ravaged over time by massive fault lines, upthrust ranges, dropped basins, volcanic intrusions, droughts, and water damage, the landscape today encompasses desert, canyons, soaring mesas, buttes and spires, rolling plains, dry lake beds, and coastal bays, bayous, and beaches. But some clear differences separate the area into three primary subregions: the Texas Gulf Coastal Plain, the High Plains, and the Basin and Range Province.

On the east, running in a huge sweeping arc, are the bays, wetlands, beaches, and coastal prairies of the *Texas Gulf Coastal Plain*. The *High Plains* grasslands, also known as the Southern Plains, dominate the regional midsection, rising from central Texas in a slow climb toward the distant Front Ranges (eastern edge) of the Rocky Mountains in central New Mexico—the Sangre de Cristos. Third, occupying the region's western lands from the Rio Grande in New Mexico to the Sierra Nevadas of California, is the *Basin and Range Province,* a landscape of wide valleys (often harboring deserts) bisected by mountain ranges—some exceeding 13,000 feet in elevation.

Within these three subregions are other distinct geographical features.

Portions of all four of North America's major deserts are found in the Basin and Range lands. Along the subregion's southern edge lies the Chihuahuan Desert of New Mexico and west Texas and the Sonoran Desert of Arizona—both extending far southward into Mexico. At the subregion's southwestern fringe is the

Crystal Hill, Kofa NWR

Mojave Desert, while the Great Basin Desert fills central Nevada and extends in pockets as far east as central New Mexico.

You might think the Basin and Range is desert land. Indeed, it can be extremely dry, and its major rivers—including the Humboldt, Rio Grande, Pecos, Gila, Salt, Verde, and even the Colorado—are more slender than voluminous. Yet a river in the arid Southwest is a doubly precious entity, a life-giving oasis stubbornly carving its way through rock and sand.

The Basin and Range also includes substantial mountain chains, finger ranges of the Rocky Mountains extending southward. Arizona harbors many isolated peaks, riding like ships in a desert sea; New Mexico is bisected by the tall Sangre de Cristos; and even Nevada's desert flats are laced with mountain chains. The backbone of North America, the Continental Divide runs north and south through western New Mexico, splitting the continent into its Pacific and Atlantic watersheds.

Parallel to the divide is a major (though currently inactive) fault, the Rio Grande Rift. This fault—and many others underlying Nevada, Arizona, and New Mexico—is associated with the volcanic activity that created many southwestern mountain ranges. Volcanic forces lifted and dropped the entire subregion many times over hundreds of millions of years, repeating cycles of sea-flooded lowlands followed by mountain-building and erosion. The forces of these tectonic plates (large blocks of the earth's crust) continue to have an effect today in Basin and Range hot springs, which the locals call "los ojos de dios" (the eyes of god).

As the snowmelt and rain flow off the summits and plateaus toward the distant Pacific and Atlantic oceans, they slowly but inexorably cut and carve immense canyons, basins, arches, and thousands of other land features into a fantastic realm of rock.

The Great Plains, or High Plains, present an entirely different southwestern face: Huge rolling prairie lands shorn of trees, occasionally broken along the Texas–New Mexico border by rocky escarpments and mesas. This is a land where the sky dominates, where precious water collects in potholes and *playas* (shallow, broad, ephemeral water bodies in natural bowls).

The Southwest's third major physiographic subregion, the Texas Gulf Coastal Plain, is divided by some substantial rivers—including the Nueces, San Antonio, Guadalupe, Colorado (of Texas), and Brazos. Swamplike bayous associated with Mississippian ecosystems dot the upper coastline near the Louisiana border. The middle and lower Gulf coast of Texas is fringed by some of the world's largest barrier islands, including Matagorda, Mustang, and North and South Padre, and long sandy peninsulas protecting Texas's extensive coastal marshes and lagoons. A handful of federal refuges strung along the Gulf, from Anahuac to the mouth of the Rio Grande, take shelter behind these barrier islands.

CLIMATE

Altitude is everything in the Southwest's Basin and Range subregion. You can hike a dry desert canyon that hasn't seen any appreciable moisture for months, and an hour away and a mile higher you'll be snowshoeing atop 10 feet of snow. Because mountain ranges trap storms and cloud-laden moisture, the climate there is moist, cool, and pleasant, even in the dog days of summer. Conversely, summer days at Ash Meadows NWR, Nevada, on the scorching Mojave Desert lowlands, can be

18

Elko

Reno

Carson
City

Nevada

Elko

12

13

14

11

10

9

Las Vegas

5

1

4

6 7

3

2

8

Flagstaff

Arizona

Phoenix

Yuma

Tucson

Albuquerque

Las Cruces

El Paso

SOUTHWEST

SOUTHWEST

ARIZONA
1 Bill Williams River NWR
2 Buenos Aires NWR
3 Cabeza Prieta NWR
4 Cibola NWR
5 Havasu NWR
6 Imperial NWR
7 Kofa NWR
8 San Bernardino NWR

NEVADA
9 Ash Meadows NWR
10 Desert NW Range
11 Pahranagat NWR
12 Ruby Lake NWR
13 Sheldon NWR
14 Stillwater NWR

NEW MEXICO
15 Bitter Lake NWR
16 Bosque del Apache NWR
17 Las Vegas NWR
18 Maxwell NWR
19 Sevilleta NWR

TEXAS
20 Anahuac NWR
21 Aransas NWR
22 Attwater Prairie Chicken NWR
23 Brazoria NWR
24 Buffalo Lake NWR
25 Hagerman NWR
26 Laguna Atascosa NWR
27 Lower Rio Grande Valley NWR
28 McFaddin and Texas Point NWRs
29 Muleshoe NWR
30 San Bernard NWR
31 Santa Ana NWR

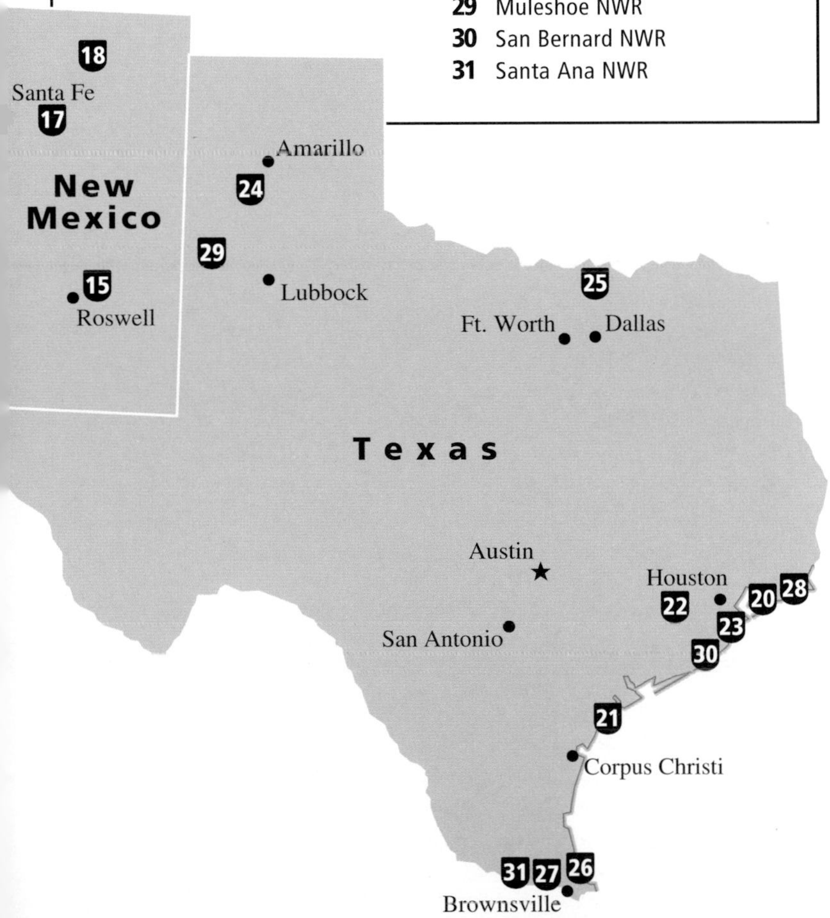
18
Santa Fe
17
New Mexico
15
Roswell
Amarillo
24
29
Lubbock
25
Ft. Worth
Dallas
Texas
Austin
Houston
22
20
28
23
30
San Antonio
21
Corpus Christi
31
27
26
Brownsville

among the world's harshest, with temperatures often topping 110 degrees. Expect significant temperature swings in the Basin and Range subregion—between winter and summer, and day and night.

Winter storms crossing the Basin and Range states generally arrive out of the northwest and west, bringing colder temperatures, rain at lower altitudes, and snow at middle to high elevations. Southern Arizona and, to a lesser degree, New Mexico are also significantly affected by moisture moving in off the Sea of Cortez (Gulf of California), which falls mostly during brief but intense summer monsoon showers.

In the desert lowlands, moisture is a hit-or-miss proposition. Certain spots can go years between rainfalls, while a few miles away average to good moisture pushes up fields of wildflowers.

Climate is more consistent along the Texas Coastal Plain, moderated by the effects of the warm Gulf waters (ranging from 52 to 85 degrees over the year at Texas locations). Here January lows average 46 degrees in Corpus Cristi, while summer highs average 94 degrees. Winter storms sweep out of the north occasionally, however, bringing high winds and near-freezing temperatures to the coast. Powerful thunderstorms also pound the coastal zone in summer and fall, dumping heavy rains and creating steaming humidity. In fact, the area around McFaddin NWR in east Texas averages 52 inches of rain a year! Occasional summer and fall hurricanes along the Gulf Coast are also a nasty fact of life.

High Plains weather is affected by both Basin and Range and Gulf Coast patterns. Particularly in summer, major fronts move off the Gulf and push northwestward into the Southern Plains, bringing hard rains that fill the *playas*. Winter storms often arrive from the west and northwest, rapidly dropping temperatures and ushering in fierce blizzards.

These widely divergent regional weather patterns and resultant soil moisture and climate conditions contribute significantly to the evolution of the Southwest's variegated flora and fauna.

PLANT COMMUNITIES

Sitting directly north of Meso-America and balanced on the spine of the Western Hemisphere, the Rocky Mountains, the Southwest is a north-south conduit for flora and fauna. But the geography of the Basin and Range subregion also isolates species from one other. Temperatures may vary tremendously in places only miles apart because of differences in sun exposure and altitude. Some Southwestern plants evolved by adapting to specific local conditions. The result is a broad range of flora, from cactus to tundra flowers.

These factors, in addition to a gradual drying-out of the landscape over time, encouraged the emergence of many endemics (species found only at one location), including the Ash Meadows blazing star, at Ash Meadows NWR, Nevada. A desert canyon of Kofa NWR, Arizona, provides a toehold for the largest known population of Arizona's only native palm.

Probably the most common plant of the Southwest's lowland deserts is creosote (see sidebar, Bitter Lake NWR). At slightly higher elevations are countless acres of chamisa (also known as rabbitbush), dozens of varieties of cactus, and cottonwood-lined rivers invaded by the exotic tamarisk (see sidebar, Bosque del

Apache NWR). These well-populated species, however, can't compete in the pop-ularity polls with the long and tall saguaro cactus—perhaps the preeminent sym-bol of the Sonoran Desert; you will see it at Cabeza Prieta NWR, Arizona.

The Sonoran is the warmest of the region's four deserts. Generally having an altitude of less than 3,000 feet, it rarely has hard freezes, and as a result the land-scape supports the most abundant plant life of any desert by far, including the beautiful yellow-flowering palo verde, tough ironwood, and dozens of other cacti.

The Chihuahuan Desert, in which lie both the Bosque del Apache and Bitter Lake refuges, receives only 8 to 10 inches of rain a year and is noted for its flower-ing yuccas, agaves, and mesquite along dry arroyos. Here, elevations climb from 3,500 to 5,000 feet, yielding occasional winter freezes and less profuse flora than in the Sonoran Desert.

Baddest of the bad, though beautiful as well, the Mojave Desert is cut off from Pacific storms by the high Sierra Nevadas. The Mojave languishes in high heat and at low elevations (from below sea level to 4,000 feet), with scant rainfall and rare dustings of snow in the mountains. The Joshua tree is most emblematic of this desert's flora, but bursage, creosote, and saltbush are also common.

Pahranagat and Stillwater NWRs in Nevada include parcels of the Great Basin Desert (4,500 feet to 6,200 feet). With hard winters, little rainfall, and high summer temperatures, the Great Basin is a harsh place to scratch out a living. Sage, a durable plant, is typical here.

But climb to the top of the highest mountains of the Basin and Range states, and things change rapidly: at the extremes, the equiva-lent of a trip from the Mex-ican border to Canada's Hudson Bay. From sea level to 4,500 feet, deserts pre-dominate in the Lower Sonoran Zone. Then, from 4,500 feet to 7,000 feet, the Upper Sonoran Zone is

Brittlebush (aster family), Kofa NWR

marked by piñon-juniper forests (see sidebar, Ruby Lake NWR) interspersed with grasslands. Next on the altitude ladder, from 7,000 feet to 8,500 feet, the Transition Zone welcomes in the larger ponderosa pine as the major species, with pockets of fir and spruce in cooler, wetter, north-facing hillside pockets, and Gambel's oak on hotter, south-facing slopes. Above 8,500 feet, moisture can jump to more than 30 inches a year. In the Mixed Conifer (or Canadian) Zone, Douglas fir, white fir, quaking aspen, and ferns flourish. Still higher, from 9,500 feet to 11,000 feet, the subalpine (or Hudsonian) Zone, sustains only hardy trees like Engleman spruce, corkbark fir, and stands of 3,500-year-old bristlecone pines, tough survivors of high winds, bitter cold, and deep snowfalls. Above 11,000 feet, in the Alpine Zone's harsh, tundralike conditions, a few pygmy trees, lichens, fine grasses, and short-lived wildflowers maintain a tenuous toehold. There are no NWRs at these elevations.

Reaching up into the subalpine Zone is Desert NWR, Nevada; Bosque del Apache and Maxwell NWRs, in New Mexico; Ruby Lake, Ash Meadows, and Sheldon, in Nevada; and Buenos Aires in Arizona approach this zone.

Riparian areas flanking streams and rivers slice through and connect these Basin and Range life zones, supporting cottonwoods (see sidebar, Bill Williams River NWR), box elders, the Goodding willow of Nevada, the Arizona sycamore, and many other deciduous trees and shrubs critically needed as habitat for almost all the subregion's vertebrate fauna.

The Gulf Coastal Plain displays an almost entirely different flora on its hundreds of thousands of acres of tidal flats, estuaries, marshes, and other wetlands. Here cordgrass, seashore saltgrass, sedges, cattails, and bulrush grow on slightly higher ground amid occasional stands of trees. The landscape grows increasingly wetter and greener as you move along the coast. While cactus is a common plant at Laguna Atascosa NWR (near Mexico), rice is commonly grown at Anahuac NWR (closer to the Mississippi Delta). Just inland from the coast are the "upland" prairies. Attwater Prairie Chicken NWR, in the heart of the Texas coastal tallgrass prairie in Colorado County, is a fine example of a healthy grassland, with more than 250 varieties of flowering plants.

Also in Texas is the richest biological subarea in the entire United States—the Lower Valley of the Rio Grande—flush against the Mexican border at the same latitude as the Florida Keys. It's the only place in the nation where native North American tropical flora and fauna grow: Florida's tropical plants are the same as those in the Caribbean Basin. Stands of manzanita, rare Texas ebony and sabal palm, and Montezuma bald cypress wave between quiet *resacas* (oxbow lakes) teaming with microscopic lifeforms and dense vegetation at water's edge. Spanish moss drapes forest limbs. Various pockets in the valley support coastal brushlands, thorn forests and scrublands, riparian woodlands, and coastal clay dune vegetation, including many endemic and endangered plants, such as Palmer's bloodleaf. With a 330-day growing season, the valley also supports immense citrus plantations and other farms.

The High Plains subregion shelters still other plants and grasses. Buffalo Lake NWR, Texas, protects one of the nation's best examples of original shortgrass prairie, while Bitter Lake NWR, New Mexico, mixes grassland plants with Chihuahuan Desert flora.

ANIMALS

Like the southwestern flora, the region's animal life is amazingly diverse. These range from alligators on Texas's Gulf Coast to the fleet-footed but endangered Sonoran pronghorn antelope at Cabeza Prieta NWR—not to mention exquisite rare butterflies and frogs that seem to bark.

Eons ago birds established flyways north and south across the Southwest's great spaces, migrating between summer territories in what is today the northern United States and Canada and winter grounds in southern states and Central and South America. Branches of three of the nation's four primary flyways cross the region today. The Texas Gulf coast welcomes birds traveling the Mississippi and the Central flyways, while the High Plains lie under the Central flyway. Migratory birds of New Mexico travel both the Great Plains branch of the Central flyway and another

Central flyway branch along the eastern face and intermountain valleys of the Rocky Mountains. Nevada and most of Arizona lie under stems of the Pacific flyway. Birds move to their own rhythms, however, and by traveling east or west they can begin their trips on one primary migratory flyway and end up on another. Some birds, such as blue geese, are also known to fly south on one flyway and north on another.

Each Southwest subregion has its own particular strengths regarding birds. The mudflats, marshes, beaches, and coastal plains of the Gulf Coast favor waders, waterfowl, and shorebirds. The upper Texas coast also sees more than 200 species of songbirds—including cerulean warbler, ruby-throated hummingbird, and wood thrush—which arrive by the hundreds of thousands on their fall and spring migrations over the Gulf of Mexico.

Texas's Lower Rio Grande Valley—home of Santa Ana, Rio Grande Valley, and Laguna Atascosa NWRs—has the greatest range of birdlife of any locale in the United States (more than 400 species), with overlapping varieties of North American and Meso-American birds, including such rarities as the green jay and the flashy altamira oriole.

High Plains refuges—including Las Vegas and Bitter Lake in New Mexico and Buffalo Lake and Hagerman in Texas—attract large numbers of lesser sandhill cranes, as well as hundreds of thousands of waterfowl. Migratory songbirds also pass through briefly, with some species staying to nest. Total bird species recorded on the High Plains is also impressive: 344 to date at Maxwell NWR, New Mexico, for instance.

Basin and Range New Mexico, Arizona, and Nevada accommodates both high altitude and desert birds not commonly seen elsewhere in the region, as well as countless migratory ducks, waders, and other water birds and songbirds in spring and fall. Year-round and nesting inhabitants include the desert-dwelling roadrunner and the omnivorous and talkative raven, which favors higher elevations and is often spotted along roadsides, scanning for roadkill jackrabbits.

Southwestern NWRs offer sanctuary to several endangered bird species: Yuma clapper rail (at Cibola NWR, Arizona); Southwest willow flycatcher (at Pahranagat NWR, Nevada; Bosque del Apache NWR, New Mexico; and elsewhere); prairie

Sandhill cranes, Bosque del Apache NWR

chicken (Attwater NWR, Texas); and the magnificent whooping crane (see sidebar, Aransas NWR).

Mammals in the Southwest come in all shapes and sizes. The thick subtropical forest and underbrush of the Lower Rio Grande Valley protect two endangered felines: the jaguarundi and ocelot. Piglike javelina jog around in packs from the Texas coast westward to southern Arizona, while antelope, elk, and mule deer favor the High Plains and the Basin and Range subregions. There are ring-tailed cats, desert bighorn sheep, kit fox, coati, kangaroo rats, ground squirrels, muskrats, and desert cottontail, beaver, gray fox, cougars, prairie dogs, armadillo, and coyote. Along the Gulf Coast endangered manatees and dolphins swim, and Texas alone is home to 33 of the nation's 43 species of bats!

The region's federal refuges also shelter an abundance of reptiles and amphibians, from the plentiful alligators of Texas's Anahuac NWR to the endangered Kemp's ridley turtle of various Gulf Coast refuges. Western diamondback rattlers inhabit large tracts of the Basin and Range subregion and the High Plains, as does the "hornytoad" (see sidebar, Havasu NWR).

As in the plant world, the Southwest's microclimates and ecosystems have encouraged the evolution of endemic fauna. Finding fish thriving in the desert may seem unfathomable, but small springs at Ash Meadows NWR in Nevada are home to four species of endangered, native finned critters, including the Ash Meadows pupfish (as well as a water beetle—the Ash Meadow nacorid); while Bitter Lake NWR in New Mexico protects more than 20 native fish species, as well as at least two "homegrown" snails and the shrimplike Noel's amphipod.

Fish of another sort, the "sport" fish of the Texas Gulf Coast, are important, too. The angling for speckled trout and redfish at Anahuac NWR is legendary, while great schools of black drum and sheephead gather in the Gulf waters of San Bernard NWR, also known for its blue crabs. Yellowfin tuna, blue marlin, tarpon, and other game fish are all caught offshore. Ruby Lake NWR, Nevada, has outstanding trout fishing, as does Sheldon NWR, Nevada.

THEN AND NOW

While the Southwest still contains wild patches of land where plants and animals flourish, it has also been exploited for centuries through grazing, hunting, industrial logging, mining, oil extraction, and large-scale agriculture (with resultant water diversion and pesticide runoff). New Mexico's Spanish explorers spoke of grass tickling their horses' bellies where today there are only dry arroyos. Mountain men and trappers raved about innumerable beaver and other fur-bearing animals. Today the grizzly bear is extirpated from the region, and beavers are not commonly seen in its mountain rivers and streams. Couriers on the Pony Express line in Nevada wrote of the skies near marshes blackened by ducks, where today dry, sun-blasted marsh beds are reminders that the waters were bled off for farming.

Along the upper Gulf Coast of Texas, major oil drilling operations and refineries have led to severe water pollution, although this condition is improving. Even more damaging has been the dredging and draining of extensive marshes that once surrounded local river deltas.

Today, fragmentation and loss of habitat are major concerns throughout the region as people settle in remote areas, suburbs leapfrog from urban centers to rural lands, and roads are cut to link new developments. The burgeoning population of the Basin and Range will likely face future battles over water rights. Will wildlife refuges be assured of adequate water in the face of rising industrial, urban, and agricultural demands?

Laughing gull, San Bernard NWR, Texas

These combined threats have pushed many regional plant and animal species to the edge of extinction. The numbers tell the sad tale: Regional species on Fish & Wildlife Service lands listed as threatened or endangered as of January 1999 included 46 animals and 27 plants in Texas; 34 animals and 17 plants in Arizona; 25 animals and 14 plants in New Mexico; and 26 animals and eight plants in Nevada—a total of 197 species. Almost no category of animal is untouched, neither birds, mammals, reptiles, amphibians, fish, invertebrates nor insects. If one of the earth's greatest biological strengths is its diversity of species, then the potential loss of these species may not portend well for the future.

But there is good news. Enlightened, dedicated, and resourceful Americans and the National Wildlife Refuge system staff are working hard to reverse the tide of shrinking biodiversity. Given the proper conditions, most flora and fauna rebound dramatically even from long periods of decline. Grasslands are being restored, forests replanted, waterways cleaned up, air pollution sources purified, unnecessary roads closed, urban sprawl better controlled, hunting better regulated. Species recovery success stories in the Southwest quite rightly boast about the return of the whooping crane, bald eagle, and peregrine falcon, plus the gumplant. In 1998, experimental wild Mexican *lobos* (gray wolf) were restored to the Southwest in Arizona's Blue Mountains, and since 1996 scores of endangered aplomado falcons (see sidebar, Laguna Atascosa NWR) have been released on south Texas refuges.

Many more promising ecosystem, flora, and fauna recovery projects are in various stages of implementation on southwestern NWRs. These efforts, along with the underlying beauty and fascination of the region's habitats and landscapes, make visiting the Southwest's National Wildlife Refuges a stimulating, heartening, and refreshing activity any time of year. Pack a lunch, lace up some sturdy walking shoes, grab the binoculars and a road map, and come out to enjoy and appreciate these wild, beautiful places.

Bill Williams River NWR
Parker, Arizona

Refuge wetland, Bill Williams NWR

It's not as big as its fellow southwestern parks, but this refuge packs an amazing diversity of flora and fauna within its borders. It includes the healthiest and largest native riparian woodlands left in the lower valleys of the Colorado River, a precious and endangered ecosystem that during the past 150 years has been drowned by reservoirs, clear-cut, built over, or invaded by exotic flora. Here a beaver leisurely gnaws on a cattail shoot while floating in the sparkling waters of the Bill Williams River, and the brilliant red and yellow hues of a western tanager flash from the cool cover of a cottonwood tree.

HISTORY

As one of the few dependable waterways in west-central Arizona, the Bill Williams River Valley has been a natural attraction for people for eons, including many pre-historic and historic Native cultures. An early southwestern trailblazer and moun-tain man, Old Bill Williams—said to have known the Southwest better than any man alive in the early 1800s—left his name on this refuge and river.

In the 1860s the Esquerra family established a ranch here in the vicinity of Mineral Wash and raised grapes, vegetables, melons, squash, and various fruits. The ranch was occupied until 1970.

In 1941 an enormous wildlife refuge completely encircling Lake Havasu, on the Colorado River, was established. Over the years, however, various portions were carved out for state parks, for Lake Havasu City, and for other uses. Bill Williams River NWR is one of the remnant pieces. It was created in 1991, when it was split off from Havasu NWR farther north, and was supplemented by lands along the Bill Williams River acquired from The Nature Conservancy. Compared with other southwestern refuges, it is tiny: only 6,091 acres. Some 30,000 people visit annually.

GETTING THERE

Bill Williams River NWR is located halfway between Parker and Lake Havasu City along AZ 95. Visitor Center is on AZ 95 just south of the Bill Williams River Bridge.

■ **SEASON:** Open year-round
■ **HOURS:** Refuge open daily dawn to dusk. Office open weekdays 8 a.m.–4 p.m.
■ **FEES:** Free entry.
■ **ADDRESS:** 60911 Highway 95, Parker, AZ 85344
■ **TELEPHONE:** 520/667-4144

TOURING BILL WILLIAMS

■ **BY AUTOMOBILE:** Planet Ranch Rd. runs up the Bill Williams River Valley, providing overviews of the riparian woodlands and close-up exposure of the valley floor and the river itself. The unsigned road begins on AZ 95 just 0.3 mile south of the Bill Williams Bridge (and just north of the Visitor Center), heading east up the river valley. At 3.5 miles the road becomes impassable to ordinary cars, but four-wheel-drive/high-clearance vehicles can forge through the various river crossings and continue on for another 4 miles to the road's intersection with Mineral Wash Rd. The latter continues south 25 miles to Parker via Shea Rd. Roadside vegetation might leave your vehicle with "desert pinstripping" (i.e., long scratches). The upper canyon beyond Mineral Wash is no longer accessible by car (despite old maps indicating otherwise) because of flooding.

■ **BY FOOT:** You can walk the Planet Ranch Rd. (including the section above Mineral Wash now closed to vehicles) in the riverbed when it is dry, or cross country in the desert uplands, but in general bushwhacking here is a rough proposition. There is also a short foot trail at the Visitor Center (see Activities, below).

■ **BY BICYCLE:** Mountain bikers can explore Planet Ranch Rd.

■ **BY CANOE, KAYAK, OR BOAT:** Boats are an excellent way to poke around in the large marsh at the delta of the Bill Williams River and Lake Havasu, but rental facilities are distant. No wake speeds only with power boats.

WHAT TO SEE

■ **LANDSCAPE AND CLIMATE**

Vermillion flycatcher

This refuge protects the last native riparian woodlands left in the lower Colorado River Valley, an ecosystem largely decimated (99 percent) through decades of human activity. Look for the cottonwood/willow woodlands along the Bill Williams River Valley floor.

The refuge includes a marshy delta on Lake Havasu where the Bill Williams emerges from its eastward-running canyon, a 9-mile native riparian corridor along the Bill Williams canyon floor. Flanking desert uplands rise in dramatic ledges and cliffs of sandstone, limestone, and basalt to flat-topped mesas some 400 to 1,500 feet above the river.

Before Alamo Dam was built 25 miles upstream on the Bill Williams, the river would flood violently, leaving behind large mud, gravel, and sand banks while burying cottonwood seeds, creating a mosaic of old and new trees, stream meanders, and open areas. Today refuge personnel work hard to try to re-create these conditions without nat-ural flooding, though minor flooding does still occur fol-lowing extreme summer rains. Today in the winter months the river runs occa-sionally as far downstream as the delta; it largely dries up in summer.

Cottonwood trees along the Bill Williams River

It is extremely hot here from April through October, with temperatures some-times climbing over 120°F. Winter days are mild and pleasant, averaging 45° to 60° F, though occasional cold fronts bring freezing weather. Annual precipitation averages 3 inches, most coming in intense summer storms.

■ PLANT LIFE

Wetlands A 500-acre marsh covers the Bill Williams River delta on Lake Havasu and extends up the river valley for a short distance in wet meadows. Com-mon plants here include cattail, bulrush, and sedges around the beaver ponds.

Forests Some 2,200 acres on the valley floor support a dense forest of Fremont cottonwoods soaring 100 feet above the ground in great galleries (see sidebar, next page), and three varieties of willow: the 50-foot-high Goodding (with its narrow 3- to 5-inch leaves), and shrublike sandbar (coyote) and seep willow. Together they form a diverse forest of seedlings, saplings, mature groves, and broken dead snags, each species attracting different birds and other wildlife. While these native trees are holding their own and even expanding their turf in some spots, the invasive salt cedar has made inroads here as well.

Arid lands On either side of the river valley striking desert uplands are found, covering 3,000 acres. Here you'll find two biotic communities overlapping: a diverse mixture of Mojave Desert flora living at its southeasternmost limits and Sonoran Desert flora at its northwesternmost limits. Characteristic of the Sonoran are the saguaro cactus and palo verde tree, while the Mojave is represented by var-ious cholla cactus; just north of the refuge Joshua trees are found.

Screwbean mesquite (see sidebar, Brazoria NWR) and arrowweed are found growing on slightly raised benches, and higher up honey mesquite, saltbush, and quailbush grow alongside hedgehog cactus, buckhorn cholla, and prickly pear. Following wet winters and in damp summers, carpets of wildflowers—including

THE COTTONWOOD TREE In the Southwest, a sure sign of water or water lying beneath the surface, is a colony of cottonwood trees waving their rich green tops. Life here without cottonwoods would be much impoverished. Their leafy canopy casts much-needed shade over the banks of rivers, streams, ponds, and springs, helping to cool and protect water from evaporation, guard ground-growing plants, and serve as a refuge for many animals. Mature trees can reach 100 feet in height.

Owls and other birds nest in the hollows left by falling limbs; orioles sing in their tops, and roadrunners pause at their feet while eating their catch. An old man leans a weary back against a gray, deeply furrowed truck while dangling his feet into the gurgle of water passing by. On the Hopi Mesas of Arizona, a Hopi artist carves a kachina figurine out of the relatively soft root of a cottonwood.

Several varieties are found in the region. The tall, roundish Rio Grande cottonwood grows in the central Southwest. The equally tall but more vertical Fremont is found in southern Nevada, Arizona, and southwestern New Mexico, while the even slimmer narrowleaf cottonwood is found at elevations of 5,000 to 7,000 feet across the mountain Southwest. In west Texas and eastern New Mexico the Plains or Sargeant's cottonwood thrives. Fluffy "cotton" produced by the females can create a snowlike blanket in the space beneath their branches in July—woe if you live under one!

rose globe mallow, brittlebush, various penstemon, purple lupine, gilia (a kind of phlox), and the sacred datura, with its large, creamy white blossoms—poke up from the dry earth.

■ ANIMAL LIFE

Birds The refuge's mixture of marshes, native riparian forests, flowing river water, and desert uplands create conditions favorable to a wide range of birds: 300 species have been recorded to date.

Migratory birds from Central and South America nest in the cottonwood and willow trees. They include southwestern willow flycatchers (an endangered species), plentiful and eye-catching vermillion flycatchers, yellow-billed cuckoos, and summer tanagers. The male of the latter species has a bright rose-red head and yellow body; while the cuckoo is noted for its slim brown-and-white body and the bright white spots on the underside of its long tail.

In spring and fall visiting migrants on their way to and from northern breeding grounds include Townsend's and black-throated gray warblers, western tanagers, and blue grosbeaks. The latter is a deep, dull blue with two broad cinnamon wing bars.

In the refuge's marshes, look for mallards, northern pintails, Canada geese, and, in particular, common mergansers and western least bitterns. The endangered Yuma clapper rail nests here in the spring.

Pause along the river road and listen for the descending repetitive call of the canyon wren singing out from the desert uplands. Watch for coveys of Gambel's quail scurrying through the underbrush and cactus wren settling into a saguaro nest.

In January and February you might spot Anna's or Costa's hummingbirds or the seldom-seen zone-tailed hawk.

Mammals Along the river you'll note ample evidence of beaver, who have built numerous small dams of sticks and mud, which help retain water in the valley.

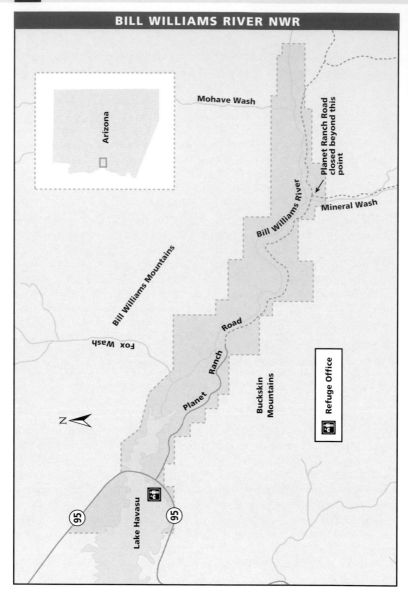

BILL WILLIAMS RIVER NWR

Muskrats enjoy the beavers' handiwork as well. Mule deer pause nervously, dipping their soft muzzles into the water, keeping an eye out for coyote or mountain lions. Look for cottontail and black-tailed jackrabbits in the grassy clearings along the river; you may even spot the backside of a bounding bobcat. Desert bighorn sheep roam the uplands alongside javelina and gray fox. Night brings out 14 bat species, including eight classified as "species of concern," or endangered, such as the Townsend's big-eared bat.

Reptiles and amphibians Some 50 species of reptiles and amphibians make their home here. Down by the river, look for garter snakes—these harmless reptiles can be easily handled—mud turtles, the lowland leopard frog (with its blotchy coloring), and collared lizards, their necks encircled by a dark ring. Poisonous reptiles include the Gila monster, the large Western diamondback, and the Mojave green rattlesnake. The latter, with its khaki tan/green coloring, is a mean-tempered, excitable snake with an incredibly venomous poison.

Fish Despite fierce competition from introduced fish, six native fish survive on the refuge. Razorback suckers and bonytail chub—both endangered— live in the delta area. Razorbacks once lived as long as 30 to 40 years and reached 20 pounds or more; the Visitor Center exhibits an old razorback in a display tank.

Invertebrates A total of 34 species of butterflies has been recorded here to date, including the rare MacNeill's sooty-winged skipper, which spends its days flitting between saltbush and mesquite on the fringes of the river valley. The refuge is the last sanctuary for 13 or 14 butterfly species once found throughout the region.

Bobcat

ACTIVITIES

■ **CAMPING:** Not allowed. Absolutely no campfires.

■ **SWIMMING:** Allowed in Lake Havasu, but not encouraged.

■ **WILDLIFE OBSERVATION:** The marsh at the mouth of the Bill Williams River on Lake Havasu looks promising for birdwatching, but the presence of anglers, boaters, and wind exposure tends to keep many birds away. There are several car pullouts along AZ 95, however, that provide good views of the marsh. Mergansers are most often seen here, but in midwinter such rarities as Barrow's golden eye and California gull have also been spotted.

The road paralleling the Bill Williams River has pullouts that provide views of a variety of habitats—wet riparian, dry riparian, and desert upland—that offer excellent birding and general wildlife viewing. Bighorns are sometimes seen on the cliffs here.

■ **HIKES AND WALKS:** A nature trail (keyed to a leaflet) runs 0.5 mile (round-trip) from the Visitor Center past a pond holding native fish and down to the edge of Lake Havasu near some marshes.

> **HUNTING AND FISHING** Hunting is allowed for **dove, quail, cottontail rabbit,** and **desert bighorn sheep**. Fishing for **striped** and **largemouth bass, catfish, bluegill,** and other species is allowed in accordance with state and federal regulations.

Eagle Slot Canyon is a popular walk. The unsigned route begins from the Bill Williams River road not far from its start: just keep an eye out for the narrow canyon slashing under the road. It drops down to the river floor.

■ **PUBLICATIONS:** Refuge brochure, trail brochure; species lists of birds, mammals, fish, butterflies, reptiles, and plants.

Buenos Aires NWR
Sasabe, Arizona

Prickly pear cactus, Buenos Aires NWR

Pronghorn antelope have free rein on the finest native grasslands of southern Arizona. At Buenos Aires National Wildlife Refuge, the sun-kissed grass undulates in golden winter waves across broad Altar Valley beneath Baboquivari Peak. Delicate watercress grows under the leafy green canopy lining the crystalline Arivaca Creek, and red-breasted vermilion flycatchers flit from tree to tree. In Brown Canyon children eagerly scamper over sheets of slickrock polished by periodic floods.

HISTORY

"As we entered the [Altar] valley from our position on its eastern border, the broad plain lay before us. Descending in a gentle slope to the center was a grassy steppe. The only other signs of life are herds of bounding antelope, or the red or gray wolf as he trots away slowly. The tracks of the great grizzly bear, the marks of the no-less ferocious panther, warn the traveler of other dangers than the Apache" (Raphael Pumpelly, 1861, *Across America and Asia*). Although the wolves, grizzly bear, and black panther are now vanquished, Buenos Aires remains a wild land with a colorful history.

Pedro Aguirre, son of a prominent mining and ranching family of Sonora, Mexico, founded the Buenos Aires (Spanish for "good air," or "fresh air") Ranch in 1864 as a stop on his Nogales-to-Tucson stagecoach route. When railroads supplanted stage travel, Aguirre turned to cattle and sheep ranching, and by 1886 Tucson papers identified him as one of the area's richest citizens. He built a public school in Arivaca (which still stands), but a seven-year drought from 1885 to 1892 wiped out more than half the grazing stock of Arizona and left the land open to severe erosion and invasion by mesquite thickets and nonnative grasses. From 1909 to 1985 a series of owners spent millions of dollars trying to reverse the grasslands' decline.

The U.S. Fish & Wildlife Service (FWS) acquired 100,000 acres in the Altar Valley in 1985, including the ranch, and subsequent land purchases along Arivaca Creek expanded the refuge to 118,000 acres. Some 30,000 people visit here annually, mostly in the winter.

GETTING THERE

Buenos Aires Visitor Center is about 60 mi. southwest of Tucson. From Tucson head west on Ajo Way (AZ 86) 22 mi. to Three Points. Then go south on AZ 286 for 38 mi. to the Visitor Center entrance road on left (follow signs for Refuge Headquarters). The refuge can also be reached from the east, off I-19 through Arivaca.

■ **SEASON:** Year-round.

■ **HOURS:** The refuge is open 24 hours daily. The Visitor Center is open sunrise to sunset daily.

■ **FEES:** Free entry, except Brown Canyon, which is $3 per person and has restricted public use.

■ **ADDRESS:** P.O. Box 109, Sasabe, AZ 85633

■ **TELEPHONE:** 520/823-4251, ext. 16

■ **VISITOR CENTER:** The Visitor Center at Buenos Aires offers a small native garden, displays on native grasses and the masked bobwhite quail, and a pleasant patio with a small fountain. A Visitor Office is also maintained in Arivaca, staffed daily in winter and on summer weekends.

TOURING BUENOS AIRES

■ **BY AUTOMOBILE:** Antelope Dr., a dirt road—suitable for 2-wheel-drive cars and RVs (except after heavy precipitation)—traverses a portion of the refuge's recovering grasslands. It begins on the Visitor Center entrance road and ends on the Mexican border at Sasabe, and loops back to its starting point to make a 10-mile round-trip. AZ 286 and the Arivaca Rd. (both paved) also cross the refuge, north to south and east to west respectively. More than 200 miles of backcountry roads are open to the public. Only a few are marked, however, and few are suitable for all types of vehicles, or in all weather. Off-road driving is prohibited. Inquire at Visitor Center.

■ **BY FOOT:** Trails access a variety of habitats at Buenos Aires. Trails and boardwalks in the Arivaca Cienega (Spanish for "one hundred springs") and Arivaca Creek areas wind through wetlands and riparian forests; both are near the town of Arivaca. Mustang Trail climbs into desert foothills. Brown Canyon also has a lovely trail, but the canyon is open only on guided tours. All the refuge roads can be walked as well. Off-road/trail hiking is allowed but is not for the faint of heart.

■ **BY BICYCLE:** All the refuge roads can be biked. The rugged terrain southeast of the Visitor Center is ideal for isolated riding. Make inquiries about remote roads.

WHAT TO SEE

■ **LANDSCAPE AND CLIMATE** Buenos Aires refuge runs 24 miles, north-south. Most of its terrain is rolling desert grasslands (also called Sonoran savannahs or upland grasslands), but flanking the refuge's western edge are the sides of a mountain range capped by the distinctively spired Boboquivari Peak. Shrines atop the 7,700-foot summit are maintained by Tohono O'Odhams and other Arizonan native peoples who have long worshipped this landmark, which rises 4,700 feet from the valley floor.

On the refuge's eastern border are the San Luis Mountains and Las Guijas Mountains. A valley dividing these two lower ranges contains a stream (Arivaca

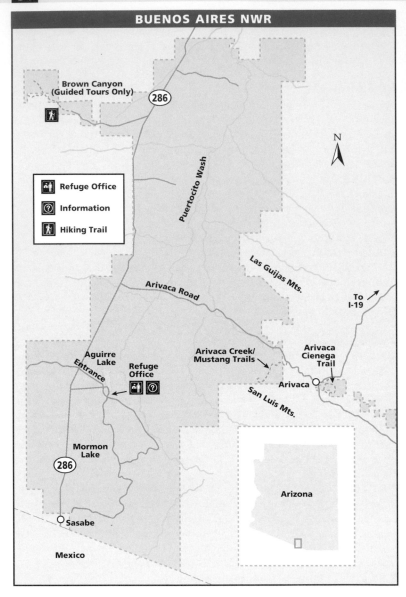

BUENOS AIRES NWR

Brown Canyon
(Guided Tours Only)

286

Puertocito Wash

Refuge Office

Information

Hiking Trail

Las Guijas Mts.

Arivaca Road

To
I-19

Aguirre
Lake

Entrance

Refuge
Office

Arivaca Creek/
Mustang Trails

Arivaca
Cienega
Trail

Arivaca

San Luis Mts.

Mormon
Lake

286

Arizona

Sasabe

Mexico

Creek) and a marsh (Arivaca Cienega) that wander along the surface for 4 miles or so before the desert reclaims them. This is the only permanent surface water found at Buenos Aires. Rancher Pedro Aguirre dug a large, shallow water body, the eponymous Aguirre Lake, near his house for watering fields and livestock, but it often goes dry between wet seasons.

Precipitation here averages 18 inches a year, although it can vary widely at different elevations. Most moisture comes in summer thunderstorms, but winters are occasionally damp. With the Sea of Cortez (Gulf of California) only 145 miles to the southwest, moisture can increase dramatically under the right conditions. Winter days are often pleasant, sunny, and warm, with highs averaging 55 to 60 degrees. Daytime highs average 90 to more than 100 degrees, May through Sept.

■ PLANT LIFE Buenos Aires' variety of ecosystems produces richly diverse flora, some 500 different species in all.

Wetlands Seven major springs in Arivaca Valley provide the nucleus of a marsh area called Arivaca Cienega. Ponds and braided streams support thriving riparian vegetation, including cattail, bulrush, sedges, and rushes. You will see water penny wort floating on the ponds' surface, its large, shiny green pads growing from a submerged stem. Monkey flower blankets the foot trail, its yellow shoot resembling a snapdragon. Look for swamproot's white flowers in May and June. Fremont cottonwood trees, 40 feet tall, dot the valley floor, tossing their shaggy tops in the breeze alongside Goodding willows.

Grasslands The immense grass savannahs of Buenos Aires are its most outstanding natural feature, comprising 80 percent of its habitat. A slew of fibers weave its earthen blanket; among them are Arizona cottontop, sideoats grama, blue grama, plains brittlegrass, sprucetop grama, hook three-awn, hairy grama, deergrass, feather fingergrass, tanglehead, sacaton (a once-abundant native grass), and green spangletop. The latter stands an amazing 40 inches high.

The predominant grass, however, is actually an introduced exotic from Africa. Lehmann's love grass forms dense clumps 15 to 18 inches tall. It is a monoculture; once it is established, it outcompetes every other grass.

Introduced grasses aren't the only element crowding out native grasslands. Grazing, combined with an extended drought in the late 19th century, stripped many of the original grasses from the valley, exposing its soil to erosion. Suppression of natural wildfires in the 20th century also helped invasive honey mesquite (see sidebar, Brazoria NWR) in its takeover of large grasslands. These impenetrable thickets of low-growing trees are easily noted along Antelope Dr.

Buenos Aires refuge is succeeding at grassland restoration through controlled

burns (destroying mesquite while rejuvenating grasses) and grass reseeding and is cooperating with neighboring land owners to restore 400,000 acres of grasslands outside the refuge in the Altar Valley. One plant to look for in recently burned areas is the poppy caltrops, which blooms in August.

Arid lands Foothills on the upper edges of the grasslands provide terrain for varieties of Sonoran Desert cactus. Most common are several types of cholla, beefy barrel cactus (blooming with an orange crown in July), and the fleshy pads of several versions of prickly pear. In March and April the spindly ocotillo produces stunning scarlet blooms (popular with hummingbirds) at the end of their long, thorn-covered gray stalks. Ocotillo looks dead most of the

Yucca, Buenos Aires NWR

year but can rapidly generate rows of leaves when moisture is present. Century plants push up a giant asparagus spear capped by delicate yellow flowers in spring and then die from exhaustion, their cycle complete.

Forests Perennial Arivaca Creek and the intermittent creek in Brown Canyon support linear riparian woodlands. Along Arivaca Creek Trail you'll notice stands of netleaf hackberry interspersed with the prevalent Fremont cottonwood and Arizona ash. The hackberry's small orange fruit is a favorite of wildlife, as is the fruit of Arizona walnut trees-also enjoying the moisture here. The holly-like bush is algerita. Watercress, tart and refreshing, grows on the edges of the stream on the water's surface.

The floor of Brown Canyon is a mosaic of Arizona sycamore, hackberry, and walnut. On its upper reaches on the steep flanks of Boboquivari Peak you can search for Kearney blue star, an endangered wildflower, plus occasional alligator juniper (its gray bark looking just like the back of a gator). Above 4,000 feet are dense stands of seven types of live oak, spreading out in a forest canopy some 30 to 40 feet high.

■ ANIMAL LIFE

Birds Buenos Aires' variety of flourishing habitats accounts for the abundance of bird species recorded here—314 to date. This refuge is the nation's only NWR with four endemic varieties of quail, including the nation's only population of masked bobwhite quail. This endangered bird prefers to scurry through grasses and thickets rather than fly, although when frightened it will burst from tall grass at your feet in a startling explosion of flapping wings. These birds disappeared from southern Arizona and northern Sonora, Mexico, around the end of the 19th century because of habitat degradation, but a remnant population was ultimately discovered on a private ranch in Sonora. Offspring from this group are being reintroduced into Buenos Aires grasslands. Initial results weren't encouraging, but the survival rate is now climbing and natural reproduction is occurring. A small population—between 300 and 500 birds—lives here today.

Masked bobwhite quail, Buenos Aires NWR

Other birds are doing well here, too. Twelve species of hummingbirds have been seen hovering about, plus 18 species of sparrows (including the rare sage sparrow), and nesting species like the rufous-winged sparrow, lark sparrow, and grasshopper sparrow. Colorful orioles, tanagers, and warblers adorn the trail at Arivaca Creek in spring and summer, while owls, woodpeckers, and sapsuckers appreciate the riparian woodlands year-round. Loggerhead shrikes, imperiled elsewhere in the West, are plentiful on Buenos Aires' rich grasslands, while the lovely singsong voice of the western meadowlark is often heard around Arivaca Cienega.

Of the plentiful raptors, the gray hawk is one of the more prized, rarely seen elsewhere in the United States. More likely are sightings of nesting white-tailed kite, American kestrel, and Cooper's and red-tailed hawk.

American pronghorn antelope, Buenos Aires NWR

Mammals The refuge grasslands support a healthy population of American pronghorn antelope. This 105- to 120-pound, brown-and-white, hoofed animal is North America's fastest land creature, capable of 55-mph bursts of speed. The bucks sport foot-tall sets of inward curling horns. With eyes the size of an elephant's on a body the size of a goat, pronghorn clearly evolved for watchfulness. Buenos Aires' original pronghorn were wiped out, but stock was transplanted here over the years, and the refuge now supports a 500-head herd.

Southern Arizona's greatest population of mule deer also lives on these grasslands, while its uplands support herds of white-tailed deer. In the base of large cactus clumps or under ledges, look for the large nests of the abundant kangaroo rats. Bobcat, coyote, javelina, and coatamundi are sometimes seen on refuge roads or trails, while mountain lion, badger, and ringtail cat are present but rarely observed.

The refuge may also shelter jaguar—a most exciting possibility! Believed to have been extirpated from the United States, positive sightings were recorded in southern Arizona in the late 1980s and the mid-1990s.

Reptiles and amphibians The poisonous but reclusive Gila monster is but one of the many lizards found at Buenos Aires. Desert tortoise, which can live 70 years, burrow as deep as 30 feet into loose soils of arroyos in the heat of summer and cold of winter and then emerge to feed on their all-vegetarian food stocks. Couche's spadefoot toads can burrow into the ground for years, protected in a chamber of damp earth, awaiting heavy rains. The booming of summer thunder brings them to the surface where they collect briefly by the thousands in ephemeral shallow pools.

ACTIVITIES

■ **CAMPING:** About 100 primitive campsites are scattered along refuge backcountry roads; stays are limited to 14 days. Basic accommodations for 16 people at the Brown Canyon Environmental Education Center cost $10 per person, plus $5 per meal. Call headquarters for details.

■ **WILDLIFE OBSERVATION:** The shrubs and feeders at the Visitor Center are popular spots for songbirds, Gambel's quail, canyon towhee, and curved-billed thrasher. Listen for the hootings of great horned owls in the pine trees next to the Visitor Center.

Visit Aguirre Lake, just north of the Visitor Center. During wet years, the water will attract migrating shorebirds and wading birds (including white-faced ibis) in April and September and waterfowl (including pintails, gadwalls, and American wigeon) in winter. At the Arivaca Cienega boardwalk, a sharp eye may get a glimpse of a sora or a Virginia rail.

Also be sure, if possible, to visit Brown Canyon (guided tours only), where birds that dwell in higher elevations—including hummingbirds, painted redstarts, sulphur-bellied flycatchers, and zone-tailed hawks—can be seen. When driving along AZ 286 through the refuge, check out the telephone poles for perching raptors, including golden eagles in January.

To view pronghorn, or possibly mule deer, explore Antelope Dr. or other roads near headquarters where the antelope gather on grassy flats: Early morning and late afternoon are best.

■ **PHOTOGRAPHY:** A dramatic panorama of roiling summer afternoon thunderheads towering over the Altar Valley, with Boboquivari Peak in the background, is a signature shot from this refuge. "Sublime" is the word for light filtering through the sycamore trees and draping the sculpted boulders and rock faces of Brown Canyon. For another entirely different look, dip into the riparian forests along Arivaca Creek. Skirt the wetlands at Cienega Marsh, where you can see barrel cactus juxtaposed with cattail. For the best photos of pronghorn, a 300mm lens or longer will help. Pan with them as they run and shoot at a fast shutter speed to capture their fleet-footedness on film.

> **HUNTING** Hunting is permitted on about 90 percent of the refuge from Sept. 1 to March 31 for **mule deer, javelina, white-tailed deer, coyote, cottontail rabbit, feral hogs, mourning** and **white-winged dove,** and **waterfowl** and **coots.** Inquire for details.

■ **HIKES AND WALKS:** Arivaca Creek Trail runs along a cottonwood-lined stream popular with aerial and terrestrial wildlife. A 0.25-mile loop stays alongside the creek. You can follow the trail downstream for another 0.25 mile, where you'll pass the abandoned home of Eva Wilber Cruce, who wrote about growing up here in her evocative book *A Beautiful Cruel Country.* The trailhead is located 2 miles west of Arivaca on Arivaca/Sasabe Rd.

Arivaca Cienega Trail (handicapped-accessible) runs 2 miles across wetlands and around various ponds. It's just over 0.2 mile to Willow Pond. The trailhead is 0.25 mile west of Arivaca on Arivaca Rd.

Aguirre Lake Trail loops around this man-made reservoir, which often dries up between wet seasons, for 0.25 mile.

Mustang Trail (5 miles roundtrip) is the refuge's most challenging hiking route, crossing Arivaca Creek and climbing to the top of a desert promontory called El Cerro. The trail forks off Arivaca Creek Trail.

Brown Canyon also has a lovely trail that slowly ascends this beautiful cleft, accessing a 47-foot-high natural stone arch in its upper reaches.

■ **SEASONAL EVENTS:** The refuge has an active education program, including a spring migration count, guided birding tours, guided geology/botany hikes in Brown Canyon, and grassland tours (every Sat., Nov. to April; free to $3).

Full-day workshops and overnight workshops (around $50) are conducted at Brown Canyon Environmental Education Center. Preregistration required for all tours and workshops.

■ **PUBLICATIONS:** Brochure, bird list, species' leaflets, program schedule.

Cabeza Prieta NWR
Ajo, Arizona

Saguaro cacti, Sonoran Desert, Cabeza Prieta NWR

One of the largest national refuges outside of Alaska is also one of the least visited. Cabeza Prieta is way off the beaten path—only 2,000 or so folks explore this wild desert terrain each year. The few who make it, however, are vastly rewarded. A glorious panorama—hills studded with towering saguaro cactus, washes lined with tough ironwood trees, rocky mountains, and huge basins—stretches as far as the eye can see. On a typical day, the breeze carries nothing more than the sweet scent of blooming palo verde trees and the calls of a pyrrhuloxia: *quink quink quink quink*. Not a soul is in sight.

HISTORY

As wild, desolate, harsh, and isolated as this region is, it actually has a long and fascinating human story dating back at least 10,000 years (see sidebar, next page). The name *Cabeza Prieta,* Spanish for "dark head," refers to one of the many knobby basaltic mountains found here. In the early 20th century, miners combed the area's mountains for mineral wealth, and the discovery of rich copper deposits in 1916 led to the opening of the Ajo mines.

   Cabeza Prieta National Wildlife Refuge's 860,000 acres were acquired by the federal government in 1939. The land was transferred in 1976 to the U.S. Fish & Wildlife Service in a farsighted move protecting a large swath of pristine desert habitat.

GETTING THERE

The refuge is located in southwestern Arizona, southwest of Globe, southeast of Yuma, and west of Ajo (pop. 3,000). You will find the Visitor Center on the west side of AZ 85 on Ajo's north side. The refuge's most accessible portion lies along the Charlie Bell Pass Rd. (see Touring, below).

■ **SEASON:** Open year-round. Cabeza Prieta, however, is located within the even-larger Barry Goldwater Air Force Range and can occasionally be closed briefly. Closures are scheduled in advance. Call for details.

■ **HOURS:** Refuge open 24 hours daily (except as noted above). Visitor Center open weekdays 7:30 a.m.–4:30 p.m.

■ **FEES:** Free entry.

■ **ADDRESS:**1611 N. Second Ave., Ajo, AZ 85321

■ **TELEPHONE:** 520/387-6483

■ **VISITOR CENTER:** Good facility with a video screening/lecture room, displays, and a small native garden.

TOURING CABEZA PRIETA

■ **BY AUTOMOBILE:** This refuge offers the nation's premier desert backcountry auto-touring experience, but it requires a 4-wheel-drive, high-clearance vehicle. Minimum drive time required for a cross-refuge outing is 10 hours. The primary backcountry road is the Camino del Diablo (see sidebar on this page), which bounces across 72 miles of desert features. It runs from south of Ajo on the Organ Pipe National Monument (adjacent to the refuge) northwest to I-8 near Wellton.

You must obtain a permit and sign a "Hold Harmless" release form to enter the refuge: The refuge was at one time a bombing range (it continues to be a training area, but no bombs are being dropped), and unexploded bombs are occasionally found out here, albeit mostly in the refuge's

CAMINO DEL DIABLO The inhospitable desert area known as Cabeza Prieta lies smack across an old primary travel route between northern Mexico and California, where long ago intrepid explorers blazed a faint trail across its tortured face. This route, El Camino del Diablo (Devil's Road), claimed hundreds of lives over several centuries of use, particularly in drought periods when the few pools of water trapped in small natural stone basins went dry. "All traces of the road are sometimes erased by the high winds . . . but death has strewn a continuos line of bleached bones and withered carcasses of horses and cattle as monuments to mark the way," wrote Lt. N. Michler in 1855.

First used by the Pinacatero and Areneno Indians, the trail was later crossed by Spanish soldier Captain Melchior Diaz in 1540 to reach the Colorado River; by the famous Jesuit Padre Eusebio Kino, between 1698 and 1670, as he set up Catholic missions; by Juan Bautista de Anza on his trek to discover San Francisco, in 1774; and by thousands of optimistic forty-niners, enroute to the California gold fields.

Today, El Camino can be traversed by well-prepared adventurers with 4WD vehicles.

northern boundaries, off the beaten path. Still, there are no regular patrols of the roads, and cell phones may not function—so be prepared for emergencies.

One refuge road, however, the Charlie Bell Pass Rd., can be undertaken by careful drivers of two-wheel vehicles—although high clearance is helpful. Drive north on AZ 85 from the Visitor Center for 0.2 mile and turn west (left) onto Rasmussen Rd. At 1.9 miles the road forks, you should veer right. At 2.9 miles the road forks again—veer left. At 4.9 miles you reach the refuge boundary entrance gate. At 8.5 miles the road passes a windmill and well on the left. The one-way distance to the end of the road at Charlie Bell Pass is 17.3 miles and requires at least 90 minutes to travel. Carry a spare tire, food, and water. Days can pass between visitors on this route.

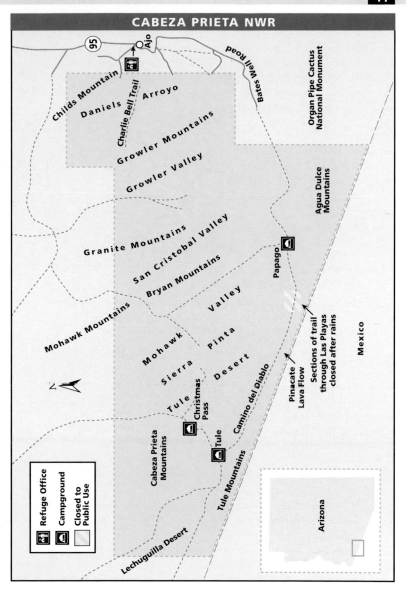

CABEZA PRIETA NWR

■ BY FOOT: The entire refuge is open to people on foot, but there are no dedicated hiking trails other than a short nature walk at the Visitor Center. Overland hiking is often over rough ground studded with rocks and cactus. The public and the service roads make for easier outings, as do the sandy arroyo beds crossing the Charlie Bell Pass Rd. Always carry water here, even on short outings. Two gallons per day per person is advised.

■ BY BICYCLE: Mountain bikes are allowed on all public roads.

WHAT TO SEE

■ LANDSCAPE AND CLIMATE Cabeza Prieta is a beautifully harsh landscape embraced by the Sonoran Desert. At relatively low elevation—ranging from

300 feet to the summit of the Growler Mountains at 3,323 feet—this is desert with a capital *D*. But within the desert is a handful of distinct subareas. A large sand-dune field extends far southward into northern Mexico, wrapping around the northern end of the Sea of Cortez in North America's harshest desert—the *Gran Dieserto*. Seven rugged major granite and basaltic mountains, including the Growlers, Tinajas Altas, and Agua Dulces, poke through the desert floor, some

harboring natural rock water tanks (*tinajas*), while huge lava flows and riparian arroyos snake out of the hills. Desert flats and broken terrain slope slowly toward the Mexican border, which runs along the refuge's southern edge for 56 miles

A huge portion, 803,000 acres (93 percent), of the refuge rests under designation as a federal wilderness area, so most of its environment should never see human-induced change (except perhaps on a macro-scale, such as global warming).

Summer air temperatures here have topped 130 degrees, and surface soil temperatures 180 degrees! Even in March a sweat collects on the forehead. Days average 90 degrees and above and higher mid-April through mid-November. Rainfall is sparse—2

Palo verde tree with early spring blossoms

to 6 inches a year. Nonetheless, winter days are very pleasant, clear and often in the 60s—a good time to visit. Hard freezes almost never occur.

■ **PLANT LIFE** Sonoran Desert vegetation exclusively characterizes the entire refuge. Even its highest mountains display desert vegetation. But Cabeza Prieta is far from barren: In fact, close to 400 plant species grow here.

Saguaro cactus is perhaps the refuge's most charismatic flora. The tall colum-nar cactus can reach 55 feet in height and may live as long as 200 years. Small arms sprouting off the main trunk form comical anthropomorphic shapes. Saguaro like to grow on *bajadas*, gently sloping terrain fronting mountain foothills and canyon mouths. Many other cacti species prosper at the feet of saguaro, including organ pipe (a multibranched columnar shape), Arizona barrel, various prickly pear, and a handful of different members of the cholla family. These include teddy bear cholla, whose golden needles and rounded shape give it a cuddly appear-ance. Even the slightest brush against it, however, will cause clumps to snap off, and small piles of discarded offspring often lie around its base. Also growing alongside saguaro are the linear ocotillo, an abundance of creosote (see sidebar, Bitter Lake NWR), and bursage—a low, rapidly growing bush that often is the first to recolonize disturbed earth.

Arroyos support plants that require slightly more water. Although these washes appear bone dry, they carry flash-flood waters after summer thunderstorms, and their sandy beds act as a sponge, holding water deep beneath the baked surface. Mesquite (see sidebar, Brazoria NWR) plants its roots into this punch bowl, producing feathery leaves, while ironwood and foothill palo verde root here as well.

The name ironwood (also called desert ironweed) is apt. It is so dense it sinks in water, and nails driven into it will often bend in defeat. Ironwood stabilizes arroyo banks and provides important shade and shelter for many kinds of wildlife. Desert mistletoe, a parasite growing on the spiny branches of ironwood, produces small white berries beloved by phainopepla. In late May ironwood's leaflets are covered with fragrant lavender blooms that are usually shed in the heat of summer.

Palo verde is another beautiful and remarkable desert tree. In March and April its mantle of yellow flowers buzzes with bees and hummingbirds. To reduce evaporation, the tree has very small green leaves and can photosynthesize sunlight through its smooth lime green trunk and branches.

Tread carefully when walking around cryptobiotic (or cryptographic) soil on desert flats. This mixture of fungi and other microorganisms serves as a thin living skin for the earth. It stands a half inch or more above adjacent wind-eroded grounds. In spring, patches of purple lupine and desert onion color the desert floor.

■ ANIMAL LIFE

Birds Despite its aridity, Cabeza Prieta sees some 150 bird species come and go annually. Warblers, phoebes, flycatchers, and swallows pass through on spring and fall migrations, while red-tailed hawk, northern flicker, turkey vulture, Gambel's quail, and mourning dove nest here and are present year-round. Listen for the plaintive and forlorn cry of the mourning dove.

Another year-round resident, the Gila woodpecker, drills holes in saguaro cacti and nests inside them; you'll see the Gilas land with impunity on the cactus, hop to their hole and vanish. When they abandon the nests, elf owls will often

move in. Common ravens are also noted frequently year-round. The large black birds are superb flyers, maneuvering in high desert winds with ease.

Mammals The refuge supports a high diversity of mammals: 40 species. Most prominent is its herd of 430 or so desert bighorn sheep (see sidebar, Desert NWR), and some 140 endangered Sonoran pronghorn antelope. But bats, squirrels, mice, rats, and gophers make up the majority of mammals here. Cabeza Prieta's 11 bats include the lesser long-nosed (formerly named Sanborn's), an endangered species. Kit fox, gray fox, and coyote represent the canine family; bobcat and mountain lion, the felines. You may spot black-tailed jackrabbit, antelope jackrabbit, or desert cottontail hopping around.

Gila woodpecker

Reptiles and amphibians This is reptile country. Forty-three species call Cabeza Prieta home, including desert iguana, rosy boa, and 11 types of rattlesnakes; of these, you may spot the Mojave and the sidewinder. The sidewinder is the most common refuge rattler, easily identified by the prominent "horns" above its eyes and its unique method of locomotion—an undulating side-to-side movement. The refuge's largest lizard, the chuckwalla, is rarely sighted but can sometimes be seen sunning itself atop large boulders in the mountain ranges. The most common amphibian here is the red-spotted toad.

ACTIVITIES

■ **CAMPING:** Camping is permitted along refuge public-use roads and dispersed locations for hikers. 4-wheel-drive car camping grounds are located on El Camino del Diablo Road. The refuge has two primitive campsites (charcoal and fuel stoves only, no campfires, no water). Camping within 0.25 mile of a water source is not allowed.

■ **WILDLIFE OBSERVATION:** Just to the west of the windmill along Charlie Bell Rd. is a water-tank with a seeper; the trickle of desert gold attracts birds and

Sidewinder rattlesnake leaving its J-shaped tracks in desert sand

other wildlife. Explore also the arroyo riparian trees; they shelter migratory and resident songbirds. Scan the ground for quail and the refuge's abundant reptilian life forms.

The rock tanks of the Tinajas Altas range (off the range on adjoining BLM lands along the Camino del Diablo) are a good spot to seek wildlife, too.

■ **PHOTOGRAPHY:** A drive along the Charlie Bell Pass Rd. provides views of a terrific variety of land forms, scenic views, flora and fauna, including close-up shots of Child's Mountain and the Growler Mountains, vistas of desert valleys and distant sawtoothed ranges, stands of saguaro combed by waving ocotillo, snakes, lizards, blooming cactus, and, in March, Anna's hummingbirds resting in the yellow bowers of a palo verde.

HUNTING Hunting is limited to five to seven **bighorn** permits issued each year.

■ **SEASONAL EVENTS:** Dec. to March: Evening lecture series at Visitor Center. Refuge guided tours, periodically.

■ **PUBLICATIONS:** Species lists: birds, mammals, amphibians and reptiles, and flora; brochure.

Cibola NWR
Cibola, Arizona

Refuge landscape, Cibola NWR

Large marshes and farm fields are fed by waters drawn from the Colorado River at Cibola NWR. Abundant flocks of ducks, geese, and sandhill cranes are drawn to the refuge by warm winters and abundant food crops; their vociferous calls, honks, and furious wingbeats fill the air. Out on the valley's desert fringes, you might see other wildlife in action, perhaps a roadrunner chasing down a chuckwalla.

HISTORY

Cibola refuge was created in 1964 to mitigate the effects on wildlife of dam construction and channelization projects on the Colorado River. Today it provides important wintering grounds for migratory waterfowl and other resident wildlife. Encompassing 17,267 acres, Cibola has an annual visitation of around 50,000, almost all in winter.

GETTING THERE

Cibola is located on the Arizona-California border 17 mi. south of Blythe, California. To get there take I-10 west 4 mi. and exit south onto Neighbor's Blvd. (CA 78), which crosses the Colorado River on Cibola Bridge. Follow refuge signs 3.5 mi. to the Visitor Center. The Visitor Center is also accessible via a long dirt road (Cibola Rd.) from the Arizona side off US 95. Lands on the west side of the Colorado River are accessible from CA 78.

■ **SEASON:** Open year-round.
■ **HOURS:** Refuge open dawn to dusk. Visitor Center open weekdays 8 a.m.–4:30 p.m.
■ **FEES:** Free entry.
■ **ADDRESS:** Rte. 2, Box 138, Cibola, AZ 85328-9801
■ **TELEPHONE:** 520/857-3253

TOURING CIBOLA

■ **BY AUTOMOBILE:** A 3-mile auto-tour route, Goose Loop, gives exposure to the Arizona side of the refuge, near the Visitor Center. The one-way route runs through farm fields favored by many waterfowl, cranes, and other wildlife in winter. Its final 0.25 mile parallels a water channel that attracts wading birds. On this road, people are required to stay in or close by their vehicles to avoid spooking the wildlife. You may also drive the refuge's extensive system of gravel roads, open to the public.

■ **BY FOOT:** The refuge recently converted 34 acres of agricultural land to native flora. A 1-mile footpath begins in upland mesquite brush, then descends into riparian willow and cottonwood woodlands to an observation tower overlooking a 20-acre pond where thousands of ducks, geese, and sandhill cranes winter. The trailhead is located along Goose Loop Drive, which is an auto-tour route only and not open to foot traffic. Most of the other public roads, however, are open to foot traffic. Several areas are closed to all public entry.

■ **BY BICYCLE:** Biking is allowed on all the public roads except Goose Loop.

■ **BY CANOE, KAYAK, OR BOAT:** Canoes, kayaks, and motorized boats are permitted on the Old River Channel, Pretty Water, Three-Finger Lake, the main Colorado River channel, and Cibola Lake (on the latter, March 15 through Labor Day, only). Nonmotorized boats may use Hart Mine Marsh from 10 a.m. to 3 p.m. daily during hunting season. All backwaters (all bodies of water other than the main Colorado River channel) are no-wake zones.

WHAT TO SEE

■ **LANDSCAPE AND CLIMATE** Situated in the historic floodplain of the Colorado River, Cibola refuge is predominately flat river bottomland fringed by low desert ridges cut by washes. The dredged river channel bisects the refuge, flanked on the west by the river channel, and 2,300 acres of wetlands, ponds, and lakes. The largest water body here is 600-acre Cibola Lake.

One-third of the refuge lies in California, the remainder in Arizona. Spanning a 12-mile section of the river, Cibola abuts Imperial NWR on its south border.

Snowy egret, Cibola NWR.

This is Sonoran Desert (at its northwesternmost limit), with a hot and dry climate, scant rainfall (only 3 to 5 inches on average), and temperatures exceeding 90 degrees for seven months. Winter days, however, are pleasant.

■ PLANT LIFE

Wetlands Growing in the refuge's extensive wetlands along the river, ponds, and lakes are cattail, bulrush, and various sedges.

Forests Also on the river bottomlands but on slightly higher ground are vast areas covered by honey and screwbean mesquite (see sidebar, Brazoria NWR) and tamarisk (see sidebar, Bosque del Apache NWR), an invasive tree that has taken over large swaths of land in the Southwest, crowding out the native cottonwoods and willows. Refuge staff are busy rolling back the tide of tamarisk by planting "reveg" plots with native flora. At ground level here you will find abundant arrowweed.

Arid lands The 785 acres or so of raised desert uplands flanking the valley floor are home to their own flora. Common plants include such desert stalwarts as creosote (see sidebar, Bitter Lake NWR), quailbush, and various cacti.

Farmlands Domestic crops, including corn, milo, millet, wheat, and alfalfa, plus native food stocks, such as grasses and aquatic plants grown on flooded sectors, are planted on 1,600 acres at Cibola for wildlife. Goose Loop drive rolls through one of these farm units.

■ ANIMAL LIFE

Birds Cibola is an important wintering area for waterfowl, in particular Canada geese and greater sandhill cranes. The geese spend summers in southern Canada, on the Great Salt Lake of Utah, and in Idaho, Montana, and Wyoming. The Great Basin subspecies frequenting Cibola is among the largest of its kind, standing 2 feet high and weighing up to 10 pounds. These birds have dark gray heads and necks, with a white throat patch. They love alfalfa, eating about a pound of green fodder a day. Peak concentrations of geese—15,000 to 20,000 birds—arrive in December and January, along with about 1,500 sandhill cranes.

Northern shoveler

The riparian zones are also home to many types of ducks, particularly mallards, northern pintails, northern shovelers, gadwall, bufflehead, common mergansers, and green-winged and cinnamon teal. The duck families reach peak concentrations in fall and winter, although some species are found here year-round.

The wetlands attract wading and shorebirds as well. Sora rails, common moorhens, least bitterns, snowy egrets, and great blue, night, and green herons all nest here and are present year-round. Avocets, stilts, plovers, and 14 species of sandpipers, phalaropes, and allies also stop over. Most abundant are spotted and least sandpipers and long-billed dowitchers. Take a walk by the marshes and you will hear many chattering red-winged and yellow-headed blackbirds.

In the fields on Goose Loop look for western meadowlarks, brown-headed

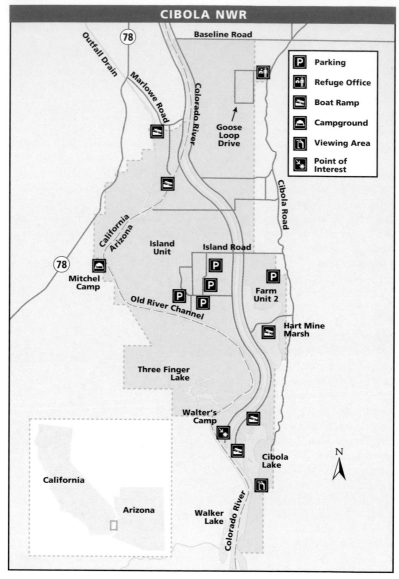

cowbirds, and northern mockingbirds. Meadowlarks have one of the more distinctive voices of any western bird: 7 to 10 gurgling notes, a *chupp* sound. This is a plump, 9-inch bird, brown with white tail patches in flight; it has a bright yellow breast with a black V across it. The mockingbird is shaped like a robin but is largely gray and displays prominent white wing patches in flight.

The desert fringes are home to white-winged dove, phainopepla, and greater roadrunner, among others. Spring and fall bring such migrant neotropical songbirds as western wood-pewee, Pacific-slope flycatcher, and lark sparrow; nesters include Lucy's warbler and the common yellowthroat.

A handful of endangered or threatened bird species appears at Cibola refuge at various times of the year, including the Southwest willow flycatcher, brown pelican, peregrine falcon, bald eagle, and Yuma clapper rail (this one favors cattail marshes and is extremely difficult to see). Birders will be impressed to know that, altogether, 249 species of birds have been recorded here at Cibola NWR.

Mammals Mule deer, coyote, bobcat, and rabbit are the mammals visitors are most likely to see on Cibola refuge.

Reptiles and amphibians Two turtle species, the wetlands-loving spiny softshell and the upland desert tortoise, reside here, along with 13 kinds of lizards, 6 toads and frogs, and 15 types of snakes, including 3 varieties of rattlesnake—the western diamondback, sidewinder, and Mojave. The Mojave is a large rattler that measures up to 4 feet long; it is distinguished by a diamond pattern and black rings on a white base around its tail (quite similar to the western diamondback). It's handsome to admire—from a respectful distance.

ACTIVITIES

■ **CAMPING:** Camping is not allowed on Cibola refuge.

■ **SWIMMING:** Swimming is permitted, but not encouraged, in the swift waters of the main river channel.

■ **WILDLIFE OBSERVATION:** Goose Loop provides excellent opportunities to watch wildlife at Cibola, because both birds and mammals are drawn to its dry and flooded farm fields in the day to feed; those you're most likely to spot include sandhill cranes, ducks, geese, and wading and shorebirds. The cranes—tall gray birds—prefer the corn and milo fields. Along the way, look to the dense stands of salt cedar, where meadowlarks, sparrows, flycatchers, and shrikes perch and seek cover. Keep an eye out, too, for kestrels hunting insects over the fields or perching on power lines. You might also see burrowing owls standing outside their burrows. An observation tower overlooks a portion of a farm unit located near the Visitor Center.

Serious birders will also want to explore three sites: the island unit (between old and new river channels—continue south past Visitor Center 4.2 miles and turn west/right); Cibola Lake (east bank of the Colorado River on the refuge's southern sector, another 5 miles or so south of Island Unit Rd.); and Three-Finger Lake (west bank of Colorado River). There is an observation point for views over Cibola Lake on the lake's south end. Drive the levee road until it veers away from the river, then follow it east for about .125 mile. Waterfowl, pelicans, and bald eagles are regularly seen from this high overlook.

You can also drive the upper and lower levee roads paralleling both Colorado River banks. Hart Mine Marsh is another prime place for spotting various birds and other wildlife (south of Island Unit Rd., on east bank of Colorado River).

Certain sections of the refuge are closed periodically to provide undisturbed waterfowl roosting areas. Check with staff about birding outside of Goose Loop. With all these options, be sure to pick up a refuge map before you go exploring.

■ **SEASONAL EVENTS:** Slide presentations, and guided tours of the Goose Loop are conducted in winter.

■ **PUBLICATIONS:** Brochure, bird list, reptile and amphibian list, auto-tour leaflet.

HUNTING AND FISHING Large- and **smallmouth bass, striped bass, channel catfish, crappie, sunfish**, and **tilapia** are all taken by anglers here. Boat ramps are found at Cibola Lake and Three Fingers Lake (no access to main river). A river boat ramp is located nearby on BLM land. Hunters stalk **mule deer, waterfowl, dove, rabbit**, and **quail**.

Havasu NWR
Lake Havasu City, Arizona, and Needles, California

Lake Havasu, along the border between California and Arizona

Water recreation is the big draw at Havasu NWR. Some 500,000 people come annually to boat, swim, and fish in Lake Havasu, the star and centerpiece of the refuge. But nature lovers will discover another, equally entrancing Havasu NWR. Look for the sunset spectacle of thousands of teal banking in the air or the last rays of light bathing the spires of the Needles in a warm red glow. Spot a kit fox emerging from its den in the rugged desert uplands, its large ears straining to detect the patter of mouse feet across the sands; see a desert bighorn commanding Topock Gorge high above the banks of the Colorado River.

HISTORY

The canyons of the Colorado River south of today's I-40 have a long human history, having seen periodic prehistoric and historic inhabitation, as attested by petroglyphs found at Picture Rock in Topock Gorge and at other sites and by relics of the 1800s mining era. In 1941, to mitigate environmental damage caused by series of dams and huge reservoirs along the lower Colorado River, a vast wildlife refuge was established encircling Lake Havasu and lands just above the lake. The name of the lake and refuge is believed to derive from an Indian term meaning "blue-green waters." Over the years various pieces were split off from the refuge for state parks, Lake Havasu City, and other uses—including creation of Bill Williams River NWR in 1991. Today Havasu NWR encompasses 37,515 acres. As an extremely popular spot for water recreation—in particular its southern sector near Lake Havasu City—the refuge entertains some 500,000 visitors a year.

GETTING THERE

Havasu refuge is strung along the Colorado River for 28 mi. between Needles, California, and Lake Havasu City, Arizona. Both its northern sector, which includes the popular birding area Topock Marsh, and its southern sector can be accessed by car. Its central section (Topock Gorge/ Needles Wilderness) is accessible only on foot or by boat.

To reach Topock Marsh, take Exit 1 off I-40 on the east bank of the Colorado River and proceed north on old Rt. 66. Sideroads branch off to access New South Dike and Catfish Paradise. Just south of the community of Golden Shores at an intersection where Rt. 66 continues north toward Oatman, bear left to reach 5 Mile Landing and Pintail Slough. Another part of the northern marsh sector—a farming unit on the refuge's west side—is reached from Needles (see "Touring" below).

The southern sector, including its popular Mesquite Bay and Castle Rock water recreation areas, is accessed via London Bridge Rd. off AZ 95 just north of Lake Havasu City.

White pelican

■ **SEASON:** Open year-round.

■ **HOURS:** Refuge open dawn to dusk; office open weekdays, 7 a.m.–3:30 p.m. in winter; 7:30 a.m.–4 p.m. otherwise.

■ **FEES:** Free entry.

■ **ADDRESS:** P.O. Box 3009, 317 Mesquite Ave., Needles, CA 92363

■ **TELEPHONE:** 760/326-3853

TOURING HAVASU

■ **BY AUTOMOBILE:** The east side of Topock Marsh is reached via automobile as described above in "Getting There." In addition, a gravel/dirt road winds 7 to 8 miles along the marsh's western edge to a large farm unit, Topock Farm. From Needles, cross over the Colorado River on K St., turn right at the second street (Levy Way), and at the T-intersection turn right onto Barrackman. Follow it until the pavement ends, then proceed 2 miles to the refuge boundary and continue south to the farm unit. You can continue on down this road several more miles until you reach a closure chain.

■ **BY FOOT:** A 4-mile loop begins and ends at the farm unit described above. Visitors can also hike along the dikes and levees throughout the refuge. The Needles/ Havasu Wilderness Areas are open exclusively to hikers, but their extremely rugged terrain and isolation should not be tackled without thorough preparation.

■ **BY BICYCLE:** All the refuge's public roads are open to mountain biking.

■ **BY CANOE, KAYAK, OR BOAT:** One of western Arizona's prime adventures is a float trip through Havasu's Topock Gorge in April, May, or early fall. The daylong, 16-mile outing begins in Topock Bay, just north of the I-40 bridge crossing of the Colorado and ends at Castle Rock. Commercial boat rentals (including drop-off and pick-up) are available. Make advance inquiries through the Visitor Center. Be aware of upriver motorized traffic. Canoes, kayaks, and no-wake boats are also allowed on Topock Marsh. A small area is always closed Oct. 1 to Jan. 31 to decrease disturbance to birds, and other areas are subject to seasonal closure. Inquire at Visitor Center. Boat ramps at Catfish Paradise, 5 Mile Landing, and North Dike.

WHAT TO SEE

■ **LANDSCAPE AND CLIMATE** Havasu National Wildlife Refuge is a three-headed entity. Spanning the Colorado River on the Arizona-California border, its northern section is composed of a flooded flat marshland, Topock Marsh—a 4,000-acre mosaic of ponds, lakes, and marsh fed by an extensive system of water diversion channels. Surrounding these wetlands are 5,000 acres of forested flats and farm fields.

The middle ground is dominated by Topock Gorge on the Colorado River, flanked on the Arizona side by Needles Wilderness Area and on the California side by Havasu Wilderness Area, a total of about 30,000 acres. Here, rugged desert mountains dominate, capped by the Needles, the dramatically sharp volcanic spires that gave a name to the California town just northwest and to the surrounding wilderness area.

In the southern sector, Topock Canyon broadens into a wide valley just north of the booming community of Lake Havasu City, a popular water recreation area packed with boaters throughout the summer.

Winter lows dip to just below freezing on occasion, while summer highs have hit a stunning 128 degrees. Rainfall is scant, averaging 4 inches annually, half coming in intense summer thunderstorms and half in gentle winter rains.

■ **PLANT LIFE** More than 200 plants make their home in the varied biomes of Havasu, including an amazing 43 members of the sunflower clan—from the Mojave aster to rabbitbrush.

Wetlands Huge expanses of cattail and alkali and American great bulrush dominate the wetlands of Topock Marsh. They grow so profusely that refuge staff must periodically burn off or otherwise retard their spread to maintain open waters within the marshes. At the edges of the marshes are a variety of sedges, from purple nut to yellow nut to spike, and various rushes. All of these are considered emergent plants—that is, emerging from water.

Forests The woodlands found on the valley floor at Topock Marsh are not

forests in the usual sense—a better description would be thickets. These are dominated by dense stands of invasive salt cedar (see sidebar in Bosque del Apache NWR). Mixed in with the vast tracts of tamarisk are occasional Fremont cottonwood and Goodding willow trees, original riparian trees of the Colorado River valleys that are almost entirely absent from the area today. The refuge has an active revegetation program, raising tree seedlings in its plant nursery at Topock Farm. Biologist Matt Connolly is experimenting with generating multiple tree shoots from single willow and cottonwood branches laid horizontally on the ground and covered with dirt, which, if successful, will greatly increase restoration efforts.

Great blue heron

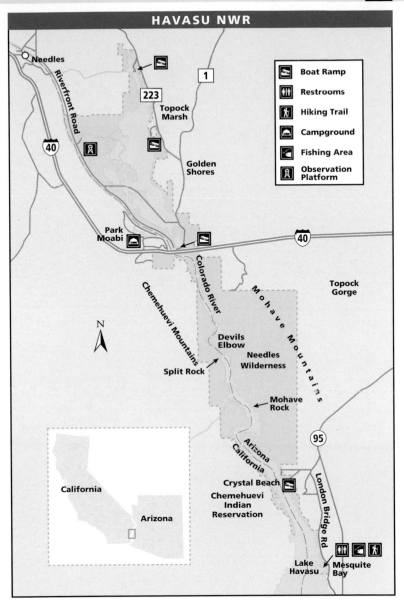

HAVASU NWR

Needles
Riverfront Road
223
1
Topock Marsh
40
Golden Shores

Legend:
- Boat Ramp
- Restrooms
- Hiking Trail
- Campground
- Fishing Area
- Observation Platform

Park Moabi
40
Colorado River
Topock Gorge
Chemehuevi Mountains
Mohave Mountains
N
Devils Elbow
Needles Wilderness
Split Rock
Mohave Rock
Arizona
California
95
Crystal Beach
Chemehuevi Indian Reservation
California
Arizona
London Bridge Rd
Lake Havasu
Mesquite Bay

Arid lands The refuge's mountainous midsection, Topock Gorge and the flanking Needles and Havasu Wilderness Area, are dominated by upland desert flora. Located at the overlapping edges of the Sonoran and Mojave Deserts, these arid places support barrel and beavertail cactus, palo verde trees, brittlebush (producing a brilliant yellow flower in March and April), and catclaw acacia. The latter is a shrublike tree growing to 10 feet in height with small olive-green leaves and an abundance of small curved spines, giving rise to its nickname, the "wait-a-minute bush." As in *Wait a minute* —before you try to pet this cat!

Farmlands To provide food for waterfowl, the refuge maintains a 210-acre farm

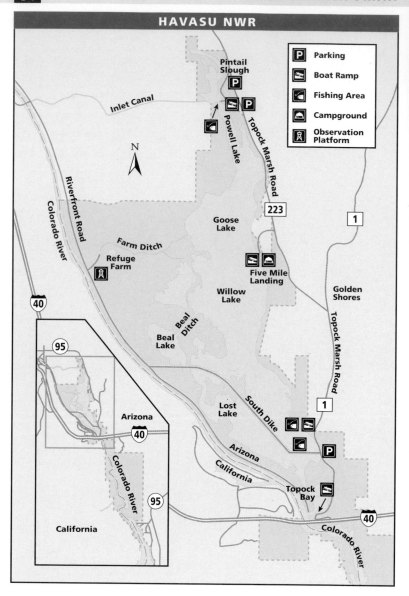

HAVASU NWR

in Topock Marsh, where Bermuda grass is grown for geese, and some moist-soil units, where native foodstocks are raised.

■ ANIMAL LIFE

Birds Havasu's marshes and associated woodlands, river canyon, and desert terrain have been good to birds and bird lovers: Of the 297 species of birds found here, 81 are nesters. Perhaps most prominent are winter concentrations of waterfowl, wading, and shorebirds. A dazzling 27 species of ducks, geese, and swans come to Havasu, including the magnificent tundra swan visiting here in fall and winter.

An early-spring drive around the Topock Marsh, on both sides of the river, can turn up blue-winged teal, cinnamon teal, eared and Clark's grebes, black-crowned herons, white pelican, and white-faced ibis. A short excursion to Teal Slough may give you sights of killdeer, western sandpiper, long-billed dowitchers, cinnamon teal, barn swallows, and great blue herons. This heron is a remarkable creature: a tall wader (more than 4 feet) with long yellow legs, a bluish-gray body, and a white head topped by a rakish black pompadour. Great blues do not like to be disturbed and will croak at you if they feel uneasy. Northern harriers skim low over fields and marsh, hovering delicately, while red-tailed hawks can be spotted throughout the refuge year-round.

In spring or fall as many as 10,000 white pelicans may descend on Topock Marsh, settling down in its lakes like a miniature navy. Present year-round are red-winged blackbirds, singing loudly from perches on cattail stalks, and marsh wrens. Bald eagles show up occasionally in autumn.

The marsh also provides shelter for two endangered birds, the Yuma clapper rail and the southwestern willow flycatcher. A small gray-green riparian-loving bird, the willow flycatcher has confounded ornithologists by nesting in the extensive tamarisk thickets infesting Topock Marsh. They normally set up housekeeping only in dense willow groves, a habitat that has undergone dramatic declines in the Southwest over the past century, contributing to the parallel decline of the bird. Some 25 pairs nested at Havasu in 1999, perhaps the largest group left in the wild.

In the drylands flanking the marshes, expect sightings of both mourning doves and the less common Inca dove. The Inca has reddish wing ends in flight and white edging on its tail, and it calls with a monotonous *coo-hoo* or *no-hope*. Also in the shrub near the marshes you can easily spot plentiful loggerhead shrikes and northern mockingbirds with their flashy black and white flight coloration.

Lastly, inhabiting the refuge's desert terrain year-round are Gila woodpeckers and greater roadrunners.

Mammals Among the refuge's 46 mammal species is a stable herd of desert bighorn sheep in the Topock Gorge area. Present but much less likely to be seen are bobcat, coyote, and kit fox, which feed on cottontail and black-tailed jack rabbits. Various mice and packrats are common here.

Reptiles and amphibians Havasu's desert lands hold some 39 species of reptiles, including the western diamondback rattlesnake, also found in Topock Marsh. You may spot a coach whip (red racer), a slender pinkish snake growing to more than 4 feet. While not poisonous, red racers are extremely aggressive, going so far as chase people! If handled, they won't hesitate to bite. The common wetlands toad is the green toad, which is actually colored mostly brown with green mottling.

Western diamondback rattlesnake, tongue extended

ACTIVITIES

■ **CAMPING:** Camping is allowed at select locations within Topock Gorge. Dispersed primitive camping is also permitted within the Needles Wilderness Area (but not within 1 mile of the river). Commercial campgrounds are located in Golden Shores near Topock Marsh. Park Moabi Campground is just off I-40 on the west side of the Colorado River.

■ **SWIMMING:** Swimming is most often pursued in Lake Havasu off Mesquite Bay and the Castle Rock area, as are skin- and scuba-diving.

■ **WILDLIFE OBSERVATION:** An observation tower on Topock Farm unit provides good views of feeding wildlife. Another tower, on the Levee Rd. south of the farm, overlooks Beal Lake. Two pairs of nesting great horned owls can be viewed at 5 Mile Landing in the massive old salt cedar trees. These owls are over 2 feet tall with prominent eartufts. Males emit five or six resonant hoots: *Hoo!, hu-hu-hu, Hoo! Hoo!*

Walking out on New South Dike offers good birding possibilities, with cottonwood and willows attracting passerine songbirds and shallow marshes drawing waterfowl and grebes.

HUNTING AND FISHING Sport fishing is permitted in all waters open to the public except those designated by sign or barrier as closed. A fishing dock is located at Catfish Paradise on the east side of Topock Marsh, as well as a boat ramp. Another boat ramp is found at 5 Mile Landing. A section of Mesquite Bay, in the refuge's southern sector, off AZ 95, is closed to boating and so has good bank fishing, including a handicapped area (and a restroom).

Hunting for **waterfowl**, **quail**, **mourning dove**, **cottontail rabbit**, and **desert bighorn sheep** (the latter by drawing) is allowed on specific days and times in select areas of Topock Marsh, along the Colorado River. Contact the refuge for details.

If you're boating through Topock Gorge, keep an eye peeled for the nesting peregrines at the Devil's Elbow, the 45 to 50 desert bighorn sheep often spotted above the Devil's Bend, and the nesting Clark's grebe along the water's edge.

■ **PHOTOGRAPHY:** Outstanding shots of the spires in the Needles Wilderness Area can be taken at sunset from the Colorado River Bridge or from east of the refuge off I-40 at daybreak. The roads about Topock Marsh offer excellent scenes of marshes and associated wildlife. Boating through Topock Gorge leads to both wildlife and landscape images well worth the voyage.

■ **HIKES AND WALKS:** A 4-mile birding trail is under construction near Topock Farm. In addition, visitors are allowed to walk all the roads open to the public, as well as throughout the two wilderness areas.

■ **SEASONAL EVENTS:** The refuge has hosted an annual Coot Festival in the early spring in the past. The purpose of the festival was to increase public awareness about the refuge; coots, the honoree, was chosen because literally thousands of these ducklike birds descend on the refuge in the spring. Call in advance for confirmation of an upcoming Coot Festival.

■ **PUBLICATIONS:** Brochure, bird and plant lists, several guides for boating Topock Gorge.

Imperial NWR
Yuma, Arizona

Refuge wetland, Imperial NWR

Although tamed in an engineering sense, the mighty Colorado River still flows powerfully inside rough canyon walls at Imperial NWR, emerging in shallow basins dotted with pocket marshes and wetlands. Here, clouds of waterfowl gather in winter, enjoying the warm, clear weather and abundant food stocks. A few feet above waterline, the desiccated landscape rolls and breaks toward stony peaks, and earthen badlands painted in pastels shimmer in the heat.

HISTORY

The prehistoric record at Imperial is extensive. Many archeological sites, some containing petroglyphs, are scattered about the refuge, but none is easily accessible. The mighty Colorado River served as a trade conduit for many centuries before modern human occupation, in spite of periodic violent flooding. Flooding was controlled in the 20th century with the construction of a series of upstream dams.

Established in 1941, Imperial NWR takes its name from nearby (downstream) Imperial Dam, an irrigation structure erected in 1937. The refuge covers 25,125 acres. Its southerly location makes it a popular destination for sun-seeking "snowbirds"; some 30,000 people visit in winter. In summer visitors come to pursue water sports.

GETTING THERE

This is extreme southwestern Arizona. From Yuma, head north on US 95 for 22.5 mi., passing the Yuma Proving Grounds artillery display. Continue 2.5 mi. farther north on US 95, turn west (left) onto Martinez Lake Rd., and proceed 10 mi. to Martinez Lake. Look for the refuge sign on your right and follow this gravel road 3.5 mi. to the Visitor Center.
■ **SEASON:** Open year-round.
■ **HOURS:** Refuge open 24 hours daily. Visitor Center open year-round, week-

days 7:30 a.m.–4 p.m. (toilets open 24 hrs.), and weekends Nov. 15 to March 31 from 9 a.m.–4 p.m.
■ **FEES:** Free entry.
■ **ADDRESS:** Martinez Lake, P.O. Box 72217, Yuma, AZ 85365
■ **TELEPHONE:** 520/783-3371
■ **VISITOR CENTER:** Good facility with new exhibitions, screened picnic area, nature bookstore.

TOURING IMPERIAL

BY AUTOMOBILE: A gravel road (Red Cloud Mine Rd.) runs 6 miles from the Visitor Center to a refuge boundary. Branching off this road are four scenic overlook points above the Colorado River: Palo Verde Pt. at 1.3 miles, Mesquite at 2.2 miles, Ironwood Pt. at 3.1 miles, and Smoke Tree Pt. at 4.2 miles. Ordinary vehicles can travel as far as Ironwood Point; beyond that, a high-clearance, 4-wheel-drive vehicle is recommended. Red Cloud Mine Rd. continues north out of the refuge across the Yuma Proving Ground and BLM land to dead end at the boundary of the refuge's northernmost wilderness section. Another road from the Visitor Center runs a short distance down to the river to Meers Point and a boat launching area.
■ **BY FOOT:** Almost all of Imperial refuge is open to hikers (farm units are closed), but there is only one designated footpath, Painted Desert Trail. It winds through the refuge's harsh but fascinating desert uplands.

HORNED LIZARD A favorite discovery of children growing up in the hot sandy wastes of the Southwest was the "hornytoad," a fierce-looking critter resembling a miniature dinosaur. This three-to-seven-inch-long reptile would flatten itself out and puff up with air, causing its sawtoothed backbone, head horns, and short body spines to stand at attention. Still, its belly skin was very soft in the hand, and most children didn't fear it. The highlight of every encounter occurred when the hornytoad had exhausted all visual defenses and would spurt a bit of blood out of its eyes. That always won a quick release!

With body coloration almost always perfectly matched to the local ground's predominant color, these lizards can be tough to spot. Their favorite food is ants, and often a darting movement to snap up a snack is the only thing that gives their presence away.

Found in deserts, grasslands, shrublands, and dry woodlands from Arkansas to California and British Columbia to Guatemala, the 14 hornytoad species are a common (though declining) denizen of the region and one of its more interesting inhabitants.

■ **BY BICYCLE:** Biking is restricted to the refuge's public roads.
■ **BY CANOE, KAYAK, OR BOAT:** Because the Colorado River is a navigable waterway, both power boats and self-propelled watercraft are allowed here. The marshy backwaters, however, are no-wake zones. A commercial company, Yuma River Tours (520/783-4400), conducts guided wildlife tours by boat. Martinez Lake Resort (520/783-9589) rents canoes and will deliver them and you to the upstream edge of the refuge, allowing an easy downriver paddle or multiday outings.

WHAT TO SEE

■ **LANDSCAPE AND CLIMATE** The Colorado River flows through the refuge from north to south in a narrow canyon, and any green vegetation is limited to a band paralleling the river. Move a few feet up in elevation, and the desert

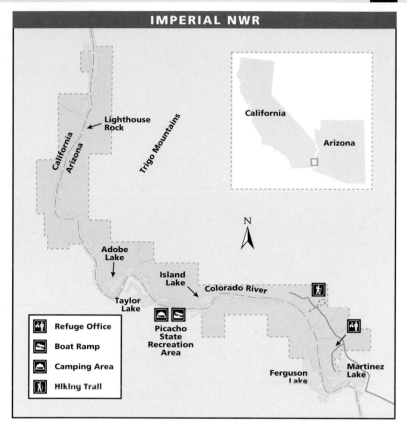

takes over. It is a truly parched landscape, where the shape and color of bare rock dominate.

At Imperial, large patches of "desert pavement"—areas of ground covered with a layer of small rocks and pebbles—support little or no vegetation. You may also notice odd curving or straight lines crisscrossing this pavement. These are pathways created by the refuge's many wild burros.

The jagged Chocolate Mountains rise along the west bank; the color of these peaks ranges from brown to a purple haze. To the north, on the east bank, are the Trigos, while lower foothills flank the refuge's eastern boundary. Rock, rock, and more rock in all colors and hues: pink, lavender, black, tan, and red. It's as if the world has just been formed and its palette of earthen colors were still young and forming.

The refuge, designed to protect the riverine environment and adjoining lands, is linear in shape, running 30 miles north to south but only a handful of miles east to west. You're in Arizona on the river's eastern bank; California, on the western bank. Waters backed up behind Imperial Dam have spilled into lowland basins at various points flanking the river, creating a series of large ponds and marshes running 30 miles upstream. These ponds range in size from a half-acre to more than 700 acres.

Low elevation, the Sonoran Desert habitat, and the southerly locale combine to produce intense heat at Imperial. Expect temperatures to exceed 90 degrees from mid-April through Oct., with truly hot days topping 120 degrees!

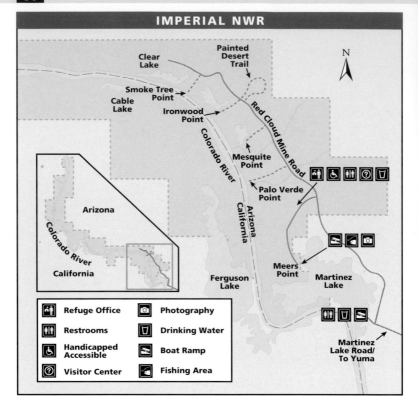

IMPERIAL NWR

■ PLANT LIFE

Marshes Refuge marshes along the edges of the Colorado River and its floodbasins cover a large area and provide critical habitat for wildlife cover, reproduction, resting, and feeding. Growing right at the water's edge are cattail, three-square bulrush, river bulrush, arrowweed, and phragmites.

On slightly raised ground, Fremont cottonwoods (see sidebar, Bill Williams NWR) and Goodding willow are found, isolated in large expanses of salt cedar (see Tamarisk sidebar, Bosque del Apache NWR). Refuge staff is actively clearing the invasive salt cedar and replanting with native cottonwood and willow, but reversing this situation will take a Herculean effort.

Arid lands Some 68 percent of Imperial refuge is classified as desert uplands, and so its predominant vegetation is of Sonoran Desert lineage. However, this portion of the Sonoran Desert is much drier than that in central and eastern Arizona, and vegetation is far sparser. The primary bush here is creosote (see sidebar, Bitter Lake NWR), growing alongside the spindly ocotillo, brittlebush (a low plant covered with brilliant yellow flowers in early spring), and various cacti. A common cacti is the beavertail, which has fleshy green pads that do indeed look like a beaver's tail. From March through June, hot pink flowers adorn the beaver's tail, ripening into fruits favored by wildlife and making a tasty jelly.

Low trees—most often screwbean and honey mesquite, or ironwood—dot the arroyo floors. When winter and spring rains come, wildflower blooms in the desert uplands can be remarkable. Along the Painted Desert Trail, look for scorpion weed (purple), evening primrose (yellow), and chuparosa (red-orange).

Farmlands The refuge also has 360 acres or so in farm production, growing sedges, rushes, millet, wheat, and barley for wildlife consumption. The farm unit is off-limits to the public.

■ ANIMAL LIFE

Birds Imperial's southerly latitude and wetlands draw some sandhill cranes and large numbers of waterfowl during the winter, in particular Canada geese and green-winged and cinnamon teals, northern shoveler, and ruddy ducks. The ruddy, with its cinnamon back, white cheek patch, black head, and blue beak, is easily distinguished. Note, too, its stiff, upright tail. In flight the ruddy's feathers make a buzzing sound.

A wide variety of wading birds and shorebirds is also present (many year-round; others, in all but hottest summer), including great blue heron, dowitchers, yellowlegs, sandpiper, black-necked stilts, white-faced ibis, avocets, various egrets, American coots, and American white pelican.

Say's phoebes are seen at Imperial in every season but summer; black phoebes are present year-round among the refuge's 16 species of flycatchers. This is also a fine place to scope out hummingbirds in winter, with Anna's, black-chinned, and Costa's all on the scene. Look in the uplands for these smaller birds.

The desert uplands support other species, including the frequently spotted Gambel's quail, phainopepla, greater roadrunner, and verdin. The verdin is a small (4 inches) and predominantly gray bird, best distinguished by its bright yellow head. Roadrunners rely on their blazing foot speed to evade predators and capture prey. The roadrunner can easily chase down lizards and will also take on rattlesnakes, jumping into the air to avoid their strikes until the snakes are exhausted and defenseless. Then they use their formidable peaks to seize their prey.

Gambel's quail

Other common refuge birds include the marsh wren, crissal thrasher, loggerhead shrike, and northern rough-winged swallow. Look for swallows dipping and darting over the river or in canyons, where they feed on concentrations of small insects.

Raptors are also plentiful at Imperial. The river attracts bald eagle, osprey, and, most commonly, northern harriers, and desert uplands are home to red-tailed hawk, Harrris's hawk, and a rare peregrine falcon or two.

Spring and fall migrations also bring songbirds through the refuge, including the blue grosbeak with its dull blue color and two contrasting reddish-tan wing bars.

Hardcore birders also enjoy the challenge of spotting a southwestern willow flycatcher or a Yuma clapper rail here. Both are endangered species. The rails hide in the dense cattail marshes and are most often recognized by their voices (a clattering *kek-kek-kek-kek* or *cha-cha-cha* than by sight. The California black rail, a species of concern, is found in bulrush patches. All told, some 271 bird species have been recorded at Imperial to date.

Mammals The refuge's highest-profile mammals—500 to 600 wild, or feral, burros—are, paradoxically, unwelcome inhabitants. These hardy animals are descended from domestic burros that were lost or abandoned in the area. They are reproducing so successfully that their browsing on trees and other vegetation has a deleterious effect on the refuge's natural ecosystem.

Imperial hosts a healthy population of desert bighorn sheep that favors the refuge's rough, mountainous terrain. Also spotted frequently is coyote (see sidebar, Ash Meadows NWR). A black-tailed jackrabbit or cottontail will frequently bound away through the desert scrub.

Reptiles and amphibians Reptiles thrive in the desert environment. Among the refuge's many species are desert tortoise, zebra-tailed lizard, chuckwalla, desert iguana, and Western whiptail lizards. The whiptail is an 8- to 12-in. slender lizard with a light tan/gray body and faint-to-distinct stripes and dots, and gray-green tail. Out and about from April to Oct. in daylight, they are especially active during the April mating season and are often seen on the Painted Desert Trail.

Western whiptail lizard

Fish The Colorado River and its associated marshes provide refuge for a number of endangered swimmers, including razorback sucker and bonytail chub. Refuge staff is creating a pond system free of nonnative fish to better care for the native species, which are often outcompeted physically by introduced fish species.

ACTIVITIES

■ **CAMPING:** Camping is not allowed on Imperial refuge, but just outside its western boundary, on the west side of the river in California, there is camping at Picacho State Recreation Area.

■ **WILDLIFE OBSERVATION:** The observation tower adjacent to the Visitor Center, open during daylight hours, provides a good view of the farm/moist soil units, a favorite feeding area for cranes, waterfowl, and wading birds in winter.

A short, unnamed trail runs across a raised dike from Mesquite Point through dense riparian vegetation to the Colorado River, providing the refuge's only on-river access other than by boat or the boat ramp at Meers Point. Many birds can be observed in the vegetation flanking the dike and river's edge.

Odd as it sounds, the best place to see desert bighorn sheep is from the waters of the Colorado River. Boaters often spot them on the hills flanking the river in the Smoke Tree area upstream from the Visitor Center. Sheep are also seen occasionally from the summit of the Painted Desert Trail on the cliffs to the east.

Good places to spot lizards and snakes are in the sandy washes along the Painted Desert Trail or other more isolated arroyos and rock outcroppings. The Palo Verde Trail provides good duck viewing.

■ **PHOTOGRAPHY:** A river outing provides a unique vantage point for photography at this refuge. Prime subjects include marsh scenes, river cliffs, and birdlife. Be sure to walk the Painted Desert Trail for fine shots of the Colorado River Valley, desert landscapes, and flora.

■ **HIKES AND WALKS:** Painted Desert Trail loops 1 mile up a gentle canyon, over a ridge, and back down another canyon, providing a fine backcountry introduction to Imperial's desert upland plants, wildlife, and land-forms—from sandy arroyos to pastel-colored stone stubs and

Blue grosbeak

badlands and jagged cliffs. From the trail's high point, hikers enjoy splendid views of the Colorado River Valley. An interpretive leaflet keyed to markers along the trail is available at the trailhead. Allow an hour for a leisurely walk. The trailhead is located 2.8 miles from the Visitor Center on Red Mine Rd.

There is also a short trail at Mesquite Point running to the Colorado River bank.

■ **BOATING:** Rental boats and other equipment are available from Martinez Lake Resort. There are no dedicated swimming areas, but people do swim off their boats.

■ **PUBLICATIONS:** Bird list, brochure, hiking leaflet.

HUNTING AND FISHING Quail, **rabbit, fox, coyote, mule deer** (archery and firearm seasons), **bighorn sheep, waterfowl,** and **dove** can all be hunted on the refuge.

Bass, crappie, sunfish, and **catfish** are most often taken by anglers. Bank fishing and a boating ramp are located at Meers Point on Lake Martinez, 1 mile from the Visitor Center.

Kofa NWR
Yuma, Arizona

Ocotillo in bloom, Kofa NWR

Rugged volcanic peaks share this sprawling refuge with hot, dry desert valleys. At Kofa NWR palm fronds rustle in the light breeze while hummingbirds dart back and forth over wildflowers blooming profusely from a slot canyon. The range of this landscape is impressive: A visitor staring down a steep cleft in canyon walls can see the desert far below, slanting away to a horizon punctuated by jagged mountain peaks.

HISTORY

Kofa refuge dates from 1939 and ranks as one of the nation's largest federal wildlife areas outside Alaska, spanning 665,400 acres—516,300 of which were designated as federal wilderness land in 1990. "Kofa," an acronym, derives from "King of Arizona Mine," a gold mine operating in the area in the late 1880s. Mineral extraction continued on the refuge until 1974, and several active claims still exist, although no mining is currently pursued. Annual visitation runs 50,000 to 60,000, almost all of it between Oct. and April.

GETTING THERE

Situated between Yuma and Quartzsite, Kofa NWR is located in southwestern Arizona (its southern boundary is 42 miles NE of Yuma). From Yuma, head north on US 95. At mile marker 55, reaching the refuge's southernmost entry road, you may then access the southern Castle Dome region. At mile marker 77, another road leaves US 95 to access the Castle Dome's north side and the King Valley. At mile marker 85.1, you'll find the road to Palm Canyon and the central Kofa Mountains (the access road runs 9 mi. to a parking area). At mile marker 92, reach the access road to the Livingston Hills and north Kofas. The northernmost road off US 95 is at mile marker 95, providing access to Crystal Hill and New Water Mountains.
■ **SEASON:** The refuge is open year-round.

■ **HOURS:** Open 24 hours daily. The office in Yuma is open weekdays 8 a.m.–noon and 1 p.m.–5 p.m.
■ **FEES:** Free entry.
■ **ADDRESS:** 356 W. 1st. St., Yuma, AZ 85364
■ **TELEPHONE:** 520/783-7861
■ **VISITOR CENTER:** No visitor facilities or services of any kind on the refuge.

TOURING KOFA

■ **BY AUTOMOBILE:** No formal auto routes exist at Kofa refuge, but 310 miles of dirt roads crisscross it, allowing auto access to all corners of the refuge. These roads vary—from those suitable for ordinary cars (including all four primary access roads noted above) to bone-jarring four-wheel/high-clearance drive tracks. Inquire for details. US 95 also runs north/south along the property's western border, serving up memorable views of Kofa's mountain ranges.
■ **BY FOOT:** Visitors may walk anywhere on the refuge, but there is only one developed hiking route, Palm Canyon Trail.
■ **BY BICYCLE:** Mountain biking on the refuge roads is allowed, but there is no off-road biking.

WHAT TO SEE

■ **LANDSCAPE AND CLIMATE** Kofa is a gigantic refuge, a roughly rectangular spread running 40 miles north-south and 27 miles east-west. Within these boundaries is an intriguing mixture of extremely rugged desert mountain chains separated by desert valleys. Most prominent are the volcanic spires of the Kofa Mountains, including Signal Peak (4,788 feet), the highest of the refuge's many isolated summits; occasionally it is dusted with snow. Neighboring peaks may be capped with snared wreaths of cloud on a late winter day, while the desert flats some 3,000 feet below bask in warm sunshine. Other refuge mountain ranges include the Palomas, Tank, New Water, and Castle Dome mountains where Castle Dome Peak rises to 3,788 feet.

Chuparosa and its blossoms

Slashing into these ridges and hills are hundreds of narrow, steep-walled canyons. Surface water on Kofa is a rarity, although tiny intermittent streams trickle through the valleys and small springs are scattered beneath the mountains.

Here, at the northwesternmost fringe of the Sonoran Desert and at low elevations, it is no surprise that Kofa broils during the hot summers. Expect temperatures exceeding 90 degrees from April through Oct. and topping 100 on many summer afternoons, with occasional highs hitting 120! Winter freezes are rare, even at the higher elevations; winter days are usually warm with highs in the 60s and 70s, lots of sun, and pleasant conditions.

The little precipitation the refuge receives—an average of 3 to 5 inches a

year—falls during summer thunderstorms or light winter rains.

■ PLANT LIFE

Arid lands Here in the Sonoran
Desert, as at nearby Imperial NWR,
vegetation is rather sparse, and
what is there is adapted to life with
little or no moisture. As elsewhere
in the desert, a widely dispersed
bush is creosote (see sidebar, Bitter
Lake NWR), which you will see frequently growing near the tall, thin
ocotillo and close by brittlebush,
bursage, and other cacti (such as
the most common one here-
abouts, beavertail). Here at their
westernmost limit are saguaro
cactus, barrel cactus, and several
varieties of cholla, including
teddy bear and staghorn. The latter has a branching structure reminiscent of deer or elk antlers,
growing 4 to 6 feet in height.

California fan palms, Kofa NWR

Low trees dot the arroyo floors.
Most often you will see screwbean
and honey mesquite (see sidebar,
Brazoria NWR), the gray-green ironwood, and palo verde.

When winter and spring rains come, blooming desert wildflowers put a lie to
the description of deserts as "barren." Springing forth in brightly colored pockets
of new growth are orange mallow, scorpion weed (purple), evening primrose
(yellow), and chuparosa (red-orange), among others.

Kofa also shelters a remarkable plant called the California fan palm. This is
Arizona's only native palm tree (despite its geographically misplaced name!)
and is found only in a few locales within the refuge, making it extremely rare.
Fan palms are likely remnants of an earlier era when the region was wetter and
cooler than it is now. The primary population—42 trees of varying ages, from
youngsters to mature palms standing 40 to 50 feet high—is located in Palm
Canyon in the Kofa Mountains.

The Kofa Mountain barberry, another rare plant native to southwestern
Arizona, is holly-like with spiky leaves. Look for it along upper sections of the
Palm Canyon Trail.

■ ANIMAL LIFE

Birds With water restricted to tiny springs, the majority of Kofa's 185 bird
species are bound to be desert lovers or migrators passing through, heading north
and south. One common resident is the white-winged dove. Similar to the
mourning dove in size, shape, and flying characteristics (about 11 inches long,
plump, and fast), the white-winged is distinguished by its prominent white wing
patches and rounded tail in flight. Other common birds you're likely to spot here
include the great roadrunner, Gambel's quail, cactus wren, phainopepla, and the

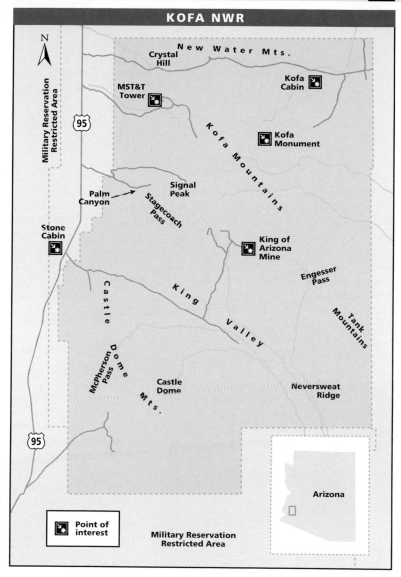

KOFA NWR

N

New Water Mts.

Crystal Hill

MST&T Tower

Kofa Cabin

US 95

Kofa Mountains

Kofa Monument

Palm Canyon

Signal Peak

Stagecoach Pass

Stone Cabin

King of Arizona Mine

Engesser Pass

Castle Mts.

McPherson Pass

Dome

King Valley

Tank Mountains

Castle Dome

Neversweat Ridge

US 95

Arizona

Point of interest

Military Reservation Restricted Area

Military Reservation Restricted Area

guilded form of the northern flicker. Like most woodpeckers, this one flies in an undulating pattern. Its voice is a strong *wick wick wick wick*, and it is colored a golden yellow under its wings and tail.

Among the raptors, the American kestrel and red-tailed hawks are often seen at Kofa; these are two of the refuge's 25 nesting species. Although not considered a local nester, sharp-shinned hawks are also observed year-round. High overhead, look for turkey vultures with their tippy, rocking glide pattern. They are present year-round at Kofa, though rarely in winter. The refuge's most common owl is the western screech owl.

Among the largest body of birds here are those in the tyrant flycatcher family, including Say's phoebe and ash-throated flycatcher (both nest at Kofa), the western wood peewee, and western flycatcher. This bird family can be distinguished by its hovering ability. Perching on tree branches, they will swoop out and pause in the air as they feed on insects and then resettle on a branch.

If you visit Kofa in fall or spring, you will hear migratory neotropical song-birds passing. Try to spot the yellow warbler, yellow-rumped (Audubon's) warbler, and orange-crowned warbler. The last one's name is disingenuous: the orange crown is rarely visible. It is distinguished by its greenish-yellow back and yellow-green underside.

Sparrows and allies comprise the refuge's largest class of birds: about 20 species, including brown towhee and both black-throated and black-chinned sparrow (all are year-round residents). The brown towhee (also called California towhee) is a ground-loving bird with a longish, dark tail and is generally found farther west.

Mammals Kofa is a prime refuge for desert bighorn sheep. Approximately 800 to 1,000 bighorns roam here, reproducing so successfully that the herd is used as a source for transplanting bighorns to other southwestern locales whose historic bighorn populations have been wiped out. Providing these sheep with dependable water sources is an important function of NWR personnel. By shading waterholes (to reduce evaporation), blasting depressions in arroyos and rock outcroppings to trap runoff waters, and equipping water tanks with trickler spouts that slowly release the precious liquid, refuge managers have substantially increased water availability on the refuge for bighorns and other wildlife.

Listen at night for the call of the coyote, one of the more common mammals here. Late in the afternoon, usually in washes, cottontail rabbits are busy moving

about. Mule deer and kit fox are frequently sighted. The fox is among the smallest of North America's canines—it's the size of a house cat—with pale coloring and black-tipped tails and large ears. Its large ears help to dissipate heat as well as maneuver in the dark, two skills the wily fox developed to improve its nocturnal hunting.

Among the kit fox's favored foods are Merriam's kangaroo rats, another common Kofa mammal resident. Occasionally seen at dawn or dusk is the larger and more common gray fox. Other burrowing mammals include round-tailed ground squirrels, Harris' antelope squirrel, and many mice species, including the Arizona pocket mouse and cactus mouse.

Bobcat and ringtail "cats" are present but rarely seen.

San Joaquin kit fox

Ringtails are actually related to the raccoon family and are strictly nocturnal. You may see their glittery eyes starring at you from the dark surrounding your campfire—a disquieting experience the first time it occurs!

Reptiles and amphibians Desert tortoises are one of Kofa's more prominent reptiles. They hibernate in the dead of winter and avoid the scorching heat of summer days. You may note their brown, highly domed shells plodding along sandy washes. Western whiptail lizards, side-blotched lizards, desert horned lizards, and desert iguana can be seen sunning themselves on rocks in the chill mornings or dashing down an arroyo later in the day. Among Kofa's three species of rattlesnakes is the 28- to 49-inch black-tailed rattler, with its faded gold and dark brown coloration and black-tipped tail. Warning: Give these handsome creatures plenty of room if you meet one on a stroll.

HUNTING Hunting for **quail**, **bighorn sheep**, **deer**, **cottontail rabbit**, **coyote**, and **fox** is allowed on the refuge in accordance with applicable state and federal laws.

ACTIVITIES

■ **CAMPING:** Primitive car, RV, and backpacking camping allowed throughout the refuge. Camping is not allowed within 0.25 mile of a waterhole; vehicles must remain within 100 feet of designated roads.

■ **WILDLIFE OBSERVATION:** A visit to Palm Canyon is a must. Keep a sharp eye out to scan the canyon's upper walls early in the morning or late in the day; this is a great way to spot desert mountain bighorns. Waterholes and springs are also prime locations for watching wildlife. Simply find a secluded, shady location overlooking a water body and settle in for an enjoyable wait. Also in Palm Canyon, look for gnatcatchers, brown towhees, and thrashers in the underbrush, and the jet-black phainopeplas swooping about for insects. Often heard but not seen are canyon wrens. This small brown bird (about six inches, with a white throat) calls out in a stream of clear notes in a typically descending scale: *te-you te-you te you tew tew tew tew,* or *tee tee tee tee tee.*

■ **PHOTOGRAPHY:** Palm Canyon is oriented to the south, and its narrow defile receives direct sunlight for only two hours or so a day, at midday. Early to midspring is best for photographing blooming ocotillo and cactus. Sweeping views of the lowland deserts are available from the mountain foothills. A telephoto lens is required for obtaining decent shots of the elusive desert bighorn sheep.

■ **HIKES AND WALKS:** Palm Canyon Trail climbs gently but persistently 300 feet over 0.5 mile, rising in a canyon at the foot of the Kofa Mountains. Huge spires of comblike rock teeth jut from the canyon ramparts as they soar upward and out of sight. Passing up a sandy arroyo and then along a ridge, the trail reaches a natural stopping point that affords a look upward into a side canyon sheltering the refuge's rare colony of native palm trees.

From this point, only climbers in good shape should attempt the ascent into the palm sanctuary. As you look up this narrow cleft, be sure to stay to the right side of a prominent spire jutting from its mouth. Here you'll find a passable route up that squeezes down at one point to less than shoulder width; you'll have to turn sideways to slip through. Then, like Alice emerging from the rabbit's hole, you'll find yourself surrounded by the clicking and rustling of palm fronds overhead. Allow two hours to the make the round-trip climb (and descent) in your car to the palm nursery.

■ **PUBLICATIONS:** Brochure, bird list, mammal list, trail leaflet.

San Bernardino NWR
Douglas, Arizona

San Bernardino NWR

Grasslands and dry hillsides of the Chihuahuan Desert slope gently southward into Mexico at San Bernardino NWR, a seemingly endless expanse of arid terrain broken by a wide valley. But all is not dry here, as green cottonwoods sprout along a stream bed, and springs harbor rare fish and endangered plants. The ponds and wetlands draw the great blue heron, its head and neck tucked as it spreads its magnificent wings up and over the desert.

HISTORY

You can stand on San Bernardino and watch trucks in Mexico lumbering along a border road. Not surprisingly, Mexican history has greatly colored this area. Jesuit priests were active here in the 1700s, and a San Bernardino Grant was created by the Mexican government in 1822. Its settlement was abandoned 10 years later because of Apache raids.

During the mid-1800s, the valley and its spring waters became a stopover for American pioneers on their way west. "Texas" John Slaughter purchased the land grant in 1887 and built his home on it (a national historic landmark, adjoining the refuge). Between 1914 and 1919, the U.S. Army cavalry encamped hereabouts to protect against attacks by Generalissimo Pancho Villa of Mexico.

Acquired in 1982, the San Bernardino refuge only opened to visitors without a permit in 1997; since then the refuge has had approximately 100 visitors a year. Another unit 18 miles away, Leslie Canyon, is still off-limits, although it can be driven through on Leslie Canyon Rd.

GETTING THERE

San Bernardino is about 17 mi. east of Douglas in Arizona's southeastern corner. Take 15th St. east from town for 2.3 mi. to where its name changes to Geronimo Trail and the road turns to gravel. Proceed 14 mi. east on Geronimo Trail. At

major split in the road (Slaughter Ranch entrance), bear left and continue 0.5 mi.
to refuge entrance on right (across from 4th power pole). Parking area is 0.5 mi.

■ **SEASON:** Year-round.
■ **HOURS:** Open 8 a.m.–4:30 p.m. weekdays.
■ **FEES:** Free entry.
■ **ADDRESS:** P.O. Box 3509, Douglas, AZ 85608
■ **TELEPHONE:** 520/364-2104
■ **VISITOR CENTER:** No office, phone, or picnic facilities on site—other than
a restroom.

TOURING SAN BERNARDINO

■ **BY AUTOMOBILE:** There is no auto route through this refuge.
■ **BY FOOT:** A trail loops 1.8 miles from the parking area, dips down into Black
Draw and passes through its riparian woodlands, and then passes Twin Pond,
providing some excellent wildlife viewing opportunities.
■ **BY BICYCLE:** Mountain biking currently is not allowed.

WHAT TO SEE

■ **LANDSCAPE AND CLIMATE** San Bernardino lies on the floor of a wide
valley at around 3,800 feet, smack on the Mexican border. This is a headwater of
the Yaqui River, draining western Chihuahua and eastern Sonora, Mexico. Here,
on the westernmost fringe of the Chihuahuan Desert, weather is generally dry
and hot (often 100 degrees in summer). Winter produces cold, windy days and an
occasional light snowfall. Most of the average 14 inches of precipitation come in
summer, but a wet winter produces a profusion of spring flowers.

The Black Draw trail winds through the center of the valley along the course
of its namesake stream, which is not much of a stream at all, as its water level is
practically nil. Water from natural seeps and artesian wells on the valley floor is
retained in marshes, ponds, and short-flowing streams that shelter rare fish.

■ **PLANT LIFE**
Forests In a desert such as this, you can't help but notice the Fremont cottonwood trees (see sidebar, Bill Williams NWR) lining Black Draw and the ponds and
springs on the valley floor. On the draw's east side is a large stand of honey
mesquite (see sidebar, Brazoria NWR). Netleaf hackberry appear here and there.
Arid lands There is fine Chihuahuan Desert habitat on a volcanic mesa flanking the entrance road. Look for the Santa Rita prickly pear, with its lavender- to
pinkish-colored pads, and the 10- to 20-foot-high whitethorn acacia, with its catclaw hooks. On desert grasslands you will most commonly find alkali sacaton and
giant sacaton.
Wetlands The aquatic habitat around the seeps and springs is home to an
endangered plant, the Huachuca water umbel—a humble-looking, low-to-the-
ground, light-green plant that grows in running water and along pond edges. Cattail, 3-square, and bulrush can also be found here.

■ **ANIMAL LIFE**
Birds Southern Arizona is one of America's best birding locales. Not surprisingly, San Bernardino counts some 290 species touching down here. Favoring the
ponds and wetlands are great blue heron, green-backed heron, Virginia rail, ringneck duck, and Mexican duck. In the riparian woods around water, look for the
magnificent Costa's hummingbird, yellow warbler, and blue grosbeaks.

Flitting about on the desert flats are phainopeplas, white-crowned sparrows, and Gila woodpeckers. Sixteen species of raptors cruise through the skies in search of prey, including gray, zone-tailed, sharp-shinned, and Swainson's hawks; golden eagles; and peregrine falcons.

Mammals Coyotes (see sidebar, Ash Meadows NWR) are one of the mammals most often seen at San Bernardino, along with cottontail and jackrabbit. But that's not all: there are many other, less obvious, mammals on the refuge, including mule deer, javelina, raccoon, antelope, and ground squirrel. Coatamundi—a dark brown member of the raccoon family with a long, pointy nose—forages for carrion, fruits, and small animals.

Gila monster

Reptiles and amphibians The wetlands and Chihuahuan Desert lands support a wide diversity of scaled and finned creatures, including the endangered Chiricahua leopard frog, Sonoran mud turtle, black-tailed and Western diamondback rattlesnake, Sonoran whipsnake, and Gila monster. The Gila sports fantastically colored black dots on a bright orange skin and is the continent's only poisonous lizard. Admire from a distance.

Fish The refuge's isolated ponds and short streams protect rare desert fish, such as the endangered Yaqui chub and the Yaqui topminnow, as well as the threatened Yaqui catfish and the beautiful shiner. All four species swim in Twin Pond on the footpath but are hard to spot: all but the Yaqui catfish are only an inch or so long.

ACTIVITIES

The refuge offers recreational birdwatching, photography, and hiking opportunities.

■ **PUBLICATIONS:** A bird list is available at the refuge office.

Ash Meadows NWR
Amargosa Valley, Nevada

Crystal Spring boardwalk, Ash Meadows NWR

The desert may know no sweeter melody than the sound of bubbling water. Even the schools of brightly colored minnows seem pleased as they dart to a spring pool's surface and back down into its turquoise depths. Water boils out of a pocket on the pool's floor, then slowly meanders down a waterway fringed by dense bulrush, cattails, sedges, and pockets of screwbean mesquite. Overhead a relentless sun beats down; a turkey vulture circles. In the middle of a frying pan of a desert, this life-giving oasis shelters an astounding number of rare fish and riparian plant species. But such is the miracle of Ash Meadows NWR.

HISTORY

Aboriginal peoples first inhabited the Ash Meadows area on a seasonal basis as early as A.D. 500 Bearing this out are the discovery of arrow and spear points, food grinding holes, and other artifacts. These prehistoric residents were followed by Paiute and Shoshone people, who came here periodically to gather abundant wild plant foods and to hunt. Forty-niners on their way to the California goldfields were the first non-Indians to settle around Ash Meadows and may have even given the area its name—a reference to its ashlike alkaline soils.

The ancient Ash Meadows ecosystem was almost destroyed in the 1960s and 1970s through pumping of the springs, water diversion, road building, earth moving, and introduction of nonnative species. In the 1980s land clearing for a proposed resort development threatened to finish it off. Concerned citizens and organizations rallied, and the refuge was established in 1984 when 13,000 acres were acquired with the help of The Nature Conservancy. In 1987 Ash Meadows was designated a wetland of international importance by RAMSAR, an intergovernmental conservation body. Today it includes more than 23,000 acres. Visitation is climbing steadily (now around 14,000 yearly), with people being drawn from nearby Death Valley National Park.

ASH MEADOWS NWR

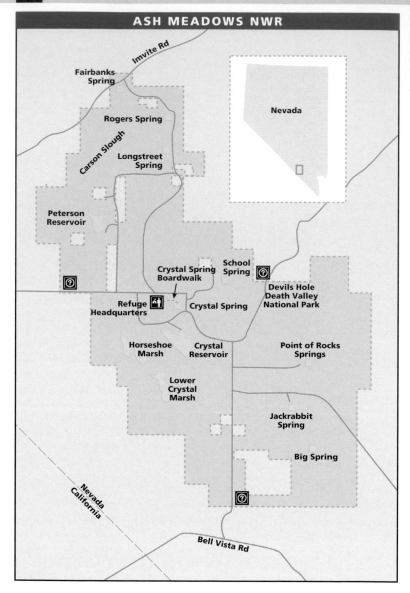

GETTING THERE

Ash Meadows is located about 90 mi. northwest of Las Vegas, Nevada, near the California border. Take I-15 south from Las Vegas to NV 160, which heads west, over the Spring Mountains into the town of Pahrump. Continue on NV 160 for another 3 mi., then turn west (left) onto Bell Vista Rd. Follow Bell Vista Rd. for 22 mi., then turn north (right) onto a gravel road marked with a refuge sign, and continue 0.25 mi. to the refuge boundary. From there proceed 6 mi. north to the office.

From the north, turn off US 95 at Lathrop Wells/Amargosa Valley onto NV 373 and proceed 13.5 mi. south. Turn east (left) onto Spring Meadows Rd.; the refuge boundary line is 3 mi. ahead, where the road turns to gravel. From there continue 3 mi. to the office.

From the west, take CA 127 through Death Valley Jct. and Stateline. After Stateline, go 1 mi., turn east (right) onto Spring Meadows Rd.; the refuge boundary is 3 mi. ahead.

Other roads access the refuge as well, but require long approaches over dirt and gravel surfaces, not recommended for visitors.

■ **SEASON:** Open year-round.

■ **HOURS:** Refuge open daily (including holidays) sunrise to sunset; office usually open weekdays 8 a.m.–4 p.m.

■ **FEES:** Entry is free.

■ **ADDRESS:** HCR 70, Box 610-Z, Amargosa Valley, NV 89020

■ **TELEPHONE:** 775/372-5435

■ **VISITOR CENTER:** There is no Visitor Center as of summer 1999 (one is proposed). Refuge headquarters has information kiosk, restroom, pay phone, covered picnic tables.

TOURING ASH MEADOWS

■ **BY AUTOMOBILE:** An extensive network of roads, some 24 miles total, crisscrosses the refuge, providing easy access to six major springs and two large reservoirs. But be aware that the northernmost roads can become impassable following winter rains. The refuge is off-limits to all terrain vehicles. ATV use in the past severely damaged portions of Ash Meadows' fragile desert soils and vegetation. Note also that about 1,000 acres of private land is located inside the refuge. Visitors must respect private property.

■ **BY FOOT:** Strolling the delightful boardwalk at Crystal Spring, adjoining refuge headquarters, is a must-do at Ash Meadows. The handicap-accessible boardwalk runs about 0.66 mile (round-trip). Short walks, of several hundred yards to 0.2 mile, are also required to see any of the other springs. Longstreet Spring is reached over flat terrain; other paths have slight uphill grades. Visitors may also walk the refuge roads and the dikes around portions of the reservoirs. Additional boardwalks are planned for Point of Rocks and Longstreet Springs.

■ **BY BICYCLE:** Bicyclists are welcome to ride on any of the refuge roads, but the boardwalk is off-limits.

■ **BY BOAT:** Boating (nonmotorized) is allowed only at Crystal and Peterson reservoirs.

WHAT TO SEE

■ **LANDSCAPE AND CLIMATE** Some 12,000 years ago glaciers covered many western mountain ranges, and their runoff flooded huge swaths of the region with interconnected lakes and rivers. This pluvial (wet) period allowed colonization of present sites by a wide range of flora and fauna. When the climate warmed and dried in a subsequent xeric (dry) phase, the glaciers vanished, and the lakes retreated and separated, isolating their plants and animals in tiny remnant spring-fed water pockets, like those found at Ash Meadows. This process explains the extraordinarily high number of endemic flora and fauna found here—24 species, including fish, plants, flowers, and a beetle.

The water flowing from the refuge's many springs emerges at an average rate of 10,000 gallons per minute. This warm water is estimated to be 2,000 to 5,000 years old. It comes from a vast underground water system stretching several hundred miles to the northeast that is recharged from mountain precipitation, which reaches the refuge via a series of underground faults and fractures. It is this water that makes Ash Meadows the place it is: essentially a desert oasis.

The springs flow out of their emergence basins in small streams and out across the desert floor. Trees and marsh vegetation flank these wandering water courses before they are swallowed up again by the desert sands. Prior to the refuge's formation, when farming was attempted here, many of the streams were redirected into cement ditches and their vegetation died away. Refuge staff are removing the ditches, allowing the flowing water to return to its original channels where it can nourish replanted native vegetation.

Geographically, Ash Meadows sits within the higher fringes of the Mojave Desert, and most of its acreage is alkaline desert habitat, basically flat, with low earthen and some rocky hills and ridges breaking the surface. Sandy dunes appear in the center of Ash Meadows.

Some desert mountain ranges flank the refuge to the southeast. In the distance higher ranges can be spotted to the west in California; and the higher slopes of the Spring Mountains form the eastern backdrop. These ranges capture occasional summer thunderstorms and winter rains, but little moisture falls on the broad

Jackrabbit Spring, Ash Meadows NWR

valley floor where the refuge lies—only 4 scant inches annually on average. Years may pass between rainfalls on specific places. Summer temperatures are brutal: 104-degree July days are average. Winter days, however, can be surprisingly cool, averaging 60 degrees in January. The best time to visit, weatherwise, is late March to early April.

■ PLANT LIFE

Wetlands The 15 major springs on the Ash Meadows refuge each support a wide variety of riparian and marshland flora. Insects hum here in warmer months, birds sing out, the wind stirs through the rushes and trees, and the air carries the earthy smell of rotting vegetation. Along the edges of the springs and their streams grow juncus rush, a low grasslike plant, as well as sawgrass, bulrush, and cattails. Tall clusters (more than 12 feet high) of elegant phragmites, or reedgrass, stand at attention.

Along the Crystal Spring boardwalk, look for the common spring-loving century, with its tiny pink bipetaled flowers. You'll also encounter mojave thistle; yerba mansa (lizard tail), a low reddish plant with green leaves and white flowers; and Ash Meadows gumplant, another of the endangered (and endemic) flora. Growing in moist clay soils and borders of scrub woodlands, the gumplant displays lemon-yellow flowers (June to Oct.) covered with a gummy substance, and leathery, dark green leaves. Popular with quail, who scurry among its dense undergrowth, is the well-named quailbush, reaching 7 feet high in the riparian area's dry soils.

Ash Meadows' variety of trees includes leather-leaf ash and screwbean mesquite. The latter, with its hooked plump pods stuffed with nutritious beans, is popular with wildlife.

Arid lands Just a few feet from lush wetlands the habitat switches to full-on Mojave Desert and, in fact, dry uplands are the predominant landscape of Ash Meadows. Here you'll find creosote, saltbush, and some trees. Note the honey mesquite growing on the dunes along a stretch of the Crystal Spring boardwalk. Here, too, on flats and knolls of hard, dry alkaline soils, are other endemic plants: the Ash Meadows milk-vetch with its pink-purple flowers (March to May) and fuzzy gray-green leaves, and the Ash

Yerba mansa blossom

Meadows sunray, distinguished by its yellow flowers (April and May) and fuzzy grayish green, ruffled-corrugate leaves growing from a clump.

The hillsides are home to many varieties of cactus, such as the pretty cotton-top, a type of barrel cactus with tufts of white flowers growing out of their red tops. Admire, but don't touch the desert holly—it will prick you!

At four refuge locations on undisturbed soils in dry arroyos and canyons the Ash Meadows blazing star, another native, blossoms. From June to Sept., you'll see its bright yellow flowers contrasting with sandpaperlike, grayish green leaves.

Carson Slough, on the refuge's northwest side, was once the largest marsh in southern Nevada, with high concentrations of water birds and endemic aquatic plants and animals. It was drained and mined for peat in the 1960s and today is essentially a dry wash lined with large thickets of invasive salt cedar. This nonnative tree provides few benefits for native wildlife and is being gradually removed, then replaced by planted native vegetation. One day the slough will again hear the quacking of ducks and the swoosh of wind rattling through cattails and sedges.

Open water The refuge's four reservoirs cover 180 acres.

■ ANIMAL LIFE

Birds A winter stroll at Ash Meadows might turn up Gambel's quail, white crowned sparrow, phainopepla, red-winged blackbird, and American coot. In summer look for pied-billed and eared grebes, mallard ducks, osprey, Virginia rail, western sandpiper, marsh wren, blue grosbeak, and the handsome lazuli bunting.

Spring migration in April and May delivers the greatest variety of birds here, when you might spot the western kingbird, yellow-headed blackbird, northern rough-winged swallow, western bluebird, and verdin. But in fall and winter the marshes and reservoirs fill with a variety of water birds, including ring-billed gull and 21 types of waterfowl such as Canada goose, canvasback, ruddy duck, and bufflehead. Tundra swan, geese, cinnamon teal, gadwall, and other water and wading birds gather on the reservoirs.

In the skies a diverse range of raptors—17 in all, including white-tailed kite, the common northern harrier, golden and bald eagles, and the endangered peregrine—are on patrol. Some 210 species of birds have been identified at Ash Meadows, along with 17 accidentals.

Mammals Most commonly seen on the refuge are black-tailed jackrabbits, desert cottontail, and coyote, but 27 species have been recorded to date, including three bats (like the Townsend big-eared), ringtail cats, and mountain lion. Desert bighorn sheep are sometimes spotted on the slopes above Point of Rocks: 96 were counted at one time.

Reptiles and amphibians Five amphibians and 20 reptiles reside at Ash Meadows. In spring, woodhouse toads sing around the springs in chorus to attract mates. Look for chuckwalla lizards on the rocky slopes at Devil's Hole in the early spring.

Yellow-headed blackbird

Fish The Ash Meadows pupfish, one of the refuge's four species of native and endangered fish, swims in ten refuge springs, including Crystal, King's, Jackrabbit, and Longstreet. A type of minnow, the pupfish's importance is not measured by its 1- to 3-inch length. It generally stays on the bottoms of the pools, but the males, which turn a bright silvery blue with black vertical bars and a black tail band when mating, can be seen occasionally. It remains in its spring pools from March through Oct., when it enters the spring's moving water system to complete another essential life cycle function.

The Devil's Hole pupfish, another pupfish variety, probably has the most restricted habitat of any vertebrate on earth. It is found only in the wild in one spring pool here, where a population of 200 to 500 individuals hangs on for dear life. The breeding males are silvery blue with a black tail band, while the females are greenish; their entire lifespan is only 6 to 12 months. Protected status came to this fish in 1952, when Devil's Hole became a satellite unit of Death Valley National Park.

Ash Meadows's staff maintain two tiny refugiums (simple covered concrete pools) on the refuge, each preserving small "back up" populations of the Devil's Hole pupfish, in case an accident ever befalls their native spring.

Four springs, including Jackrabbit, are home to the endemic and endangered Ash Meadows speckled dace. This fish is 3 to 4 inches long, with a brown stripe.

Unfortunately, nonnative exotics were introduced into many of the springs (including Crystal) in the past; sailfin mollies and mosquito fish (which come to the surface to sip mosquito larvae) prey on the native fish, contributing to their decline.

Invertebrates The refuge's small streams are home to yet another unique critter: the threatened Ash Meadow naucorid, a small beetle. At one time its habitat was reduced to only one refuge stream, but it has been reintroduced to other waterways here and is recovering well.

ACTIVITIES

■ **CAMPING:** Camping is not allowed on the refuge. The nearest public campsites are at Death Valley National Park, 30 miles away. Pahrump, 22 miles southeast of Ash Meadows, offers several commercial campgrounds.

■ **SWIMMING:** Swimming in the springs is strictly forbidden, as it can harm the rare fish found here, but swimming is allowed at the 50-acre Crystal Reservoir.

■ **WILDLIFE OBSERVATION:** Crystal Spring provides the refuge's best birdwatching. An attractive boardwalk lined with occasional interpretive panels runs from the parking area at headquarters along a stream and marsh to the spring. This habitat and flanking desert land attract plentiful wildlife at all times of the year.

The mesquite and ash tree groves at headquarters and Point of Rocks shelter have resident and migratory songbirds year-round, including the Crissal thrasher, verdin, phainopepla, and Lucy's warbler. Visit the reservoirs to observe wading birds and waterfowl. Year-round, a pair of golden eagles is often seen near King's Spring.

LONELY COYOTE Maligned a million times in cartoons; shot, trapped, poisoned, and cursed by ranchers, feared by cat-owners moving to the country or city suburbs across the nation; and the butt of many Native American oral stories whose prime character is devious and untrustworthy—the coyote would seem to face a perilous future.

But, in fact, the coyote is thriving. Once restricted to lands west of the Mississippi, it has significantly expanded its range today, turning up even in New York's Central Park, mixing with dogs and other canine species in the process. And that's a good thing: coyotes play a valuable role in maintaining a balanced ecosystem, filling a niche left by wolves.

Equal-opportunity grazers, coyotes will eat jackrabbits or dog food, will occasionally bring down deer when hunting in a pack, and will dine on grasshoppers, juniper berries, and they even display a fondness for ripe watermelons!

Desert coyote subspecies, with gray, tan, and reddish tints, weigh some 20 pounds; mountain varieties can top 50 pounds while sporting thicker, darker coats.

Coyotes are social animals. The eerie yowls, yips, barks, and wails of coyote groups can be heard across southwestern deserts and mountain foothills every evening as they gather to go scavenging. Coyotes are occasionally seen trotting across a road or clearing—often stopping to check *you* out, plotting, no doubt, some nefarious scheme.

ASH MEADOWS HUNTING SEASONS

Hunting (Seasons may vary)	Jan	Feb	Mar	Apr	May	Jun	Jul	Aug	Sep	Oct	Nov	Dec
cottontail rabbit	■									■	■	■
jackrabbit	■									■	■	■
geese	■									■	■	■
ducks	■									■	■	■
coot	■									■	■	■
moorhen	■									■	■	■
snipe	■									■	■	■
dove									■			
quail	■									■	■	■

Hunting of geese, ducks, moorhens, snipe, dove, quail, jackrabbits, and cottontails is allowed in accordance with current state and federal regulations. Hunting is restricted around the refuge headquarters and other areas. Contact the refuge for further details.

■ **PHOTOGRAPHY:** Wonderful chances for photography exist along the Crystal Springs boardwalk, including the spring itself, the rich marsh, and fringing desert scenes.

■ **HIKES AND WALKS:** The only dedicated walking path is the boardwalk at Crystal Spring, but you can walk anywhere on the refuge (barring small areas closed at hunting season). If time permits visit at least one other spring. At Point of Rocks, stroll back into the low hills just above the spring, bearing southeast, to find odd holes 9 inches or so wide at the mouth and a foot deep. They were made by native peoples grinding and mashing nuts and seeds like screwbean mesquite using a hand pestle or pole.

Also be sure to visit Devil's Hole to see the pupfish described earlier. The hole has been fenced, but with a little scrambling to the left as you face the hole, you can reach a vantage point for a view down into the deep, rocky crevice.

■ **PUBLICATIONS** Brochure and wildlife lists (birds, mammals, reptiles, amphibians, fish).

Desert NW Range
Las Vegas, Nevada

Joshua tree, Desert National Wildlife Range

Though it lies only a half hour away from booming Las Vegas, Desert NWR is a world apart: Endless desert flats with nary a tract home in sight sizzle under the summer sun; quiet, seldom-visited canyons corkscrew back into high, rugged, forested mountains; and rough roads wander where you may not see another soul for hours. The only fast food here is the sandwich you brought with you; the only gambling is on whether or not you have enough water to sustain the day's explorations. Not far away the nation's atomic weapons were once tested, but here in this remote wilderness the ancient laws rule.

HISTORY

Desert NWR was established in 1936 with the primary objective of protecting desert bighorn sheep. It was formerly called the Desert Game Range—the R in its name still stands for Range, not Refuge. At a whopping 1.5 million acres (more than 2,200 square miles), it is the largest wildlife refuge in the nation outside Alaska. However, 845,000 acres are overlain by Nellis Air Force Range, and a small portion are used for bombing and gunnery practice; this section of the refuge is off-limits to the public. As archaeological sites on the refuge attest, its mid-elevations were used occasionally by transient native peoples and Euro-American immigrants to collect food, water, and other resources. The large springs at Corn Creek were particularly favored, used over the centuries as camping grounds by prehistoric and Paiute Indians, and as a stagecoach stop and ranch. Some 45,000 people a year visit Desert NWR, concentrating mostly around Corn Creek Field Station.

GETTING THERE

The refuge is located about 28 mi. northwest of Las Vegas. Most visitors enter at Corn Creek Field Station. From the city, head north on US 95 to milepost 101, and turn east (right) at the small brown refuge sign onto a gravel road; proceed 4 mi. to the field station. The refuge's main office is in Las Vegas.

■ **SEASON:** Open year-round.

■ **HOURS:** Refuge is open 24 hours daily (except the Nellis AFR portion). Corn Creek Field Station restrooms and hiking trails open daily sunrise to sunset.

■ **FEES:** Entry is free.

■ **ADDRESS:** 1500 N. Decatur Blvd., Las Vegas, NV 89108

■ **TELEPHONE:** 702/646-3401

■ **VISITOR CENTER:** No Visitor Center, but Corn Creek Field Station, when staffed, has an emergency phone.

TOURING DESERT

■ **BY AUTOMOBILE:** On a refuge this big, the only way to see its various parts is to drive. It's best to have a high-clearance, 4-wheel-drive vehicle to access the better part of the preserve. Before heading into the backcountry at Desert, make sure you have a spare tire, a full gas tank, and plenty of water. All motor vehicles on the refuge must be legal to drive on the street.

All vehicles can access Corn Creek Field Station. The 4-mile gravel entrance road from US 95 to Corn Creek crosses a broad flat through Mojave Desert habitat.

Desert cottontail rabbit

Ordinary vehicles in good weather with competent drivers can also negotiate Mormon Well Rd., which runs 48 miles (three to four hours one-way) between US 95 and US 93 along the east side of the Sheep Mountains (call refuge in advance for road conditions). Follow the handy refuge brochure keyed to certain points along this road, including two historic sites: a prehistoric agave roasting pit and Mormon Well Corral—once a stopover point on a stage line. The corral (and its spring) are located about .33 mile off Mormon Rd. to the west on a gated road open for walking.

Ordinary cars should avoid the 70-mile Alamo Rd., which also runs between US 95 and NV 93, but along the west face of the Sheep Mountains. Rocky ridges along its northern stretches can disable standard vehicles, but it is negotiable as far north as Hidden Forest Rd., providing access to many of the Sheep Range's west-facing canyons. It takes six to seven hours typically to drive the entire Alamo route one-way.

■ **BY FOOT:** The entire refuge is open to hiking. Miles of foot and horse trails lace the property, particularly the mountain canyons, where the shade of rock walls and tree cover keep the heat tolerable during the shoulder seasons of fall and spring. Begin walking early in the day to avoid midday heat, and always carry water.

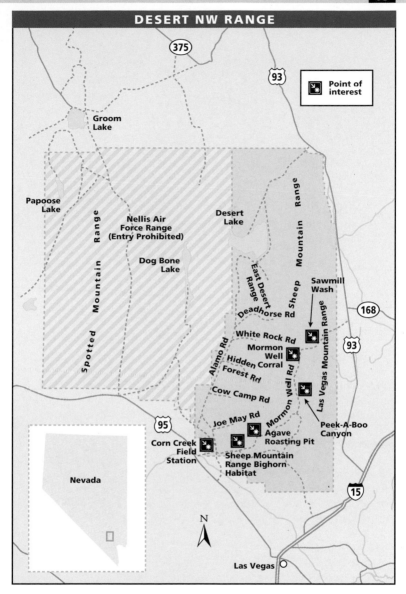

DESERT NW RANGE

Point of interest

Groom Lake

Papoose Lake

Nellis Air Force Range (Entry Prohibited)

Desert Lake

Dog Bone Lake

Spotted Mountain Range

East Desert Range

Sheep Mountain Range

Sawmill Wash

Deadhorse Rd

White Rock Rd

Alamo Rd

Mormon Well

Hidden Corral

Hidden Forest Rd

Las Vegas Mountain Range

Cow Camp Rd

Mormon Well Rd

Peek-A-Boo Canyon

Joe May Rd

Agave Roasting Pit

Corn Creek Field Station

Sheep Mountain Range Bighorn Habitat

Nevada

N

Las Vegas

Some of the best birding is found on the short (under 1 mile), pleasant trail network around the ponds and orchards of Corn Creek Field Station. One loop climbs some low hills, but another branch is essentially flat. Trails are open sunrise to sunset.

BY BICYCLE: Bicycles are allowed on all refuge roads. Bike entry is prohibited in a proposed high mountain wilderness area and on all foot trails.

WHAT TO SEE

■ **LANDSCAPE AND CLIMATE** Desert NWR encompasses six mountain ranges; the highest, Sheep Range, rises from 2,500 feet to 9,920 feet at Hayford Peak. Steep canyons with many small perennial springs bore back into these

Desert bighorn sheep

ranges. A combination of alluvial fans (spreading out and downward from the mountain canyons) and Mojave Desert uplands dominate the lower elevations. The valley floors are absolutely flat; they are the bottoms of former lakebeds.

Visitors encounter several climates on the refuge, though few people reach the higher elevations. Heat, not cold, is the element to contend with, because temperatures frequently climb to 100 degrees at Corn Creek Field Station and into the 80s at higher elevations. Winter, however, does have a distinct bite: Lows can dip into the 20s even at Corn Creek, and much lower at higher elevations. Late fall and spring make the best visiting periods, though winter days can be quite pleasant, and summer mornings are tolerable.

■ PLANT LIFE

Wetlands Corn Creek Field Station area has three small ponds, which are bordered by marshes fed by nearby spring waters channeled through small irrigation ditches; this is the extent of the refuge's wetlands. Around the water grow cattails and bulrush; cottonwoods, willows, and a small orchard of almond, pecan, mulberry, and other fruit trees complete the oasis.

Arid lands Arid terrain composes the bulk of Desert's landscape, particularly its lower elevations. The Mojave Desert scrub community is dominated by creosote bush, white bursage, and saltbush. A few thousand feet higher in elevation, Mojave yucca and various cactus, including the pretty red cottontop, take over. Still higher grow blackbrush and Joshua tree. This zone, and the zone above it, are splashed with color from spring through late summer from many varieties of wildflowers, including desert marigold, larkspur, Mojave aster, Indian paintbrush, and fleabane.

Mountains High desert woodlands of Utah juniper and single-leaf piñon

BIGHORN SHEEP Among the world's best climbers, sentinels of summits, and symbol of the wild West, bighorn sheep are a hardy and inspiring animal. Much revered by prehistoric peoples of the American Southwest, as seen in many petroglyph depictions, the rams' magnificent curling horns (which take seven to eight years to complete a full circle) are prized today among big-game hunters.

Two species inhabit the region: the desert bighorn, which prefers arid land, rocky cliffs and canyons, and the Rocky Mountain bighorn, which lives in the high alpine environment. Both are big—5 feet to 6 feet in length, with horns measuring up to 4 feet—and were once fairly numerous, but hunting, introduction of diseases from domesticated sheep, and loss of habitat have severely curtailed their populations. Remnant populations hang on in pockets, some doing well enough to allow limited capture and transplanting to other, safer sites.

Desert bighorns can obtain all their water from their forage of grasses and shrubs during droughts and can withstand extreme dehydration—up to 20 percent of their body weight. They need to spend minimal time at watering holes, the favored ambush points for predators like mountain lions.

interspersed with big sagebrush and bunchgrasses are found above 6,000 feet. From 7,000 feet to 9,000 feet, where snow lingers and additional rain falls, conifer forests thrive: mostly ponderosa and white fir. At the highest elevations, just under 10,000 feet, bristlecone pine have a foothold in one of only four places in Nevada where this tough, age-defying tree can grow.

■ **ANIMAL LIFE**
Birds In the desert, the standing water and vegetation of Corn Creek Field Station are a bird magnet. Add species drawn to high-mountain terrain to birds favoring arid lands, and you'll find Desert NWR has a surprising range of flyers, both migrating and nesting birds (some 280 species). Look for water-lovers like grebes, herons (including the green-backed), egrets, 18 species of waterfowl, gulls and terns, and waders like the greater yellowlegs. You may also spot desert-lovers like the roadrunner, horned larks, Le Conte's thrasher, sage sparrow, and cactus wren.

At higher elevations, such as Peek-a-Boo Canyon, expect to see spotted towhee, ash-throated flycatchers, Bullock's and Scott's orioles, blue-gray gnatcatcher, and Say's phoebe among the songbirds.

Nesting birds at Desert refuge include the western screech owl, the lesser nighthawk, mourning dove, sharp-shinned hawk, calliope hummingbird, many flycatchers (including the dusky and Say's phoebe), three jay species, numerous warblers, and the yellow-bellied sapsucker.

Mammals In the past the refuge has supported 1,500 to 1,800 desert bighorn sheep. Today this number has fallen to about 800, but this is still among the largest populations in the world. Other large mammals here, among 52 mammal species known to be on the refuge, include mountain lion, bobcats, foxes (gray, kit, and red), badgers, and coyote. Most are nocturnal, however. Your best chance to see them is at dawn and dusk. During the day a quick eye is more likely to glimpse the blacktailed jackrabbit or desert cottontail.

Twelve bat species swoop through evening skies here, including the Mexican freetailed bat and Yuma bat. The western pipistrel bat is the common bat of the refuge below the ponderosa pine zone.

Mice, squirrels, chipmunks, rats, and gophers at Desert refuge number an impressive 22 species.

Reptiles The refuge shelters numerous snakes and lizards, including the collard lizard, leopard lizard, and banded gecko—26 species in all. The gecko is nocturnal and is typically found under rocks and fallen yuccas in the spring at elevations below 4,000 feet. Two species of nocturnal rattlesnakes can also be encountered: the speckled and the sidewinder. The threatened desert tortoise is commonly seen here between March and Sept. on flats and surrounding foothills.

Fish In 1971 some 29 Pahrump poolfish (an endangered, minnow-sized, endemic species) were placed in Corn Creek ponds when their original habitat was destroyed. They first flourished, but in 1994 predatory nonnative crayfish were illegally introduced in the ponds, and the poolfish population plummeted. Its status is now uncertain.

ACTIVITIES

■ **CAMPING:** Free camping year-round is permitted on this refuge. Roadside camping is popular along Mormon Well Rd., but there are no developed sites or facilities. You must camp within 100 feet of the road—look for pullouts. Dispersed, backcountry camping for backpackers is also allowed, but camping within sight of or .25 mile of a spring is forbidden, to give wildlife undisturbed access to water. Campfires are permitted, but only downed wood may be burned.

Desert vegetation with cloud-studded Sheep Range, Desert NW Range

■ **WILDLIFE OBSERVATION:** The wide elevation range at Desert NWR creates habitat and climate niches for a diverse body of wildlife. Some species overlap the various life zones, while others are specific to certain locales, requiring a visitor intent on seeing a wide variety to roam among several refuge sites. For instance, pinyon jay, common bushtit, and broad-tailed hummers frequent the desert woodlands, while Clark's nutcrackers, white-breasted nuthatch, and gray-headed junco are found in the coniferous forests.

Birds and other wildlife in general congregate around the refuge's perennial springs, which are a visitor's best chance for wildlife observation. The waters of Corn Creek Field Station and nearby flora, shade trees, and small orchard create a primary birding area. Even in the dead of winter you might find red-shafted flickers, ruby-crowned kinglets, American coot, mallards, and phainopepla. Other species regularly seen here include the Audubon warbler, Western tanager, and northern oriole. April's blooming mulberry trees are a beacon for many migratory songbirds. Sept. and Oct. are also good birding months as migrants move south.

But it is the Sheep Range that supports the refuge's greatest diversity of flora and fauna. A good place to look for mule deer in midsummer to early fall is at Mormon Well, where a spring provides precious water for wildlife. The southern end of the Sheep Range, on the north face of Yucca Gap along Mormon Well Rd., is excellent bighorn habitat. Precipitous terrain protects them from predators, while shrub-covered ledges and slopes provide good forage. They occupy this area from late fall to early spring but can be difficult to spot, even with powerful binoculars or a scope. Better chances for observing bighorns come in July or Aug. further north in the range when they concentrate around the few springs.

HUNTING Hunting for **bighorn sheep** is allowed on certain portions of the refuge (including tracts on the Nellis AFR) in Nov., Dec., and early Jan., according to federal and state regulations. Contact the refuge for further details.

■ **PHOTOGRAPHY:** There is an interesting range of scenes to photograph at Desert in addition to wildlife: ponds and historic cabins at Corn Creek; historic corral at Mormon Well; flowering cactus; Joshua tree forests; rugged, rocky canyons; and colorful sunsets.

■ **HIKES AND WALKS:** The short trails at Corn Creek Field Station make for enjoyable, if brief, walks. The hillside trail along the station's northern edge provides access to a historic blacksmith shop and railroad tie shop later absorbed by a ranch run by the Richardsons of Utah. Timbers bear the marks of the hand-held adz used to square them off. The family's fruit and nut trees still grow in the small orchard.

Higher sections of Sheep Range (Mormon Well Rd. reaches just the 6,000-foot mark) are reached only on foot. Look for trailheads on side roads off Mormon Well Rd. and Alamo Rd.

Most popular among the refuge's many mountain hiking routes are Hidden Forest Canyon and Sawmill Canyon trails. Both end in heavy woods at springs. Each trail is about five miles (one-way) with substantial climbing.

■ **PUBLICATIONS:** An informative brochure and lists of birds, mammals, and reptiles.

Pahranagat NWR
Alamo, Nevada

Refuge wetland, Pahranagat NWR

Pahranagat NWR is a land of striking contrasts. On the valley floor, waves lap at the shore of a deep blue lake, the shoreline fringed with silvery cottonwoods, orange bulrush, and yellow cattails. Dry alluvial plains slope down toward the valley floor from brown and black volcanic mesas, their north faces draped with light snow. In the distance rise blue mountain slopes. A bald eagle scans the waters from a cottonwood perch, then flaps off with sure, powerful strokes.

HISTORY

Pahranagat NWR was established in 1964 when its 5,380 acres were purchased with funds collected from the Federal Duck Stamp Program, a conservation program enacted to raise monies used in preserving waterfowl habitat. (The program, begun in 1934, required all waterfowl hunters 16 years and older to buy a duck stamp annually.) The name of the refuge is derived from a Paiute word meaning "place of many waters." Surrounded by endless miles of the Great Basin and Mojave deserts, marshes here were a magnet for prehistoric and historic native cultures drawn to the area for both food gathering and ceremonial purposes. Petroglyphs, drawings or inscriptions carved by ancient populations into rock, and even rarer pictographs, ancient drawings or paintings on rock walls, can be found on the refuge. Around 11,000 people visit annually.

GETTING THERE

Pahranagat is about 90 mi. north of Las Vegas and 4 mi. south of the small town of Alamo. From Las Vegas, take I-15 north some 20 mi.; turn north onto NV 93 and proceed about 70 mi. to the refuge. Headquarters is located off NV 93 in the northern third of the refuge.
■ **SEASON:** Open year-round.
■ **HOURS:** Refuge open sunrise to sunset. Office: 6 a.m.–4:30 p.m. weekdays.

■ **FEES:** Entry is free.
■ **ADDRESS:** P.O. Box 510, Alamo, NV 89001
■ **TELEPHONE:** 775/725-3417
■ **VISITOR CENTER:** No Visitor Center, but headquarters has toilets and an emergency phone. Bring food and drink.

TOURING PAHRANAGAT

■ **BY AUTOMOBILE:** A 2-mile auto-tour route with some interpretive panels skirts the east shore of North Marsh/Upper Lake, a prime wildlife area. Access this route via NV 93 at the north end of the North Marsh. Roads open to the public also leave NV 93 to wind along the eastern edges of Middle Pond for two miles, and Lower Lake for 1.5 miles. These roads, of deteriorating asphalt, are rough in spots but passable for ordinary vehicles and RVs. Each road overlooks a water body, marshes, and open landscape, providing outstanding wildlife viewing opportunities.

■ **BY FOOT:** A number of refuge roads and trails, totaling some 7 miles, are available for walking. In addition to the auto routes, footpaths encircle Upper Lake and the south and west sides of Middle Pond. Some areas, however, are seasonally closed to protect nesting birds.

■ **BY BICYCLE:** The primary refuge roads and the hiking trail around Middle Pond's east, south, and west sides are open to biking. Don't ride along NV 93, however: The semis will blow you off the road.

■ **BY CANOE, KAYAK, OR BOAT:** Nonmotorized boats and boats with electric motors are allowed on Upper Lake, Middle Lake, and Lower Lake, year-round. Upper Marsh is closed to boating of any kind. There are no boat ramps available on the refuge.

WHAT TO SEE

■ LANDSCAPE AND CLIMATE

The refuge lies in a 10-mile stretch of Pahranagat Valley, hard on the Mojave Desert and Great Basin regions of southern Nevada. Elevations range only between 3,200 and 3,400 feet, but uplands flank the valley, rising in alluvial fans and mesas to distant mountain slopes. Springs on the valley floor a few miles north of the refuge feed its three man-made impoundments and marshes. The lakes cover approximately 410 acres when full.

Climate at Pahranagat varies widely. For a few weeks in summer, temperatures can top 100 degrees but can drop to 10 degrees in winter. Annual precipitation is low, usually under 7 inches a year. Spring and late fall commonly bring high winds, while summer serves up powerful thunderstorms.

■ PLANT LIFE

Wetlands Marshes cover 420 acres, about 8 percent, of the refuge. Flourishing on the marsh edges are cattail, bulrush, and sedges.

Grasslands Grasslands and wet meadows span another 510 acres. At the northern end of Northern Marsh look for yerba mansa, a medicinal herb. The yerba mansa, with 2-inch-wide flower heads, has spreading root systems that help create well-compacted soil—soil that native Indians and the Spanish favored as building material. Some native grasslands in excellent shape are found south of Lower Lake. Here you can see Great Basin wild rye, once an important food plant for native peoples. The grasslands and nearby drier uplands also produce bountiful wildflowers after a wet winter and spring.

Arid lands Dry uplands—about half the refuge—are covered with a mix of both Great Basin (greasewood and saltbush) and Mojave Desert (creosote and bursage) scrub vegetation.

Riparian forest In the fall you will see splashes of bright color in stands of cottonwood along the eastern shore of Upper Lake and on the northern edge of North Marsh, where there is also a healthy grove of Goodding's willow. Both trees provide excellent cover for birds.

Farmlands To provide feed for sandhill cranes, geese, shorebirds, and other wildlife, about 180 acres of the refuge, including lands north of Middle Pond and near the refuge headquarters, are farmed.

■ ANIMAL LIFE

Birds Because of Pahranagat's standing water, it is a beacon for both resident and migratory birds. Perhaps the best birding season is March and April, when both waterfowl and migratory songbirds congregate. More than 100 species of perching birds set down here, utilizing riparian, wetland, and dry upland habitats. Much of the music in the air comes from warblers, such as orioles, finches, and sparrows, vermilion flycatchers, and western tanagers.

As an important stop on a branch of the Pacific flyway, the refuge is frequented by 19 species of waterfowl, peaking usually near the end of Oct. and lasting through mid-Dec., with some 10,000 ducks on site—predominately pintails and green-winged teal, as well as mallard and American wigeon.

Geese are most prevalent during any of the winter months, typically Dec. and Jan., with populations running as high as 1,950 birds. Some 2,000 of the Lower Colorado River's population of greater sandhill cranes (almost one-quarter of this subgroup) are often found here in March and to a lesser degree in Oct.. The refuge also shelters Nevada's largest nesting population of the endangered southwestern willow flycatcher and yellow-billed cuckoos. All told, 240 bird species have been recorded at Pahranagat.

Mammals Coyote can be seen all over the refuge, while the farmlands and large desert washes are popular with kit fox and mule deer. Moist native grasslands are home to the endemic Pahranagat Valley montane vole.

Pintail ducks in flight

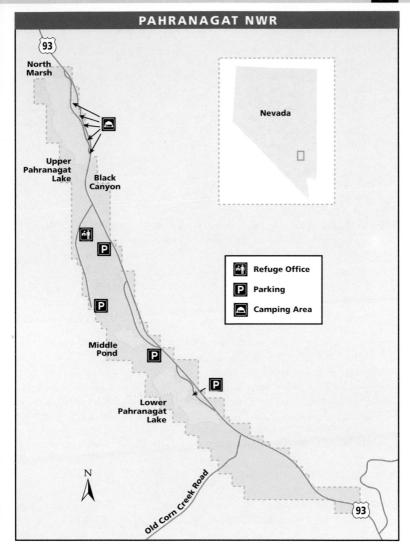

Reptiles and amphibians The slow-moving desert tortoise, a threatened species, inhabits the refuge's desert uplands. A foot long, the tortoise digs long tunnels with its unusually flat front limbs.

ACTIVITIES

■ **CAMPING:** Free camping (tables, firepits, outhouses; 14-day limit) is allowed only along sites on the eastern shoreline of Upper Lake on a first-come basis.

■ **SWIMMING:** Not allowed.

■ **WILDLIFE OBSERVATION:** The favored birding area on the refuge is around Upper Lake and North Marsh, with its open waters, marshes, meadows, and forests. Great blue herons, geese, and cormorants nest around its northern end. Waterfowl gather on the lake in fall and winter, while the shoreline trees harbor many songbirds in spring and summer and perching raptors, including bald eagles and red tail hawks, in the dead of winter. Scan the trees along the shore for

PAHRANAGAT HUNTING AND FISHING SEASONS

Hunting
(Seasons may vary)

	Jan	Feb	Mar	Apr	May	Jun	Jul	Aug	Sep	Oct	Nov	Dec
cottontail rabbit	■									■	■	■
mourning dove									■			
Gambel's quail	■									■	■	■
ducks	■									■	■	■
mergansers	■									■	■	■
moorhen	■									■	■	■
coots	■									■	■	■
common snipe	■									■	■	■
Canada geese	■									■	■	■
white-fronted geese	■									■	■	■

Fishing is allowed year-round at North Marsh/Upper Lake, Middle Pond, and Lower Lake. Common fish caught include **largemouth bass**, **green sunfish**, and **catfish**. State and federal regulations apply. Hunting for **waterfowl, dove, rabbit,** and **quail** is permitted in the public hunting area south of the refuge headquarters on specified days during hunting season, which follows Nevada state regulations.

raptors as you drive or walk the shore road. Migratory seasons are best for viewing a variety of raptors, but nesting occurs in summer. Mountain lion have even been spotted here in the thick woods at the north end of North Marsh.

Black Canyon is another prime birding area. Its marshes shelter lots of pintail ducks and other waterfowl in winter, and the trees support songbirds in spring and summer. Lower Lake is ephemeral, and its shallows provide good habitat for dabbling ducks and the graceful tundra swan in winter and migratory waders—including lesser yellowlegs, spotted sandpiper, and marbled godwit—in fall and spring, Greater sandhill cranes can be spotted in the fields and small impoundments just south of the refuge headquarters. The surrounding uplands may provide views of roadrunners, Gambel's quail, and mourning dove.

■ **HIKES AND WALKS:** Upper Lake is encircled by a 2.5-mile, easygoing combination road and trail. You can also walk the road along North Marsh and Upper Lake's eastern edge and out across the two dikes across the lake at its middle and its south end. Another short trail runs about 0.25 mile along the western edge of North Marsh from the north dike. A road, accessible from NV 93, cuts through a stretch of open marshland just north of and past Middle Pond. Hikers can also walk a trail on the east, south, and north shores of Middle Pond or stroll the road beside Lower Lake's east shore.

Refugee staff and representatives of the Southern Paiute people are discussing possibilities for limited viewing of prehistoric petroglyphs in Black Canyon (south of Upper Lake on the east side of NV 93). Ancient low stone walls built to provide some protection from the elements, the existence of sacred plants growing here, and hundreds of images etched in stone attest to this site's importance to the ancestors of today's Paiutes. Visitors should treat this area with the utmost respect. From the mesa sides you can look up and down the Pahranagat Valley and into a side canyon popular with wildlife.

■ **PUBLICATIONS:** Brochure, bird list.

Ruby Lake NWR
Ruby Valley, Nevada

Canada geese on snow with Ruby Mountains on horizon

Ruby Lake NWR is a fish out of water. It is essentially a valley surrounded by icy alpine terrain—all set down in the Great Basin Desert. Yet this remnant marsh, a sparkling picture of white on white, teems with life. Trumpeter swans bob on the water, upending themselves, dunking for roots and shoots. Others rest on the snow-covered ice, heads tucked under a wing, snakish necks draped over white shoulders. These messengers of the Arctic winds speak a language all their own—and, wary of man, they keep their distance. A brilliant sun glints off the high peaks of the Ruby Mountains, which rise abruptly from the valley. Fishermen wade and cast in a pocket of ice-rimmed open water, while clusters of horned larks skip along a dry levee, scratching for seeds.

HISTORY

In the pleistocene epoch, a 470-square-mile lake more than 200 feet deep covered a long valley in the area now occupied by this refuge. As the climate warmed, the lake largely dried up, leaving behind the remnant marsh, now Ruby Lake NWR. A rich natural resource, it has drawn people here for eons. Evidence of prehistoric people who roamed throughout northeastern Nevada can be found all along the west side of the refuge at the foot of the mountains. In 1859 Captain J. H. Simpson explored the valley as an alternative route to the West coast. He wrote, "Large numbers of Sho-sho-nees winter in Ruby Valley, on account of it being warmer than the other valleys around. . . . As many as 1500 must have staid here last winter."

The Ruby Valley was also an important stop on the Pony Express route, and from 1862 to 1869 the valley was the site of Fort Ruby. Nothing on the refuge remains of these structures, but visitors can take a close look at a pioneer cabin built in 1880 by Pennsylvanian Jacob Bressman. In 1938 President Franklin Roosevelt set aside 37,632 acres for the refuge. Ruby Valley averages 45,000 visitors a year, although this changes in response to the fishing quality.

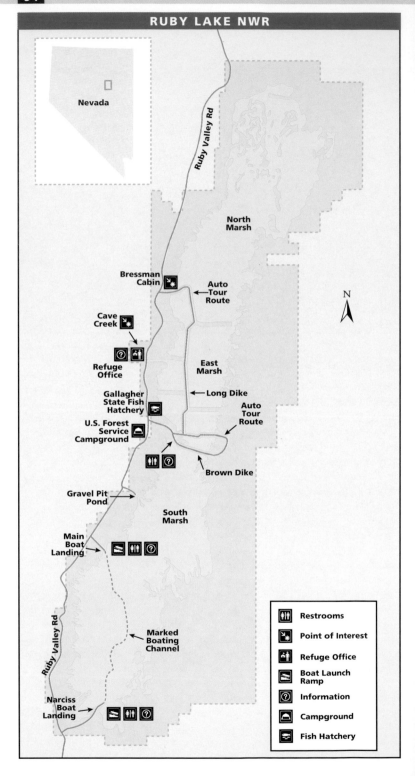

RUBY LAKE NWR

Nevada

North Marsh

Ruby Valley Rd

Bressman Cabin

Auto Tour Route

Cave Creek

Refuge Office

East Marsh

Gallagher State Fish Hatchery

Long Dike

Auto Tour Route

U.S. Forest Service Campground

Brown Dike

Gravel Pit Pond

South Marsh

Main Boat Landing

Ruby Valley Rd

Marked Boating Channel

Narciss Boat Landing

N

Restrooms

Point of Interest

Refuge Office

Boat Launch Ramp

Information

Campground

Fish Hatchery

GETTING THERE

Isolated Ruby Lake NWR is in northeastern Nevada, southeast of Elko and northwest of Ely. From Elko, take NV 227 south to NV 228 and proceed through Jiggs to Forest Service Rd. 113 (dirt) for 10 mi. over Harrison Pass. At its junction with Ruby Valley Rd. (gravel), turn south (right) and proceed 8 mi. to the refuge Visitor Center. Note: Harrison Pass is not suitable for RVs and is closed from late fall through mid-spring. In winter from Elko proceed east on I-80 to NV 229 at Halleck, then southward through Arthur to the Ruby Valley Rd. This later route spans 65 mi. From Ely, head west on US 50 for 32 mi. to the Long Valley Rd. (gravel and dirt) and turn north (right). Proceed 35 mi. to the refuge Visitor Center. This route covers 96 mi. Note: While signed, this route should be attempted only with a detailed map and in good weather—winter travel via this route is discouraged. In general, call ahead for road conditions Nov. through May.

■ **SEASON:** Open year-round.

■ **HOURS:** The refuge is open daily one hour before sunrise to two hours after sunset. The Visitor Center is open Mon. through Fri. 7 a.m.–4 p.m. (except during occasional winter storms and on major holidays). Note: Unlike most of Nevada, which is on Pacific time, the refuge operates on Mountain Standard Time year-round.

■ **FEES:** Entry is free.

■ **ADDRESS:** HC 60, Box 860, Ruby Valley, NV 89833-9802

■ **TELEPHONE:** 775/779-2237

■ **VISITOR CENTER:** A Visitor Center with small displays, some literature, staff, and emergency phone is located on Ruby Valley Rd. Nearest fuel and food, however, are 13 miles north at Ruby Lake Resort.

TOURING RUBY LAKE

■ **BY AUTOMOBILE:** Wending through a portion of the refuge's marsh bottomlands is a 7.5-mile dirt-gravel auto-tour route built atop long dikes. The northern end is on Ruby Valley Rd., 1.5 miles north of the Visitor Center. Short side roads branch off this main stem, which returns to the main road just south of Gallagher State Fish Hatchery. The route is well marked, including identification of various water bodies. Historic Bressman Cabin is located just off Ruby Valley Rd. at the auto route's north end. The cabin, which was built in the 1880s, is not open to the public.

Snow or heavy rain can briefly shut down the tour route, but it is suitable for ordinary cars in most conditions and for RVs up to 25 feet. ATVs are prohibited on the refuge; all vehicles must be licensed.

Ruby Valley Rd., running 16 miles north and south through the refuge, also provides additional vantage points for seeing wildlife. A mature bald eagle flew off a sign on this road, giving us the yellow eye during our visit.

■ **BY FOOT:** All the roads open to public access, including the auto route and its spurs, are also open to people on foot. Some levees separating marsh units not open to car traffic can also be walked. In addition, there is a 1.2-mile (round-trip) hiking trail along a stretch of Cave Creek, which climbs westward into the Rubies, and walking on the banks of the 6.5-mile-long Collection Ditch is allowed. However, entry into many marshes is prohibited to protect nesting waterfowl.

■ **BY BICYCLE:** Bicyclists will find nice going here along the auto-tour route. Ruby Valley Rd. is also available for bikers, but watch for vehicles. The Harrison Pass Rd., just outside the refuge, offers a true biking challenge.

PIÑON-JUNIPER WOODLANDS What creosote is to the Southwest's deserts, the evergreen cousins *juniper* and *piñon* are to the region's mid-elevations. While piñon-juniper woodlands are always common in the region, intensive livestock grazing and modern fire suppression, which reduced or eliminated grasslands, has led to an explosive growth of piñon-juniper woodlands on mountain slopes and mesas between the elevations of 4,500 feet and 8,000 feet.

Five juniper species and several varieties of piñon grow in the Southwest. They often take root side by side, although piñon occupy the higher elevations of their range.

Filled with pitch, piñon is valued as an aromatic fuel wood, while mature trees produce perhaps the world's most costly nut—the pine nut, a sweet, delicious little morsel laboriously collected mainly in western and northern New Mexico. Pine nuts are used in Italian cooking to make pesto sauce (with basil) and a pignoli (pine-nut) dessert. Tart, purple-to-gray-green juniper "berries" flavor gin and dried meat, while woodrats, bear, coyote, bluebirds, and other wildlife love to eat the berries raw.

Piñon and juniper are very slow growing, eking out existence in often marginal conditions—rocky soils, intensive cold, heat, and periodic droughts. But their patience is rewarded: They can live as long as 400 years.

■ **BY CANOE, KAYAK, OR BOAT:** No boating Jan. 1 through June 14. From June 15 through Jul. 31, motorless and battery-powered boats are allowed south of Brown Dike. Between Aug. 1 and Dec. 31, motorless- and boats with motors 10 HP or less are allowed in the South Marsh. There are two launch sites: Main Boat Landing and Narciss Boat Landing. Cartop boats can be launched also at Gravel Pit Pond and Brown Dike. Life jackets are required. It's easy to get lost in the tall bulrush of South Marsh; novices beware!

WHAT TO SEE

■ **LANDSCAPE AND CLIMATE** Ruby Lake NWR is breathtakingly beautiful and, at 16 miles by 3 miles, big. Situated in the domain of Great Basin Desert, it is nonetheless essentially a mountain preserve. Running along the western border are the impressive Ruby Mountains, whose 11,000-foot summits rise above treeline in vast expanses of silver and gray rock spires, and whose canyons' lower slopes support huge forests of various pine, juniper, and aspen.

To the east of the refuge is another large mountain complex, the Maverick Springs Range, and at the valley's northern end is still another lofty range. Thus, Ruby Valley is almost entirely surrounded by alpine terrain.

Precipitation trapped by the mountains descends in many streams to collect in large marshes on the valley floor, including South Marsh (7,000 acres) and North Marsh (3,000 acres). Marsh water levels on the refuge are regulated by a system of crisscrossing dikes and ditches. Some 160 springs create additional pools of open water. Surrounding these wetlands are some 20,600 acres of meadows, grasslands, alkali playas, and shrub-steppe uplands.

At a 6,000-foot elevation, winters here can be long and hard; there are only 60 frost-free days a year on average. The typical winter low is 13 degrees, but in 1991 the thermometer bottomed out at 45 degrees below zero. Summer highs are moderate for Nevada, around 88 degrees. Average precipitation is 13 inches. Each season at Ruby Lake has something to recommend it, though winter can be a challenge. Staff members say the most scenic month is May, when snow lingers high on the Rubies and the valley refuge bursts with new greenery and wildflowers.

■ PLANT LIFE

Wetlands The refuge protects 17,000 acres of marshes, a mosaic of open water, dense stands of bulrush, cattails, and small islands. Pools at the refuge's many springs support pockets of riparian vegetation.

Grasslands Dominating the transition zone between marsh and upland habitats are sedges, rushes, grasses, and many species of wildflowers. In general, the southeastern end of the refuge is drier than the north end and contains its best grasslands.

Open waters Cave Creek and several other small streams run out of the mountains onto the refuge, and they are graced with narrow riparian ribbons of deciduous and evergreen trees, bushes, and annual and perennial flowers.

Arid lands For an interesting contrast, explore the vegetation along the refuge's uplands on its western edge. Here it's of Great Basin Desert lineage, reflecting the broader local geography despite the refuge's alpinelike character. In the uplands, the dominant color is bluish-gray sagebrush, *the* Great Basin's defining plant, mixed with the common grass—Great Basin wild rye.

Forests At the upper edge on the western boundary of Ruby Lake refuge you will find some stands of piñon pine and west-

Trumpeter swans

ern juniper. Higher on the slopes of the Rubies, outside the refuge, are dense forests of limber pine, bristlecone pine, and aspen. A fire in 1979 burned a large tract of this forest directly above the refuge; today it attracts cavity-dwelling birds.

■ ANIMAL LIFE

Birds Serving as a crossroads for migratory species on both the Pacific and Central flyways, Ruby Lake is regularly visited by more than 220 bird species. This includes the greatest concentration of nesting canvasback ducks in western North America, large numbers of redheads, and 13 other waterfowl species, as well as coots, grebes, herons, egrets, white-faced ibis, avocets, and marsh wrens. Sept. and Oct. bring concentrations of up to 50,000 waterfowl and coots.

High on the bird beauty list is the trumpeter swan. This regal, formerly endangered bird was originally transplanted here from Red Rock Lakes NWR in

Montana between 1947 and 1958. Trumpeters have done well at Ruby Lake; some eight pairs stay year-round raising their young, and as many as 55 can be found overwintering from fall through late spring. They are joined by 50 to 60 other robust bird species, including some bald eagles, horned larks, plentiful marsh hawks, and chukar.

May and June are the best months to observe nesting and migrating songbirds. Greater sandhill cranes can also be spotted on the refuge, and some 20 pairs nest here. Willet, spotted sandpiper, and long-billed curlew nest at Ruby Lake, among the 13 shorebirds found in the valley marshlands. The drier uplands support sage grouse, dusky flycatcher, and burrowing owls.

Large contingents of sparrows—19 species in all, including green-tailed towhee, sage sparrow, and grasshopper sparrow—flit around the refuge, particularly its uplands.

Mammals Mule deer and coyote are the large mammals most frequently seen. Also present, but observable only occasionally at dawn or dusk, are bobcats. Easily spotted swimming in the marshes are muskrats, whose houses and feeding platforms provide resting and nesting sites for waterfowl. Of the refuge's four rabbit species, black-tailed jackrabbit pop into view most often. Still other mammals include weasels, badgers, beaver, and many species of mice, rats, voles, and the pocket gopher.

Reptiles and amphibians During the summer, Great Basin rattlesnakes often cross the main valley road, while garter snakes keep to the marsh areas. The leopard frog is the only amphibian on the refuge.

ACTIVITIES

■ **CAMPING:** There is a campground in adjoining Humboldt National Forest, located on Ruby Valley Rd., midpoint in the refuge (open Memorial Day to mid-Oct.).

■ **SWIMMING:** Swimming is prohibited.

■ **WILDLIFE OBSERVATION:** The auto-tour route and its associated marshes and levees provide fine sites for birding. South Marsh is prime territory, sheltering large numbers of nesting canvasback and redhead ducks. Even in winter,

Mule deer

RUBY LAKE HUNTING AND FISHING SEASONS

Hunting
(Seasons may vary)

	Jan	Feb	Mar	Apr	May	Jun	Jul	Aug	Sep	Oct	Nov	Dec
ducks	■									■	■	■
coot	■									■	■	■
snipe	■									■	■	■
geese	■									■	■	■

Fishing
(Seasons may vary)

	Jan	Feb	Mar	Apr	May	Jun	Jul	Aug	Sep	Oct	Nov	Dec
largemouth bass							■	■		■		
trout	■	■	■	■	■	■			■	■	■	■

Parts of the refuge are open to fishing year-round, including the Collection Ditch, marsh units north of Brown Dike, the spring ponds, and South Marsh. Wading, bank fishing, and float fishing are allowed in specific locations and seasons. Fish taken here include **largemouth bass, and rainbow, eastern brook**, and **brown trout**. In some winters, ice fishing is possible. Possession of bait fish is illegal. Limited **waterfowl** hunting (by boat and some walk-in terrain) is allowed on the refuge during the season established by the state of Nevada.

when much of the marsh freezes over, there is open water in South Marsh where the Collection Ditch empties into it and in the larger spring ponds. Here you will find overwintering waterfowl.

If you're out in the morning before the anglers, the banks, brush, and waters of the Collection Ditch can also reveal plentiful birdlife year-round, including wading species, waterfowl, and songbirds.

To view shorebirds and dabbling ducks, head to East Marsh, where the shallow water depth is to their liking. Riparian habitat along Cave Creek is another ecological niche appealing particularly to songbirds—several first-occurrence records for Nevada have been recorded here.

Mule deer are most commonly noted in winter as they move from the foothills down to grasslands and the marsh waters. In summer pronghorn speed around the refuge's southern and eastern edges, but they are hard to spot.

■ **PHOTOGRAPHY:** The weathered exterior of Bressman cabin speaks of its age and Ruby Valley's rough climate. Mornings provide the best exposure for photographing the Ruby Mountains along the refuge's western boundary. Summer greenery doesn't really come on until June, but even the dead of winter here produces some extraordinarily beautiful scenes.

■ **HIKES AND WALKS:** Cave Creek Trail makes for a pleasant walk, paralleling the stream for 1.2 miles. The trail provides great views of the valley and a closer look at riparian vegetation along many streams tumbling out of the mountains. The trail begins where the creek runs under the Ruby Valley Rd., immediately to the south of the Visitor Center.

■ **PUBLICATIONS:** Brochure; bird and mammal list; fishing, hunting, boating guidelines.

Sheldon NWR
Northwestern Nevada

Pronghorn antelope, Sheldon NWR

These are the high semidesert lands of the northern Great Basin, where only a century ago cattle and sheep grazed by the thousands on sprawling ranches. Sheldon NWR has seven historic ranching sites from those days, including Last Chance Ranch and Kinney Camp. Encompassing almost 575,000 acres, Sheldon has scant annual visitation of only 15,000—which works out to 38 acres per person, plenty of room for you and the wildlife to roam.

HISTORY

Evidence of humanity on the refuge extends back at least 12,000 years, and petroglyphs as old as 7,000 years have been found. About 1,500 years ago, ancestors of today's Northern Paiute and Shoshone Indians occupied the area. In the early 1800s white trappers and explorers blazed through, followed by wagon trains of settlers. Vast cattle and sheep ranches were established, but overgrazing eventually contributed to their collapse.

The refuge was founded in 1931 by the Boone and Crockett Club and the National Audubon Society, and it is named after Charles Sheldon—avid sportsman, explorer, and conservationist. In 1976 the property transferred to the U.S. Fish & Wildlife Service.

GETTING THERE

The refuge lies in northwestern Nevada, bordering the Oregon line. From Winnemucca, NV, take US 95 north 31 mi. to NV 140, turn west (left) and proceed 68 mi. to Denio Junction. Go west (left) on NV 140 for another 17 mi. to the refuge's eastern boundary. NV 140 cuts across the refuge's northeastern corner, into Oregon. Pick up a refuge brochure, available another 12 mi. along this road.

From Lakeview, OR, head north 5 mi. to OR 140, turn east (right) and proceed 65 mi. southeast to Sheldon's northern entrance.

You can also enter the refuge on long, graded dirt roads from the west and south, but 4-wheel-drive/high-clearance vehicles are strongly advised.

■ **SEASON:** Open year-round, but refuge roads (other than NV 140) are not maintained in winter.

■ **HOURS:** Refuge open 24 hours daily.

■ **FEES:** Free entry.

■ **ADDRESS:** P.O. Box 111, Lakeview, OR 97630

■ **TELEPHONE:** 541/947-3315

■ **VISITOR CENTER:** No visitor facilities or services of any kind on the refuge, except primitive campgrounds. Emergency phone available at field office, when manned. Refuge brochures and maps (including campground locations) are available at north entrance and Virgin Valley Campground.

TOURING SHELDON

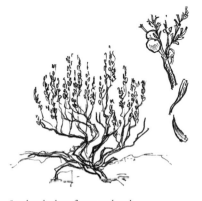

■ **BY AUTOMOBILE:** NV 140 slices across Sheldon's northeast corner. The refuge also maintains about 100 miles of graded dirt roads and comparable miles of jeep trails. Graded roads are passable for ordinary vehicles in dry weather.

■ **BY FOOT:** All parts of the refuge are open to hiking, but there are no established, maintained trails. Closed roads are used for hiking.

■ **BY BICYCLE:** Mountain biking is allowed on all open refuge roads.

Sagebrush plant, flower, and seed

WHAT TO SEE

■ **LANDSCAPE AND CLIMATE** Flat, open tablelands and rolling hills are cut by narrow canyons and by wider valleys with borders of precipitous rocky rims. Each major canyon contains a creek, and many drain into Virgin Creek, which over the years has carved a deep, vertical-walled canyon called Thousand Creek Gorge. Several mountains poke above the tablelands and canyons. Elevations run from 4,100 to 7,200 feet.

Precipitation is sparse, averaging 14 to 17 inches a year. Temperatures vary radically, season to season and day to night, with lows of -30 degrees and highs exceeding 100. Winters are harsh, with drifting snow and high winds. Sheldon is best visited from late spring through mid-fall.

■ PLANT LIFE

Wetlands A variety of emergent plants, such as cattails, roundstem bulrush, black rush, and various sedges, grow around the refuge marshes, alkaline lakes, wet meadows, ponds, and fresh lakes.

Shrublands Sagebrush is a signature plant of the Great Basin, particularly its colder northern half. Sagebrush ecosystems cover the largest area of any plant community in the nation, more than half the acreage of the 11 western states. Big sagebrush grows 2 to 7 feet high and has silvery blue-green ever-present leaves and dark gray bark. Low sagebrush features a darker leaf, grows to less than 18 inches, and prefers higher elevations. Sagebrush is the food of choice for pronghorn antelope, contributing up to 90 percent of their diet in fall and winter.

Mountainous areas Common to hillsides above 6,000 feet is the deciduous bush mountain mahogany, a slow-growing plant (to 10 feet) with small dark green leaves. Close by is bitterbrush (2 to 6 feet), a favorite browse of mule deer. Stands of juniper populate Sheldon's western edge.

■ ANIMAL LIFE

Birds Some 192 bird species are seen on the refuge. Spring and fall are good times to observe birds here, with both migrating waterfowl and neotropicals, but summer also finds many birds nesting at Sheldon, including at least 10 species of waterfowl—among them Canada geese, mallards, teal, redheads, and ruddy ducks. When water levels fall in the lakes and ponds, shorebirds move in to feed on the exposed shorelines.

HUNTING AND FISHING Fishing at the five Duferrena ponds, Big Springs Reservoir, and Catnip Reservoir is good to excellent. The Nevada state records for **bluegill** and **yellow perch** came out of the Duferrena ponds. Also taken are **Lahontan cutthroat trout**, **rainbow trout**, **cutbows**, **white crappie**, and **largemouth bass**. Hunting of **pronghorn antelope**, **mule deer**, **bighorn sheep**, **California quail**, and **chukar** is allowed. Some areas subject to closure.

The increasingly rare sage grouse, a large chickenlike bird that prefers mixed big and low sagebrush habitat, also favors Sheldon refuge.

Mammals Sheldon was set up initially to protect pronghorn antelope. They remain important residents, with their numbers peaking in winter. But California bighorn sheep also enjoy life on the refuge. Native to the area, they were extirpated in the 1930s but reintroduced in 1968. Some 150 reside here today. You will see abundant mule deer as well as some pesky squatters: wild burros and horses, fast-producing nonnatives whose overgrazing threatens the balance of the native ecosystem.

Note: A fire in the summer of 1999 burned some 42,000 acres of the refuge. This fire is expected to have a significant effect on the habitats of the mule deer and sage grouse.

Fish The refuge shelters Lahontan cutthroat trout (a threatened species), as well as native Alvord chub and Sheldon tui chub.

Reptiles and amphibians Look for the native Pacific treefrog or Great Basin spadefoot toad at almost any Sheldon body of water; these compete against the introduced and rapacious bullfrog. Found throughout the refuge is its only poisonous viper, the western rattlesnake.

ACTIVITIES

■ **CAMPING:** Fourteen primitive campgrounds, including six with handicapped-accessible restrooms. A private campground nearby has RV hookups. Refuge maps contain campground locations.

■ **SWIMMING:** No designated swimming areas, but explore the hot springs pool at Virgin Valley Campground.

■ **WILDLIFE OBSERVATION:** Swan Lake and the area known as Little Sheldon provide good pronghorn viewing. These sites can usually be reached by ordinary vehicles, but call ahead to check road conditions. Of the refuge's 15 reptiles, 12 are found in the Virgin Valley, Bog Hot, or Jackass Flats areas. Deer normally summer on Bald Mountain.

■ **PUBLICATIONS:** Refuge brochure; all-animals species brochure.

Stillwater NWR
Fallon, Nevada

Stillwater NWR

In the midst of a vast desert basin, two thousand tundra swans, like a flotilla of sailboats, float on the waters of a cobalt blue lake. High above, winter snow lingers on mountain summits. When the sun sets, it casts a veil of color over the marsh waters fringed by tall hedges of spiky cattails. It's quiet here—the name Stillwater is apt. But this is a place of much activity, both past and present, all spawned by the incongruous presence of water in the desert.

HISTORY

Stillwater has a long history of human use. For at least 3,000 years people have resided around its marshes, living off abundant plant and animal resources. Paleolithic hunter-gatherers called Marsh People were followed by the Toedokado culture (also known as the Toidikadi or Stillwater Paiute), who occupied the area when the first Euro-American settlers arrived in the mid-1800s.

The Carson River was dammed in the early 1900s, reducing water flow into the marshes to a trickle. In 1948 an effort to stem the loss of this precious resource was undertaken with the creation of the Stillwater Wildlife Management Area. In 1990, 77,500 acres of this management area were set aside as Stillwater NWR. Studies are under way regarding the incorporation of additional management-area acreage as well as select acreage of nearby Fallon NWR into Stillwater. Because of poor road conditions, Fallon is basically inaccessible to the public. Stillwater, however, draws about 35,000 people annually.

GETTING THERE

The refuge is located northeast of the town of Fallon in west-central Nevada. From the corner of Williams Ave. (US 50) and Maine St. (US 95), head east out of Fallon for 4.6 mi. and turn north (left) onto Stillwater Rd. (NV 116). It zigs and zags north and east 12.3 mi. to the refuge entrance.

■ **SEASON:** Open year-round.

■ **HOURS:** The refuge is open 24 hours daily (refuge office in Fallon, open 8 a.m.–4 p.m. weekdays).

■ **FEES:** Free entry.

■ **ADDRESS:** P.O. Box 1236, Fallon, NV 89407. Refuge office: 1,000 Auction Rd., Fallon (off US 50, next to Walmart).

■ **TELEPHONE:** 775/423-5128

■ **VISITOR CENTER:** No facilities on the refuge; bring water and food.

TOURING STILLWATER

■ **BY AUTOMOBILE:** There is a 15-mile auto-tour route on the refuge. It begins east of the refuge entrance on Stillwater Rd. near Stillwater Point Reservoir and runs north on Hunter Rd., and then in a loop between numerous marshes and lakes. A profusion of other roads branch off this main route, offering additional wildlife viewing opportunities. If you venture off the beaten track, carefully note landmarks and road signs—you can get lost out here! There's an astonishing 175 miles of roads open to the public on the refuge, but only the auto route is consistently signed.

■ **BY FOOT:** This sprawling refuge doesn't lend itself to exploration on foot— large waterless tracts separate many of the marshes. There are no dedicated foot trails. Visitors may walk any open refuge roads, however, and only one small section of the refuge is off-limits to the public.

■ **BY BICYCLE:** Bike travel on open refuge roads is authorized but is not very practical because of the large distances to be covered between marshes.

■ **BY CANOE, KAYAK, OR BOAT:** Boats with motors up to 10 hp are allowed in refuge waters. There are 16 launch sites scattered throughout the central section of the refuge.

WHAT TO SEE

■ **LANDSCAPE AND CLIMATE** Stillwater lies on the floor of a huge basin called the Carson Sink, hemmed in on the west by the distant Sierra Nevada mountains and by the Stillwater Range immediately to the east. Twelve thousand years ago Lake Lahontan, a giant lake created by melting glaciers in the mountain, filled the valleys of western Nevada. The lake's wave action can be noted in the notches in the hillsides on the refuge's south border. As the climate warmed and the glaciers largely disappeared, the lake dried up, leaving remnant marsh complexes such as Stillwater. Today, hundreds of large and small bodies of water are circled by flourishing marshes and large areas of mudflats.

A Great Basin Desert ecosystem predominates around the refuge marshes, including a section of silt dunes on its northern edge covering 30 to 40 square miles. Stillwater is almost treeless, although cottonwoods and tamarisk rim most of the lakes in the Indian Lakes section of the adjoining Stillwater Wildlife Management Area.

Most amazing are the wet years, such as 1986, when snowmelt brought prodigious volumes of water down the Carson River and flooded Stillwater and other sectors of the Carson Sink. It was so wet you could ride an airboat across Carson Sink for 35 miles, and old Lake Lahontan showed signs of returning. This wet period was followed by a drought, and by 1992 fewer than 100 acres of wetlands remained on Stillwater.

Temperatures here can be daunting: up to 105 degrees in the summer, with winter lows of 10 degrees. And, there's little precipitation: 5 inches a year, average.

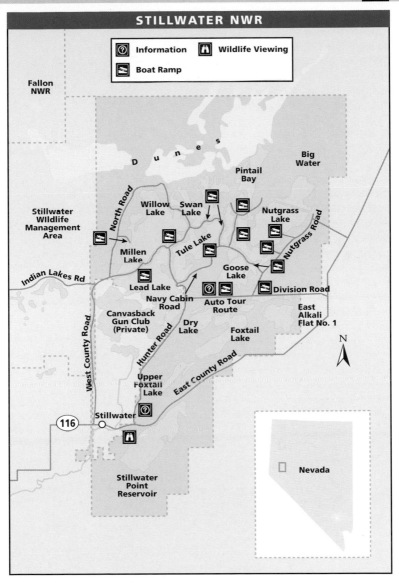

May and June are probably the best months to visit: The combination of weather
and the number of bird species present make it ideal.

■ PLANT LIFE:

Wetlands Although water flow can be erratic at Stillwater, the refuge attempts
to keep 14,000 acres classified as marsh and open water. Freshwater marshes contain cattail and hardstem bulrush and, in deeper water, a favorite waterfowl
food—sago pondweed. The leaching of minerals from surrounding hills, agricultural runoff, and evaporation create many alkaline and somewhat salty ponds
dominated by beds of alkali bulrush and, in deeper water, musk grass. Occasional
high runoffs in the Carson River fill sloughs, creating some 250 to 500 acres a year
of salt grass meadows. Infrequently, mass flooding causes huge swaths of land to

disappear under a few feet of water, which slowly drain off, creating immense, if temporary, wetlands.

Arid lands Greasewood holds down patches of sandy soils scattered through-out the refuge. It was on these "islands" that the Marsh People made their homes and raised their families. The hot-burning greasewood provided them with excellent firewood for cooking and warmth. Here, too, are found native herbs, wild-flowers, and some native grasses.

■ ANIMAL LIFE

Birds Stillwater attracts 250,000 to 350,000 swans, ducks, and geese annually, including extensive flocks of tundra swans and large numbers of pintail, green-winged teal, shovelers, and canvasback ducks—roughly 25 percent of the entire Pacific Flyway population of the latter species. The southward fall waterfowl migration peaks in Oct. and Nov., but March and April also bring large numbers of ducks (primarily redheads) heading north. Some mallard, pintail, and wood ducks are year-round residents, as are black-billed magpies.

Aug. and Sept. shorebird migrations, with up to 350,000 birds, are also spec-tacular—so much so that Stillwater was designated a unit of the Western Hemisphere Shorebird Network in 1988, one of a series of sites of critical value to shorebirds running from Alaska to Tierra del Fuego. Most common are avocets, black-necked stilts, Wilson's phalaropes, and long-billed dowitchers. Great blue and black-crowned night herons and several egret species nest here in summer.

Twelve species of vultures, hawks, and falcons fly at Stillwater, including the more common marsh hawk, red-tail, and Swainson's hawk—which all nest locally—as well as ferruginous hawk, golden and bald eagles, short-eared owls, and prairie falcon.

Fall and spring also see the influx of large numbers of migratory songbirds, including western kingbirds, sage thrasher, and yellow-rumped warbler, into the refuge. Stillwater shelters a sizable number of white pelicans as well, particularly in the summer and fall months. In all, some 250 bird species have been recorded at Stillwater refuge.

Cinnamon teal duck

Mammals Mule deer are sometimes seen at Stillwater, but you're more likely to spot muskrats swimming in the marsh edges or coyote prowling about. The dry uplands are home to many animals, but only a few, including black-tailed jackrabbits and antelope ground squirrel, are active by day. At night, kangaroo rats, pocket mice, and voles emerge from their burrows and are hunted by kit fox and badgers.

Reptiles and amphibians Collard and leopard lizards frequent the dry uplands, along with bull snakes. Great Basin rattlesnakes are rarely found on the refuge.

Fish The Tui chub, native to these waters and once an important food to the Marsh People, still occupy some marshes but at a fraction of their former numbers. Carp, introduced in the 1890s, are believed to be a contributing factor to the chubs' demise.

ACTIVITIES

■ **CAMPING:** Free camping throughout the refuge is allowed but seldom done due to the inhospitable landscape and climate. Most campers congregate around Indian Lakes on the adjoining Stillwater Wildlife Management Area where shaded sites are available.

■ **WILDLIFE OBSERVATION:** Driving the auto route provides the best chances for seeing a variety of wildlife on this mazelike refuge. Some of the best birding is out along the levee separating Nutgrass unit from Goose Lake. The canal along Navy Cabin Rd. is generally very active with grebes, coots, and ruddy ducks in spring. Hunter Rd. offers good chances to see golden eagles, rough-legged hawks, and an occasional peregrine falcon.

> **HUNTING AND FISHING**
> Limited **waterfowl**-only hunting on the refuge from Division Rd. north is allowed from mid-Oct. through mid-Jan. Contact the refuge for details. Fishing is allowed, but no fish are stocked.

The refuge's extensive mudflats are popular with wading birds, such as avocet and black-necked stilt, which feed on the brine flies and aquatic insects.

For the best chance to see mule deer, scan the fields to the west as you head north on Hunter Rd. Also watch the trees and power poles as you drive toward the refuge along Stillwater Rd.; there you may spot more than a few raptors and perching birds.

■ **PHOTOGRAPHY:** Some interesting photo possibilities can be found just at sunset by shooting reflective scenes with water and the beautiful Stillwater Range to the east.

■ **HIKES AND WALKS:** Stillwater does not offer designated hiking trails; however, all open roads are available. The places noted for good wildlife viewing are best bets for parking the car on the road shoulder and stretching your legs. Certain areas are open for hunting in the fall and winter, so be on the lookout for any closure signs during those seasons.

■ **SEASONAL EVENTS:** In mid-May, over a three-day period, the refuge hosts the annual Spring Wings Bird Festival with workshops, guided tours, a wildlife art show, and a banquet with keynote speaker.

■ **PUBLICATIONS:** Brochure and bird list.

Bitter Lake NWR
Roswell, New Mexico

Bitter Lake NWR

It appears first as a harsh, alien land, with sinkholes and salt-encrusted mudflats pockmarking a largely treeless face. But down among the marsh bulrushes, a Pecos pupfish changes color as it enters its mating phase. A bobcat pads warily from behind the brilliant red rimrock and descends towards the roosting grounds of thousands of sandhill cranes. A crescent moon rises over winter's yellow grasslands. Here, at the juncture of the Great Plains and the Chihuahuan Desert, it's a good night to hunt.

HISTORY

The majority of Bitter Lake's 24,536 acres was acquired in 1937 to provide nesting and feeding grounds for waterbirds, marshbirds, and shorebirds on an important Central Flyway. The refuge's largest natural body of water, Bitter Lake, is a large, shallow playa with brackish water that often goes dry in the summer, leaving a white alkaline bed. Iodinebush, growing abundantly but inconspicuously around the refuge's many playa lakes, was once raised by Pima Indians in Arizona for its seeds (used for the staple food *pinole*), so it's probable that native people gathered here to hunt, though not for long-term settlement. Today 40,000 people a year visit Bitter Lake's natural wonderland, home to some 24 animal species listed as threatened or endangered and many endemic species.

The refuge is divided into four areas: North Tract, the Salt Creek Wilderness Area, Middle Tract (including the refuge ponds and auto route), and South Tract.

GETTING THERE

The refuge is located 13 mi. northeast of Roswell, NM, in the Pecos River Valley of southeastern New Mexico. From the intersection of US 285 and US 380, head north 4 mi. on US 285, turn east (right) onto East Pine Lodge Rd. and proceed 9 mi. to the refuge headquarters.

■ **SEASON:** Refuge open year-round.

■ **HOURS:** Open daily from one hour before sunrise until one hour after sunset, unless otherwise posted.

■ **FEES:** Free entry.

■ **ADDRESS:** P.O. Box 7, Roswell, NM 88202

■ **TELEPHONE:** 505/622-6755

■ **VISITOR CENTER:** The refuge headquarters has a small visitor contact station with an interesting display on Bitter Lake's endemic fish, a staff member, and restroom. Open 7:30 a.m.–4 p.m.; closed major holidays.

TOURING BITTER LAKE

■ **BY AUTOMOBILE:** An 8.5-mile self-guiding gravel-road auto tour winds around the six man-made lakes on the refuge's Middle Tract, providing a good overview of the marshlands and desert uplands. Rare winter blizzards and drenching summer rains may close this road. In addition, a paved road running north of the refuge headquarters provides a view of Bitter Lake itself, and US 70 looks out on the Salt Creek Wilderness Area—a refuge subsection.

■ **BY FOOT:** There is one short, dedicated foot trail on the refuge's Middle Tract, and 8.5 miles of gravel roads are also open to the public for walking. The entire Salt Creek Wilderness Area is accessible only on foot.

■ **BY BICYCLE:** Biking is allowed on the 8.5-mile auto tour route, but no dedicated bike trails exist.

WHAT TO SEE

■ **LANDSCAPE AND CLIMATE** Bitter Lake reflects a complex overlapping of the rolling shortgrass prairie of the Southern Great Plains and the drier upland terrain of the Chihuahua Desert's northernmost reaches. But there's more. Natural aquifers and underlying limestone and gypsum deposits—remnants of the Permian Sea that once covered this region—have produced 60 sinkholes linked by creeks on the refuge harboring many native life forms. Water impoundments and natural marshes on the edges of the Pecos River create wetlands, while ephemeral shallow playas come and go depending on rainfall. There are some extensive dune fields in the 10,000-acre Salt Creek Wilderness Area and red-rimmed plateaus along the Pecos River's eastern bank.

With an elevation of 3,500 feet, Bitter Lake's winters are generally mild. Spring days vary from perfect to windy and cold or windy and hot. Fall weather is generally wonderful here, while summer days can be oppressively hot.

■ **PLANT LIFE**
**Wetlands and water-
ways** Spring water and
seeps retained behind con-
structed dikes, natural
sinkholes linked by small
waterways, playas, and the
banks of the Pecos River
combine to create a robust,
water-loving plant com-
munity at Bitter Lake. Bulrushes and cattails cluster
along marsh edges, while
tall marsh cane, kochia,

Coyote

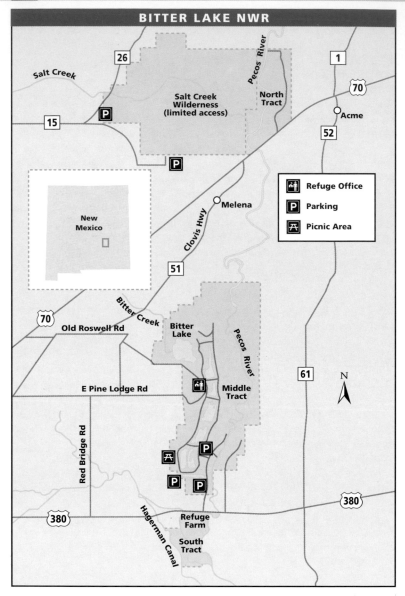

BITTER LAKE NWR

Salt Creek

26

Pecos River

1

70

Salt Creek
Wilderness
(limited access)

North
Tract

Acme

15

52

New
Mexico

Melena

Clovis Hwy

	Refuge Office
P	Parking
	Picnic Area

51

Bitter Creek

70

Old Roswell Rd

Bitter
Lake

Pecos River

E Pine Lodge Rd

Middle
Tract

61

N

Red Bridge Rd

P

P

P

380

380

Hagerman Canal

Refuge
Farm

South
Tract

and sunflowers favor slightly higher ground around the ponds and marshes. The Pecos puzzle sunflower, which flowers here in late Aug. and Sept., is one of the world's rarest sunflowers, growing in saline wetlands. How it has adapted to such conditions in contrast to other sunflowers is a puzzle. It is found only here, a handful of other locations in New Mexico, and one site in Texas.

Some of the refuge's bodies of water also support mats of aquatic vegetation called musk grass, a lime-colored algae providing important cover for native fish and food for ducks, and a few of the sinkholes sustain a species of marine algae otherwise found only in the Gulf of Mexico! The 700-acre area of the sinks is open only to scientific or educational groups with advance notice.

The invasive exotic salt cedar was first noticed in the refuge's bottomlands in

1915 and has since spread over much of the Southwest's lowlands. The refuge is eliminating it but is leaving some stands as important windbreaks and cover for wildlife.

Grasslands Rolling grasslands cover the majority of the refuge. When first "discovered" by American cattlemen like the legendary Texan John Chisum, the entire Pecos River Valley was prime rangeland. From 1866 to 1869 some 300,000 head of cattle were raised here and driven north to railheads in Colorado; the land is still recovering. Today Bitter Lake's grasssland is dominated by a tough bunch grass called alkali sacaton, as well as gyp grama.

Uplands Creosote, tarbush, fourwing saltbush, and mesquite predominate on the Chihuahuan Desert uplands. Where the soil is well drained and lower in salt concentrations, mixed stands of prickly pear cactus, cholla cactus, and Mormon tea are common.

■ ANIMAL LIFE

Birds Protection of the lesser sandhill crane, other marshbirds, waterbirds, and shorebirds provided the impetus for the establishment of Bitter Lake refuge, and they have done extremely well here. Between 5,000 and 15,000 lesser sandhill cranes normally roost on the refuge from Nov. to Feb., but as many as 70,000 have been recorded at times! This is a significant portion of the world's population of this species. Upwards of 20,000 ducks—including wigeon, pintail, and ruddy—and 40,000 geese—mostly snow but some Canada—visit here during fall migration. Some 30 species of waterfowl have been seen on the refuge.

A prominent migratory waterbird is the white pelican. Spring migration brings thousands of shorebirds to the muddy playas. Bitter Lake itself is home to nesting snowy plovers, a threatened shorebird. Other warm-weather residents include killdeer, avocet, black-necked stilt, and the endangered interior least tern, which has chosen this refuge as its only nesting area in New Mexico. In the uplands are found roadrunner, scaled quail, and pheasant. Raptors are also common—20 species have been recorded. In all, more than 350 bird species have been spotted here.

Black-necked stilt

Mammals Upland residents include bobcats, mule deer, coyote, badgers, pronghorn, and abundant cottontails and black-tailed jackrabbits. A total of 57 mammals are known to frequent the refuge, some far more shy than others. Coyotes are most often heard howling at night; bobcats are secretive; but rabbits and deer are frequently visible.

Reptiles and amphibians Barking frogs—native to three southern New Mexico counties—hide in limestone crevices or gypsum soils: You'll hear their yapping chorus in June and July. Other herps include prairie and western diamondback rattlers, desert massasauga, their enemy the desert kingsnake, New

THE MIGHTY CREOSOTE BUSH Creosote is one tough plant. A resident of some of the harshest terrain in North America—the Sonoran, Chihuahuan, and Mojave deserts—it secretes an armory of volatile oils, resins, and waxes that reduces its water loss to evaporation and repels grazing animals. So powerful and off-putting is its array of foul tastes and odors that the Mexicans call it *hediondilla* ("little stinker"). The plant has no relation, however, to the toxic wood preservative "creosote."

This desert plant's ability to cope with little moisture and to ward off would-be diners have served it well. Since the end of the last Ice Age, creosote has successfully colonized a huge swath of North America's deserts, covering most of northern Mexico and 70,000 square miles elsewhere in the Southwest. Creosote's yellow-green, small leaves (produced year-round) paint the predominate color of the Southwest's arid lands, particularly in well-drained soils of plains and slopes below 4,000 feet. Inch-wide yellow flowers dot the bush following rains, producing cottonball-like fruits.

Although animals find the plant repugnant, its widespread occurrence has led to the evolution of a variety of insects that live only within creosote's protective cover, including several types of grasshoppers, praying mantis, moths, and beetles. Nor are these insects its only friends: The plant's complex chemical properties were appreciated by preindustrial peoples who used it to make soothing poultices of its leaves and stems, and brewed creosote teas to treat a variety of ailments, such as the common cold.

Mexico spadefoot toad, and collared lizard. Altogether, 52 species of reptiles and amphibians reside here.

Fish It's odd that a semidesert landscape would shelter some of the world's rarest fish, but here's proof. In fact, most of the refuge's 24 fish species are native to these, or nearby, sinkholes and small creeks, including the Pecos gambusia, the western mosquito fish, the Mexican tetra, the green-throated darter, the plains killifish, rainwater killifish, and the Pecos pupfish, whose males change magically from dull brown to iridescent blue to attract females in the breeding season.

Invertebrates The sinkholes in the northern section of the refuge's Middle Tract might be compared to biological test tubes harboring unique life forms. The shrimplike half-inch Noel's amphipod is only found in three refuge springs. Koster's spring snail, a dark brown critter only one-tenth of an inch in diameter, has been found in four refuge springs and off-refuge at only one other location, as has the Roswell spring snail.

ACTIVITIES

■ **CAMPING:** Educational group camping, Oct. to March, by special use permit. Primitive camping year-round by special use permit in the Salt Creek Wilderness Area. Picnic tables at several sites overlooking the lakes.

■ **WILDLIFE OBSERVATION:** The auto-tour route provides a fine means of checking out the prolific birdlife here. A prime time is late November and early December, when lesser sandhill crane and geese populations reach their height. Good viewing spots include Lake 6, the preferred midday and overnight roost for arctic nesting snow geese, and the dike between Lakes 15 and 16 is a favorite spot for loafing geese and cranes. Lake 7 is the largest and deepest lake, and during the fall and winter thousands of diving ducks and geese can be viewed here.

Creosote bushes

Cormorants, white pelicans, and various grebes also favor Lake 7. An observation platform to the east of Lake 6 overlooks refuge farmlands crowded with feeding birds during the day.

A large marsh is located off the southeast corner of the auto route, sheltering rails, bitterns, egrets, avocets, stilts, herons, and many other wading and shorebirds. Winding into the marsh is a foot trail. Precious shade trees around refuge headquarters make a good spot to catch May migrants.

HUNTING AND FISHING Deer, rabbit, upland game birds, sandhill crane, and **waterfowl** can all be hunted on the refuge in accordance with state, federal, and refuge regulations. Contact the refuge for further details.

■ **PHOTOGRAPHY:** Although there are many fine sites for photography (given the variety of habitats), there are no photo blinds at Bitter Lake. Your car will have to serve. The red bluffs to the northeast of the refuge make for especially striking pictures in the fading afternoon light.

■ **HIKES AND WALKS:** The nature trail starts next to the restroom on the southeast corner of the auto tour route and is less than 0.25 mile in length. It weaves along the edge of an old river oxbow popular with ducks and shorebirds. Look for the native Pecos puzzle flower. Or explore anywhere in the Salt Creek Wilderness Area and on the North Tract. Use established parking areas on either side of the Pecos River Bridge on US 70.

■ **PUBLICATIONS:** A free bird list and auto-tour brochure.

Bosque del Apache NWR
San Antonio, New Mexico

Snow geese, Bosque del Apache NWR

As the sun's first gold-orange rays slant over the San Pascual Mountains, tens of thousands of snow geese, sandhill cranes, and other waterfowl rise on the morning breeze. With a clamorous din and a blur of flapping wings, the creatures rise from their overnight roosts on the marshes of the Bosque del Apache. This is what the world must have been like ages ago—a profusion of seemingly inexhaustible natural wealth. Later, the powerful New Mexico sun goes to work coloring the surrounding green-tinged Chihuahuan desert uplands and distant mountains. Raptors float languidly on air currents. In the shadows of cottonwood *bosques*, or riverside forests, the winding Rio Grande cuts a life-giving swath through the desert landscape.

HISTORY

Piro Indians settled this stretch of the Rio Grande Valley more than 700 years ago. Late in the 16th century, Spanish explorers and colonists traveling between Mexico and what is now northern New Mexico established America's first "highway," the *Camino Real* ("Royal Road"), up the valley. In the process of befriending the native Piro, colonists introduced decimating diseases. Surviving Piros fled New Mexico with the Spanish during the Pueblo Revolt of 1680 and never returned. Remnants of the Camino Real and Piro villages can be found today within Bosque del Apache NWR. The Apache frequented the area as well, raiding both the Piro villages and the Spanish caravans, and inspired the refuge's name ("woods of the Apache").

President Franklin Roosevelt declared the area a wildlife preserve in 1939, the same year a large Civilian Conservation Corps crew built the first dikes, ponds, and drainage and irrigation canals to control water levels in this intensively managed, 57,191-acre refuge. Today, more than 160,000 people visit the refuge annually.

GETTING THERE

Bosque del Apache is located 18 mi. south of Socorro, near San Antonio. From the north, leave I-25 at Exit 139, head east 0.25 mi. on US 380 to the flashing signal in San Antonio, turn south (right) onto NM 1. Proceed 8 mi. to the Visitor Center. From the south, leave I-25 at Exit 124 (San Marcial), turn east (right) on NM 178 for 1 mi., and then north (left) on NM 1 for 11 mi. to the Visitor Center.

■ **SEASON:** Refuge open year-round.

■ **HOURS:** Open daily (including holidays) from one hour before sunrise to one hour after sunset. Visitor Center open 7:30 a.m.–4 p.m. weekdays, and 8 a.m.–4:30 p.m. weekends; closed Thanksgiving, Christmas, and New Year's Day.

■ **FEES:** Entry $3 per car, $25 per commercial vehicle.

■ **ADDRESS:** P.O. Box 1246, Socorro, NM 87801

■ **TELEPHONE:** 505/835-1828

■ **VISITOR CENTER:** The Bosque del Apache Visitor Center itself is an attraction, with a good 15 minute video (played on request), exhibitions and displays, a fine bookstore, and a gift shop with handmade crafts and artwork. Binocular rentals available for full- or half-day.

TOURING BOSQUE DEL APACHE

■ **BY AUTOMOBILE:** A 15-mile auto-tour route splits into two one-way sections: The southern Marsh Loop (7 miles) and the northern Farm Loop (6 miles), linked by a two-way road (1 mile), allows for a shorter tour if desired. From April through Sept., an additional seasonal tour road is open. Wildlife along the route are accustomed to vehicles, so expect to get some close-up looks. An audio cassette keyed to numbered sites along the route provides interpretive information ($5 at the Visitor Center). Along NM 1, the refuge approach from the north, there are also some fine views of the landscape.

■ **BY FOOT:** The auto-tour roads are open to people on foot, as are other select, well-marked roads. Five trails totaling 18 miles are designed specifically for hiking, with some trails crossing marshlands, one flanking the Rio Grande, and two more accessing the surrounding upland desert.

■ **BY BICYCLE:** The auto-tour route and other marked roads are open to bicyclists. With a mountain bike, you may also ride on the Marsh Overlook Trail (though not up the spur overlook itself). This trail is closed to all foot and bike traffic during the Festival of the Cranes (see Seasonal Events, below).

WHAT TO SEE

■ **LANDSCAPE AND CLIMATE** The dominant land feature of Bosque del Apache is the Rio Grande, although many people visit here and never see it. The river is hidden on the wide, flat valley floor by sinuous cottonwood *bosques* (forests) and choking thickets of tamarisk (salt cedar). The river's waters are drawn out through a complex system of irrigation canals and ditches into ponds, marshes, sloughs, and old oxbows, mimicking what nature used to do through periodic floods.

Lush wetlands—1,600 acres worth—are the primary attraction here for both birds and people, but flanking these bottomlands on the refuge are almost 25,000 acres of Chihuahuan desert mesas and foothills and another 25,000 acres of grasslands. Some 30,850 acres of Bosque's desert terrain and grasslands are protected in three national wilderness areas: Chupadera and Indian Well to the west and Little San Pascual to the east. Elevations run from 4,500 feet to 6,272 feet.

Winter is by far the preferred season here for visitors because of the refuge's great concentrations of waterfowl and cranes. Although most winter days are mild, morning temperatures can dip into the low teens. Spring frequently brings dry winds, while summer afternoon temperatures regularly climb into the 90s. Fall is glorious: clear, calm, and warm.

■ PLANT LIFE

Wetlands The diversion of Rio Grande water and its careful use by refuge staff has created an oasis in the desert. Sunsets flash brilliantly over a liquid sheen of ponds, marshes, and wet meadows supporting a rich profusion of plant life. Most conspicuous in the marshes are cattail, smartweed, and bulrush, fringed by coyote and black willow—which can reach heights of 30 to 50 feet. The coyote willow, a bushy southwestern tree growing 6 feet tall or so, loves water. Its dense red-plum-colored branches, about the thickness of a man's finger, always grow around water in thickets, just the place to hide a wary coyote or two. Look also for a tall, plumed plant, the exotic phragmites, locally called carrizo.

Soils with high salt concentrations favor saltgrass. Summer brings out wild-flowers (spring is too cool in the high desert), including abundant annual sun-flowers. Here also you'll find immense thickets of the exotic invader tamarisk (see sidebar, below), which refuge managers are slowly replacing with native trees and plants. Walk along the Rio Viejo Trail to see their plantings of screwbean mesquite, New Mexico olive, and seep willow, the later covered with dandelion-like seeds in the winter.

Arid lands Above the valley floor rise low mesas and foothills of the Chihuahuan Desert, reaching its northernmost limit in this area. The contrast between the green and wet valley and the arid uplands—a study in browns and beige—is striking. Here you'll find fourwing saltbush, mesquite, hardy evergreen

---

TAMARISK: FROM EURASIA WITH A VENGEANCE Call it the Eurasian invader. Although it has its appealing side—able to survive as an ornamental tree with no watering, beautiful in summer when it sprouts long pink flowering stalks, and eye-catching in fall and winter when it glows a coppery red—the tough tamarisk has done considerable damage to Southwestern ecosystems.

In less than a century—in some areas, in less than two decades—several species of this exotic tree (also known as salt cedar) have taken over huge chunks of the Southwest, particularly around arid land waterways, in many cases completely pushing out native trees and shrubs and the animals dependent upon them.

However, in an odd case of nature finding a way, in at least two NWRs—Pahranagat, Nevada, and Hake Havasu, Arizona—the endangered southwestern willow flycatcher is now nesting in dense stands of tamarisk that have overgrown its dense native willow stands.

Bosque del Apache NWR is a pioneer in the efforts to eradicate invasive tamarisk. A combination of tractors dragging disc tillers and root cutters, plus controlled fire and the judicious use of herbicides (followed by replanting of native flora), is converting large tamarisk tracts to more productive naturally occurring vegetation that, in turn, repopulates with native wildlife.

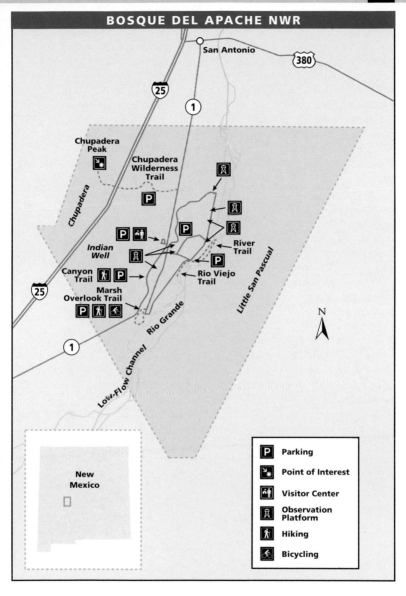

juniper, prickly pear cactus and tree cholla, spiky yucca, Mormon tea, and the most common resident, creosote (see sidebar in Bitter Lake NWR). Summer monsoon rains bring a surprising outburst of many different wildflowers, including desert primrose, aster, and sand penstemon.

Forests The stately cottonwood forests lining the banks of the Rio Grande spread onto high ground near the Farm Loop Rd. Cottonwoods turn a buttery yellow and finally a pale brown as fall slides into winter, their trunks twisting skyward in a graceful chorus. In summer the female trees produce clouds of a fine, cotton-like fluff. Here, too, are the invading tamarisk and Russian olive. A major fire in 1996 burned significant mature cottonwood bosques.

Farmlands To prevent massive raiding by refuge wildlife on neighboring private farms, the Bosque del Apache NWR raises corn, alfalfa, winter wheat, and sorghum on 1,300 acres. The refuge has also become a pioneering expert in "wet-soil" management. By raising and lowering water levels in marshes, extensive native crops of smartweed, millet, chufa, and sedges are produced for wildlife.

■ ANIMAL LIFE

Birds Abundant snow geese and sandhill cranes (mostly greater sandhills) are the signature wildlife of Bosque del Apache. In 1941 there were only 17 of these magnificent cranes, an archaic bird, recorded on the refuge; recent years have seen as many as 17,000 show up for a winter visit. Joining them are more than 12 species of ducks, topping 60,000 individuals at times—including green-winged teal, mallard, and gadwall—as well as snipe, and pie-billed and eared grebe.

Here, too, one has a good chance to spot the extremely rare whooping crane—North America's tallest bird, growing up to 5 feet. The whoopers are slightly larger than the sandhill cranes, but what really gives them away is their bright white color; sandhills are a brownish-gray. In flight whooping cranes also display black primary feathers at the tips of their wings, which are hidden when they are grounded. As many as 34 whoopers overwintered here in the 1980s, and it appeared that a viable population to supplement the flock that frequents Aransas NWR in Texas was taking wing, but drought, disease, unproductive sex and age ratios, and other hazards had reduced the Bosque flock to unsustainable numbers by 1999.

Birders will be busy with scores of other species as well. Significant winter residents include bald and a few golden eagles, as well as squadrons of other raptors, including red-tailed hawk, Cooper's hawk, sharp-shinned hawk, kestrel, and the peregrine falcon. If you're lucky, you may see an eagle lock talons in mid-air with an aggressive hawk. Winter waders include great blue heron, black-crowned night heron, and greater yellowlegs.

A wide range of neotropical migrants—plentiful black-chinned hummers, solitary and warbling vireos are a few—plus shorebirds and white pelicans pass through the refuge in spring and fall. Summer along the River and Rio Viejo trails finds nesting songbirds, such as loggerhead shrikes, who have the odd habit of sticking captured grasshoppers on screwbean mesquite barbs to save for snacking later on. Plying the summer marshes are waders, such as the white-faced ibis, shorebirds including American avocet and black-legged stilt, and a wide variety of ducks. Other summer residents at Bosque del Apache are belted kingfisher, summer tanager, blue grosbeaks, and yellow-breasted chat.

Throughout the year expect to see American coot,

Greater sandhill cranes, Bosque del Apache NWR

ring-necked pheasant, Canada goose, Say's phoebe, Chihuahua and common raven, Rio Grande turkey, roadrunner, and many duck species.

Along the two trails winding into the upland mesas visitors may look and listen for sage sparrows, lesser goldfinch, Crissal thrashers, ladder-backed woodpeckers, and cliff swallows.

In all, over 320 bird species have been reported here since record-keeping began.

Mammals Mule deer wander through the more secluded and drier bottomlands, along with the occasional bobcat and wily coyote, both hunting geese. Scan cotton-wood trees for porcupine and the marsh edges for muskrat and beaver. In the desert uplands desert cottontail rabbit and black-tailed

Black-tailed jackrabbit

jackrabbit skitter about, along with Ord kangaroo rat and rock squirrel. The nocturnal Mexican freetail bat and occult little brown bats roost in desert canyon overhangs and cracks. A patient observer can find some 50 species of large and small mammals roaming the refuge.

Reptiles and amphibians Scattered in different refuge habitats, reptiles and amphibians at Bosque del Apache are most active in spring through early fall. In the wetlands expect to see western painted and spiny soft shelled turtles, and the all too common bullfrog. In drier terrain look for the Sonoran gopher snake, desert box turtles, and two species of rattlesnake: the western diamondback and western prairie. Wildlife experts have noted about 60 species of reptiles and amphibians on the refuge.

ACTIVITIES

■ **CAMPING:** Camping on the refuge, for educational and volunteer groups only, can be arranged with advance notice. A private campground is located just north of the refuge (505/835-1366)

■ **WILDLIFE OBSERVATION:** The sandhill crane population peaks between mid-Nov. and mid-Dec., but the birds are present from early Nov. through mid-Feb. The same time frame finds the greatest concentrations of the vociferous snow- and Ross's geese. These are best seen along the marsh auto-tour route during the morning fly-out and evening fly-in when the birds come and go en masse. During midday they concentrate in the fields along the Farm Loop, where you'll also most likely find the refuge's whoopers.

The auto-tour route offers raised viewing platforms, some with spotting scopes. You may stop at any point along the route; just be sure to pull to the side of the road. To see a wider range of wildlife, take a stroll on one of the foot trails.

The feeding station at the Visitor Center is a surprisingly good place to observe birds. A large window provides face-to-beak encounters, and an outdoor microphone picks up the birds' varied calls clearly. Typical winter visitors include rufous-sided towhee, white-crowned sparrow, Gambel's quail, red-winged blackbird, house finch, and pyrrhuloxia.

■ **PHOTOGRAPHY:** The refuge has no photo blinds, but several hiking trails providing a range of photo opportunities. Come early and stay late—the desert landscape serves up memorable Technicolor skies and brilliant reflections off the marsh waters. In winter, look for the contrasting colors and surfaces among willows, grasses, desert uplands, and distant mountains.

■ **HIKES AND WALKS:** Several good options await the visitor at Bosque del Apache, but bear in mind that in late spring and summer, trails here may sometimes be closed because of flooding.

Marsh Overlook Trail (a 1.5-mile loop with a 0.25-mile spur to the top of a knoll) presents a great overview of the refuge and Rio Grande Valley. It circles around a large old oxbow lake fringed with prolific plantlife filled with chattering blackbirds. Raptors nest along some overhanging slopes. Except for the optional spur, the trail is flat and easily traversed. Closed during Festival of the Cranes.

River Trail (a 2.2-mile loop) actually brings you face to face with the source of all this waterful bounty— the Rio Grande. The chocolate-colored river is choked with silt; it was Will Rogers who quipped that the Rio Grande was the only river he'd seen that needed irrigation. It is fringed by stately stands of mature cottonwoods, as well as the pesky tamarisk and other invasive exotics.

Rio Viejo Trail (2 miles) follows an old course on the river through lovely cottonwood bosques and small open clearings. Here you may chance upon a mule deer, coyote, or even a bobcat.

Canyon Trail (2.5-mile loop) leads into another realm, the dry but hardly lifeless Chihuahuan Desert. The moderately strenuous trail heads up a sandy arroyo dotted with summer wildflowers. Here you'll find serpentine Solitude Canyon with its artistically sculpted walls, and a high point with sweeping views—the Sandias near Albuquerque some 90 miles to the north, the snow-flecked summits of Sierra Blanca to the east, and mountain chains marching south toward Mexico. Canyon Trail provides access to the Indian Well Wilderness Area.

Chupadera Trail (9.5 miles long with a vertical rise of 1,700 feet), is the most strenuous walk in the refuge, traversing washes and foothills of the Chihuahuan Desert. With little shade and no water, hikers should come prepared for a five- to

Snow geese observation, Bosque del Apache NWR

BOSQUE DEL APACHE HUNTING AND FISHING SEASONS

Hunting
(Seasons may vary)

white-tailed deer (using following hunting methods)

	Jan	Feb	Mar	Apr	May	Jun	Jul	Aug	Sep	Oct	Nov	Dec
bow	■								■			
firearm										■	■	
mourning dove									■			■
white-winged dove									■			
quail	■	■									■	■
rabbit	■	■	■	■	■	■	■	■	■	■	■	■

Fishing
(Seasons may vary)

	Jan	Feb	Mar	Apr	May	Jun	Jul	Aug	Sep	Oct	Nov	Dec
carp				■	■	■	■	■	■			
channel catfish				■	■	■	■	■	■			
flathead catfish				■	■	■	■	■	■			

The season for **quail** runs from the 15th of Nov. to the 15th of Feb. Fishing is permitted in accordance with all applicable state and federal regulations from April 1 through Sept. 30. Species include **carp, channel catfish,** and **flathead catfish**.

six-hour outing on this route. The trail accesses the Chupadera National Wilderness Area. Possible sightings of javelina, flowering prickly pear cactus, golden eagles, and stunning views from its 6,190-foot summit makes this an enticing walk.

Excellent trail guides are available at the Visitor Center.

■ **SEASONAL EVENTS:** Festival of the Cranes, in the third week in Nov., is one of the more popular events in the wildlife refuge system. This four-day affair features speakers, slide shows, art exhibitions, book signings, guided tours to areas normally closed on the refuge and to interesting nearby off-refuge sites, and social events that draw thousands of people from far and wide. Contact Socorro Chamber of Commerce: P.O. Box 743, Socorro, NM 87801, 505/835-0424.

The refuge also conducts three-hour guided birding tours most weekends between mid-Nov. and the end of Feb. Reservations required. Guided tours for educational groups can be arranged year-round with advance notice.

■ **PUBLICATIONS:** A free annual guide called *Habitat*, refuge brochure, bird list, trail guides; *Bosque del Apache National Wildlife Refuge*, by Stephen Mauer (Southwest Natural and Cultural Heritage Association, 1994, $6); and three video guides: *Birds of the Bosque* (N.M. Cooperative Extension Service, 1991, 15 minutes, $19.95); *An Oasis for Wildlife* (U.S.F.W.S., 17 minutes, $12); and *Magic Moments from Bosque del Apache* (Steve Wems, 52 minutes, $22).

Las Vegas NWR
Las Vegas, New Mexico

Pond, plain, and Sangre de Cristo Mountains, Las Vegas NWR

Las Vegas NWR is located where the prairies of the Great Plains rise up to meet the descending southernmost leg of the Rocky Mountains. Beneath an immense sky, waterfowl congregate in ponds, marshes, and lakes as bald eagles hover above the native grasslands in search of their next meal. On the Gallinas Walking Trail, under a juniper tree, songbirds dip down to drink at a small stream pool.

HISTORY

Native Americans hunted and gathered for wild foods in this region long before the first European explorers and colonists arrived in the 16th and 17th centuries. The nearby town of Las Vegas—Spanish for "the meadows" and not to be confused with the more glitzy Las Vegas, Nevada—was founded in 1835, and small *ranchitos* sprung up to support cattle grazing. The refuge today contains the remains of weathered rock homes and corrals dating to the early 1900s. The refuge was established in 1965, expanding to 8,672 acres today, and welcomes some 35,000 people annually.

GETTING THERE

The refuge is located 6 mi. southeast of Las Vegas. Head east out of town on NM 104 for 1.5 miles, turn south (right) onto NM 281, and proceed south for 4.5 miles to the refuge office.
- **SEASON:** Open year-round.
- **HOURS:** Auto-tour route open 24 hours daily; Visitor Center/office open weekdays (excluding major holidays) 8 a.m.–4:30 p.m.
- **FEES:** Entry is free.
- **ADDRESS:** Rt. 1, Box 399, Las Vegas, NM 87701
- **TELEPHONE:** 505/425-3581

TOURING LAS VEGAS

■ **BY AUTOMOBILE:** A year-round, 8-mile auto-tour route loops through the heart of the refuge, passing ponds, lakes, marshes, grasslands, mature tree stands, and brush thickets offering excellent wildlife viewing. Half of the route is paved NM 281; the other half (County Road C22C) is a mix of dirt and gravel. Road conditions may be impassable for ordinary vehicles following winter snowstorms and major summer thunderstorms.

In addition, on Sunday afternoons in Nov. only, another gravel-dirt road, the Fall Wildlife Drive, is opened. Running 4.5 miles, it leaves the main auto route at the refuge office and swings by several more remote bodies of water, some native prairie, and croplands before returning to the main auto route. Traffic on this supplemental route is one-way.

The county roads just outside the refuge also provide fine birding, particularly during fall and spring songbird migrations.

■ **BY FOOT:** The tour road system is open to walkers. In addition, the Gallinas Walking Trail winds 0.33 mile (round-trip) off the rolling grasslands into a canyon on the refuge's southwest corner. A free permit, available at the refuge headquarters weekdays only, is required.

■ **BY BICYCLE:** The auto-tour road is also available for biking, but bikes are forbidden on Gallinas Trail.

■ **BY CANOE, KAYAK, OR BOAT:** Nonmotorized and no-wake power boating are allowed on McAllister Lake (an inholding managed by the New Mexico Department of Game and Fish) from March 1 to Oct. 31. There are portable toilets at the lake.

WHAT TO SEE

■ **LANDSCAPE AND CLIMATE** Las Vegas NWR lies at the western edge of the Great Plains, and most of its terrain consists of gently rolling prairie. But only four miles to the west are the 12,000-foot Sangre de Cristo Mountains, including prominent Hermit's Peak, a great knob of purple stone jutting upward from thick pine forest.

Located at the southwestern fringe of the Las Vegas Plateau, the refuge is deeply cut at its west, south, and east sides by steeply sloped, heavily timbered river canyons: Gallinas River on the west and Vegosa Creek on the east.

In prehistoric times ephemeral bodies of water formed here in wet weather, trapped in large natural bowls called *playas*. Today most of the standing water is retained in artificial impoundments. Ditches convey water from Storrie Lake (north of the town of Las Vegas) to the refuge's Bentley Lake, and from there it is distributed elsewhere on the refuge—including Crane Lake, Brown's Marsh, and Middle Marshes, as well as refuge farm fields and moist soil units (artificial wetlands).

At an elevation of 6,500 feet, the refuge enjoys a pleasant climate. Summer temperatures are mild, with highs averaging in the 80s. Thundershowers from July to Sept. provide most of the 15-inch annual precipitation. Snow is common between Nov. and March, but it seldom exceeds 12 inches, and while winter night temperatures can dip down into the teens, days are generally sunny and warm.

■ **PLANT LIFE**
Wetlands Bulrush is common around the marshes. Occasionally pondweed, a favorite food of ducks and coots, is seen floating on lakes and ponds. Other predominating wetlands vegetation includes cattail and spike rush. Wetlands plants

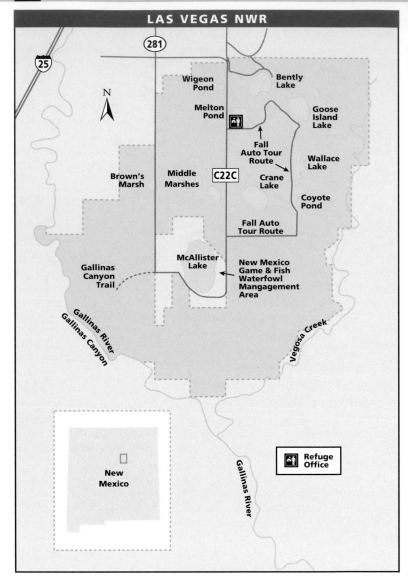

LAS VEGAS NWR

have generally adapted to their circumstances one of two ways: by growing tall rigid stems (to cope with rising water levels) or floating on the water's surface, attached to umbilical-cord-like stems beneath the water.

Grasslands A mixture of short and tall grasses, including blue grama (bluish tint in spring, golden yellow in fall, found commonly in sandy, gravelly soil) and Western wheat grass, covers the refuge's prairies.

Open waters Crane Lake is one of the largest water bodies on the refuge, covering more than 115 acres when full.

Forest Broken stands of juniper, piñon, and ponderosa pine fill the rough canyons flanking the refuge; here, too, you will find the tough deciduous scrub oak that turns a handsome gold, brown, and red in fall, when an internal clock signals it to stop making chlorophyll (the source of green in summer's leaves).

Farmlands The refuge has 760 acres of wheat, barley, corn, and peas under cultivation, which are left unharvested for wildlife.

■ ANIMAL LIFE

Birds Because of its geographic setting on a branch of the Central Flyway and at the meeting ground of the Great Plains and the Rocky Mountains, Las Vegas refuge sees a wide range of birds common to the Midwest and eastern and western United States.

Most prominent on the lakes and marshes in the late fall and winter are waterfowl—5,000 to 8,000 Canada, snow, and Ross's geese, up to 17 species of ducks totaling 10,000 or so birds, and more than 600 greater sandhill cranes. Spring and fall bring shorebirds on the shallows and mud flats. Look for long-billed curlews, an assortment of sandpipers—least and western black-necked stilts—and killdeer.

A large contingent of avian hunters keeps a close eye on all these meals on wings: up to 15 different raptor species may be found here in fall, including bald eagles, some peregrine falcons, rough-legged hawks, ferruginous hawks, the swift and high-flying prairie falcon (the official mascot of the U.S. Air Force Academy), golden eagles, and northern harrier. Up to 20 eagles overwinter here. You may see a bald eagle diving on a flying duck flock one cold winter day. It will dive repeatedly, but the birds stay bunched up. Finally a duck breaks from the pack, and the eagle drops and hits it with a puff of feathers. The hunter then sets down on some ice along a lake shore and begins to eat. To spot an eagle perching, look toward the large dead trees on the east leg of the main auto route.

In warm weather, canyon wrens are found, naturally, in the refuge's canyons, along with cliff swallows, seven varieties of woodpeckers (hairy, red-naped sapsucker, and ladderbacked among them), and the striking and vocal Steller's jay with its cobalt blue body and pitch black head crest.

Spring and fall also bring large numbers of migrant neotropicals. The mature tree stands along NM 281 inside the refuge, the trees near Lake McAllister, and ranch houses just outside the refuge are good bets for sighting yellow-billed cuckoo, lovely cedar waxwing, and the common American robin. Four varieties

Golden eagle perching

of hummingbirds flit about and hover at Las Vegas in summer, including the black-chinned and calliope. All told, 271 bird species have been recorded here since 1966.

Mammals There is plenty of action to observe among mammals at Las Vegas. Fleet herds of pronghorn antelope race on the open prairie, while tassel-eared squirrels bound through the rocky terrain of the canyons. Mule deer move up out of the canyons and feed in the fields. Also common are bobcat (more elusive) and badger. Abundant pocket gophers, voles, rodents, and ground squirrels populate the plains.

Reptiles and amphibians Of the refuge's two rattlesnakes—the western diamondback and the western rattlesnake—visitors are most likely to spot the larger diamondback as it slithers across a roadway. You may also spot a bull snake.

ACTIVITIES

■ **CAMPING:** Camping on the refuge is not permitted, although primitive camping is allowed at the Lake McAllister inholding. Camping is available in nearby Santa Fe National Forest and Storrie Lake State Park and at commercial campgrounds in Las Vegas.

> **HUNTING AND FISHING**
> Fishing for **rainbow trout** is allowed in McAllister Lake (an inholding managed by the N.M. Department of Game and Fish) from March 1 through Oct 31. Very limited **waterfowl** hunting is conducted only by permit and special drawing.

■ **WILDLIFE OBSERVATION:** The main auto-tour route provides prime wildlife observation opportunities. The west shore of Crane Lake has a viewing platform, on a short walk off the auto-tour route. Diving ducks like redheads, ring-necked, buffleheads, and ruddy all favor the lake, while its shallows draw dabbling ducks and its banks shelter sandhill cranes. Dabbling ducks—including mallards, gadwalls, wigeons, and shovelers—like the shallows at Crane Lake's south end.

Along the supplementary Fall Wildlife Drive, pronghorn antelope occasionally pop into view near Melton Pond, and mule deer can be seen in the farm fields south of Crane Lake. Look for still other wildlife found only in the refuge's rugged canyons (see "Hikes and Walks," below).

■ **PHOTOGRAPHY** Pictures of the yellow grasslands of winter backed by the deep blue Sangre de Cristos can be vivid and memorable. Along the Gallinas Trail, the stunning colors and abstract shapes of the rocky rim of the canyon makes for bold photos. The ruins of Spanish ranches offer other interesting images.

■ **HIKES AND WALKS:** Gallinas Walking Trail (0.33 mile) offers a look at the refuge's other main ecosystem—its canyons, filled with thick pine forests, springs, streams, and imposing rock faces. Under overhanging sandstone bluffs protected from the elements, careful viewing may yield sights of prehistoric pictographs of animal and geometric images. The trail begins at the south end of a parking area located on the main auto tour route on the refuge's southwest corner.

■ **PUBLICATIONS:** Brochure, bird list, Gallinas Walking Trail guide.

Maxwell NWR
Maxwell, New Mexico

Refuge wetland, Maxwell NWR

The refuge is situated at the overlapping edges of the High Plains and the southern Rocky Mountains. But Maxwell NWR is no rough-and-tumble rocky landscape, it is a gentle country, dotted with playa lakes and waterfowl farmlands that draw migratory birds by the thousands. Three reservoirs totaling 700 acres provide important roosting and feeding habitat for such waterfowl as mergansers, mallards, gadwalls, pintails, redheads, wigeon, Canada geese, eared grebe, and snow geese. In good years, Maxwell's waterfowl can peak at more than 90,000 birds in the fall.

HISTORY

Opened in 1965, the 3,800-acre refuge is named after Lucien Maxwell, a local land baron of the 1800s. Located in sparsely settled northeastern New Mexico, the refuge receives scant visitation—some 16,000 people a year—but is an ideal spot for observing birds, from waterfowl to raptors. More than 344 species have been recorded to date, more than that found on many of the more heavily visited refuges.

GETTING THERE

From Raton, take I-25 south 26 mi. to Maxwell. Head north on NM 445 for 0.8 mile, then west (left) on NM 505 for 2.5 miles Turn north (right) at entrance sign and proceed 1.5 miles to refuge headquarters. From Las Vegas, take I-25 north 81 miles to Maxwell.

■ **SEASON:** Open year-round.
■ **HOURS:** Refuge roads open 24 hours daily; office open 7:30 a.m.–4 p.m. weekdays, except major holidays.
■ **FEES:** Free entry.
■ **ADDRESS;** P.O. Box 276, Maxwell, NM 87728
■ **TELEPHONE:** 505/375-2331

TOURING MAXWELL

■ **BY AUTOMOBILE:** The refuge's two miles of quiet, graveled public roads provide an easy way to observe wildlife. Six miles of county roads also run through the refuge and along its borders.

■ **BY FOOT:** There are no dedicated foot trails here, but the refuge's roads provide plenty of room to roam on foot. Off-road hiking, however, is prohibited.

■ **BY BICYCLE:** Biking is allowed on all the refuge's public roads, but no off-road biking is allowed.

■ **BY CANOE, KAYAK, OR BOAT:** Small, no-wake watercraft are permitted on Lakes 13 and 14 between March 1 and Oct. 30. Note: No boat ramps (bring lots of muscle or a lightweight portable craft).

WHAT TO SEE

■ **LANDSCAPE AND CLIMATE** Located on the westernmost fringe of the Great Plains, Maxwell NWR has an elevation of 6,050 feet and attracts thousands of migratory birds that travel a migration corridor along the front ranges of the Rocky Mountains.

Maxwell's most pleasant season is fall. Winter has its attractions (such as tracking animals in the snow), but blizzards can roll in off the High Plains and stall against the nearby Sangre de Cristo Mountains, making travel hereabouts difficult. Spring often brings incessant winds to Maxwell's many open grasslands—to avoid the stiff breeze, visit early in the day. Summer days can range from spectacular to uncomfortably hot.

■ **PLANT LIFE**
Wetlands The irrigated playas and three artificial lakes support coyote willow that turn a brilliant crimson in fall, plus tall cattails and other marsh flora, such as the lovely flowering smartweed (look for its rosy pink petals) .

Grasslands Flanking the lakes and playas is a rich acreage of recovering blue grama, a variety of a species that fed the once-great herds of buffalo; the hardy prairie three-awn, often called needlegrass for its sharp, pointed awns; and Buffalo grass, wiry and tenacious, used by early prairie settlers to build sod homes. Buffalo grass grows 2 to 12 inches high and is distinguished by creeping surface runners; its gray-green color dries to a yellow-brown

Uplands On slopes and slightly raised uplands, which comprise the majority of the refuge's terrain, one finds fourwing saltbush and a variety of cactus. Fourwing is most commonly known in northern New Mexico as *chamisa* and also goes by the name rabbitbush. It is a gray-green shrub that grows up to 5 feet in height and is most noticeable in the fall when it produces brilliant yellow blooms.

Farmlands To discourage visiting waterfowl from destroying adjoining private farms, Maxwell raises substantial grain crops. The flatlands landscape has few trees, but groves of elm, locust, and cottonwood originally planted as windbreaks along several refuge roads now serve double duty as perches for songbirds and raptors.

■ **ANIMAL LIFE**
Birds Waterfowl are the prime draw here. Surprisingly, these inland seas of grass are also home to shorebirds in spring, summer, and fall—in particular ring-billed gulls that wander far inland of the continental coasts. There's also a sizable number of raptors, including wintering bald eagles, resident great horned owls, and pere-

grine falcons. The rare southwest willow flycatcher has been spotted at Maxwell as have Hammond's flycatcher, Swainson's thrush, warbling vireo, and indigo bunting.

Mammals Maxwell's grasslands support a modest number of white-tailed and mule deer, as well as coyote, bobcat, and badger. An active black-tail prairie dog colony concentrated near the southern edge of the refuge share their underground homes with burrowing owls. The bark of these rambunctious ground-dwelling squirrels—something like Ar-ar-ar!—is so energetic that it will some-times cause the dogs to throw themselves into the air. The prairie dog colony is marked by small piles of dirt that are heaped up around holes puncturing the prairie, which the "dog-gies" keep well-trimmed in order to monitor the approach of would-be adversaries. Also frequently seen are curious long-tailed weasels. Pronghorn antelope and elk pass through occasionally, and muskrats patrol the lake edges.

Black-tailed prairie dog

Reptiles and amphibians Prairie rattlers are one notable snake at Maxwell, although they're not often encountered.

ACTIVITIES

■ **CAMPING:** Primitive camping (no facilities) is allowed on the refuge from March 1 through October 30; there's a three-day limit.

■ **WILDLIFE OBSERVATION:** Waterfowl numbers peak in the fall and spring. Lakeside viewing is guaranteed to reward, because all the refuge lakes are devoid of trees. Be sure to drive (or walk) along the road on Lake 13's southern shore, probably the refuge's best birding viewpoint. Bald eagles frequent the cottonwoods on the north bank. Lake 12 is always off-limits to visitors, but the road that skirts it actually provides more prime birding sites. Just east of Lake 12 a black-tail prairie dog colony can be easily observed. Lake 14 sometimes

> **FISHING** Rainbow trout are stocked annually in Lakes 13 and 14. A state license is required. The season runs March 1 through October 30.

supports as many as 100 floating grebe nests. The perimeter roads to the north and east (County Roads A4 and A1 respectively), overlook feeding fields. Also keep an eye peeled for long-tailed weasels perched on fence posts!

■ **PHOTOGRAPHY:** There are no photo blinds or observation towers at Maxwell, and so the refuge roads are your best bet for good photography sites.

■ **PUBLICATIONS:** A simple flyer with map and a bird list.

Sevilleta NWR
Socorro, New Mexico

San Lorenzo Canyon, Sevilleta NWR

Called "the place where edges meet," Sevilleta is one of the largest and most diverse refuges in the nation, with a correspondingly wide range of fascinating flora and fauna. Snowcapped peaks roll out into forests of piñon pine and juniper. Far below, a thin ribbon of water glints in the bone-dry desert of the Rio Grande Valley. In between are prairie lands, marshes, wetlands, and riparian forests, all supporting a remarkable array of wildlife.

HISTORY

The New Mexico property known today as Sevilleta NWR was once part of a large Spanish land grant called *La Sevilleta de la Joya* ("The Jewel of Little Seville"), presented to the inhabitants of La Joya in 1819. The land grant survived Spanish and Mexican domination, but back taxes owed the state of New Mexico forced its sale at public auction in 1936 to General Thomas Campbell, for 5 cents an acre. The Campbell family used the land for grazing until it was largely grazed out. In 1973 Sevilleta was donated to the Nature Conservancy, which transferred its 230,000 acres to the NWR system in 1973, making it the nation's seventh largest wildlife refuge outside Alaska. Today the refuge is operated largely as a research area and is closed to the public; scheduled tours can be arranged by appointment only. The refuge hosts the University of New Mexico's Long Term Ecological Research program, and scientists from around the world come here to conduct studies.

GETTING THERE

From Albuquerque take I-25 south about 50 mi. to exit 169. At the stop sign, take an immediate right onto a dirt/gravel road and follow it for 0.25 mi. to the refuge headquarters.
■ **SEASON:** Open year-round.
■ **HOURS:** Refuge open sunrise to sunset daily; refuge office open weekdays from 6:30 a.m.–4 p.m.; call ahead for an appointment to visit.
■ **FEES:** Free entry.

■ **ADDRESS:** P.O. Box 1248, Socorro, NM 87801
■ **TELEPHONE:** 505/864-4021
■ **VISITOR CENTER:** None. Emergency phone and toilet available at office, when staffed. Bring food and drink.

TOURING SEVILLETA

This is a refuge to see on foot. The primary area open to public visitation is Cornerstone Marsh on Unit A, located 4 miles from the refuge office. From the refuge office: On the access road return to I-25 and pass beneath the highway. At mile 2, at a large canal, turn right and go 0.5 mile. Cross over the railroad tracks on the left and proceed to another canal. Turn right and follow its west bank for 1.5 miles Park at a locked gate and walk into Unit A. Biking on this route is not allowed.

WHAT TO SEE

■ **LANDSCAPE AND CLIMATE** Running across the broad Rio Grande Valley, from an altitude of more than 8,000 feet to 4,600 feet, the refuge's large land base jumps from the high, cool, and relatively wet slopes of the Ladrone and Los Piños mountain ranges down to Chihuahuan Desert terrain at its northernmost limit. Butting up against the Chihuahuan is the Great Basin Desert, which reaches southeastward from the Colorado Plateau. Great Plains prairie lands, and marshes, wetlands, and riparian forests on the valley floor round out the picture.

Moisture and temperature at Sevilleta vary widely by altitude. In the valley, average temperatures run from 52 degrees in Jan. to 91 in Aug. Annual precipitation averages 8.8 inches, with most coming as heavy summer rainfall.

■ **PLANT LIFE** A testament to Sevilleta's climatic and biotic diversity is seen in the refuge's number of flora: 1,200 species have been identified to date. The valley marshes are fringed by cottonwoods. Creosote commands the Chihuahuan Desert lands, along with ocotillo and banana yucca. Sagebrush, four-winged saltbush, and Indian ricegrass cover the Great Basin terrain. Blue and black shortgrasses carpet the refuge's grasslands.

■ **ANIMAL LIFE** Sandhill cranes, ducks, and other waterfowl congregate on the marshes in late fall and early winter. Spring and fall also bring a range of migratory songbirds, including red-winged blackbirds, as well as shorebirds. Circling overhead are red-tailed hawks and bald eagles.

Mammals also thrive at Sevilleta: 89 species have been seen. Most common are mule deer, coyote, and pronghorn antelope, but species more challenging to find—desert and Rocky Mountain bighorn sheep, elk, mountain lion, and bear—also roam the mountains. There are also 58 reptile species on this refuge. Watch for the western diamondback rattlesnake and the prairie rattler from spring to fall.

Sevilleta refuge also plays a vital role in the Fish & Wildlife Service's Mexican gray wolf (lobos) recovery program. The lobos, a critically endangered species, are held here in a large outdoor enclosure prior to their release into the wild in Arizona's Blue Range Mountains.

ACTIVITIES

■ **WILDLIFE OBSERVATION:** Visitors can circumnavigate the 125-acre Cornerstone Marsh on raised dikes in fall and spring. (The marsh is drained in summer.) Dryland species are found along the road from the office.
■ **PUBLICATIONS:** Refuge brochure, bird list.

Anahuac NWR
Anahuac, Texas

American alligator basking

Sprawling dense marshes and lovely tree-draped bayous meet the seas of Galveston Bay at Anahuac NWR on the Gulf of Mexico. American alligators lurk in the tangled cordgrass awaiting an unwary coot, while raucous flocks of snow geese feed in rice paddies and coyotes patrol the field edges. A fisherman slowly wades along the seashore casting for speckled trout.

HISTORY

The origin of the Anahuac name is lost in obscurity but appears to be related to an Aztec Indian place name in Mexico. The refuge area was once inhabited by the Atakapa and perhaps the Karankawa Indians. These tribes ate shellfish by the ton and discarded the shells at their villages along East Galveston Bay. Many of these sites, called shell middens, now dot coastal marshes, as do small groves of trees in an otherwise treeless landscape. Anahuac NWR was established in 1963 and contains more than 34,000 acres today. Some 60,000 to 70,000 people visit Anahuac each year.

GETTING THERE

The refuge is located southeast of Houston on the east side of Galveston Bay. From Houston take I-10 east to Anahuac/Hankamer exit # 812 and proceed 4 mi. south on TX 61 to a four-way stop. Continue straight through the stop onto TX 562 for some 8 mi. to a fork; bear left onto FM 1985 and proceed 4 mi. to the refuge entrance.

From Beaumont, take I-10 east to Winnie exit # 829, and proceed south on TX 124 for 11 mi. to FM 1985. Turn west (right) and proceed 10.5 mi. to the refuge entrance.

■ **SEASON:** Open year-round.

■ **HOURS:** The refuge is open 24 hours a day, with the exception of East Bay

Bayou Tract, which is open 6 a.m.–7 p.m. daily. The office is open 7:30 a.m.–4 p.m. weekdays.
- **FEES:** No entry fee.
- **ADDRESS:** P.O. Box 278, Anahuac, TX 77514
- **TELEPHONE:** 409/267-3337
- **VISITOR CENTER:** A Visitor Contact Station at the refuge's main entrance with educational displays, merchandise, and view window onto a pond is expected to be completed in spring 2000.

TOURING ANAHUAC
- **BY AUTOMOBILE:** There are 12 miles of gravel roads on the refuge. The primary visitor experience is to circle Shoveler Pond, a 2.5-mile, one-way loop. This route and other main roads can accommodate buses and recreational vehicles. Occasional wet weather can force brief road closures.
- **BY FOOT:** Only one dedicated foot trail is available on the main tract—a short jaunt starting from the visitor entrance kiosk. There is also a mile-long foot trail along East Bay Bayou. Visitors are welcome to walk the public roads, including those closed to auto traffic in accord with specific signage. But beware: Mosquitoes are fierce at times and are present during all but the coldest weather.
- **BY BICYCLE:** Biking is allowed on all the refuge's public roads.
- **BY CANOE, KAYAK, OR BOAT:** Boating is not permitted on inland refuge waters except for the boat canal. Small, nonmotorized boats may be launched along East Bay Bayou.

WHAT TO SEE
- **LANDSCAPE AND CLIMATE** It is the marshes and open waters that make the biggest impression on a visit to Anahuac. They dominate the landscape and come in several varieties: saltwater, brackish, intermediate, and freshwater. But Anahuac also contains 25 acres of native Texas upper coastal prairie and close to 6,000 acres of fields reverting to prairies. Draining these uplands is a series of linked bayous that circuitously wind to East Bay, the huge arm of even larger Galveston Bay just to the west of the refuge.

The refuge is divided into several administrative sub-parts and tracts: Wildlife watchers concentrate on the main unit, which includes Shoveler Pond. An area of particular interest to birders is East Bay Bayou Tract.

Prevailing breezes off the Gulf of Mexico bring an annual rainfall of 51 inches to Anahuac, but hurricanes like Frances in 1998 dropped 17 inches of rain in only a few hours and pushed a 5- to 7-foot wall of tidewater onto the refuge, flooding most of it. High summer temperatures and humidity can be very uncomfortable. Winter, probably the best time to visit, is generally very mild, with a handful of freezes.

PLANT LIFE
Wetlands Growing throughout the refuge's interior marshes and coastal shoreline on East Bay are smooth cordgrass, seashore saltgrass, phragmites cane, and marshhay cordgrass. Female alligators pack their nests with the latter; as it rots, the heat helps incubate the alligator eggs.
Grasslands Most of the great Texas coastal prairieland that once ran to the edge of the Gulf of Mexico is gone today, converted to productive farmland or urban and industrial sites. Anahuac protects a 25-acre remnant of this ecosystem; an additional 6,000 acres of farmlands is slowly reverting to prairie through natural

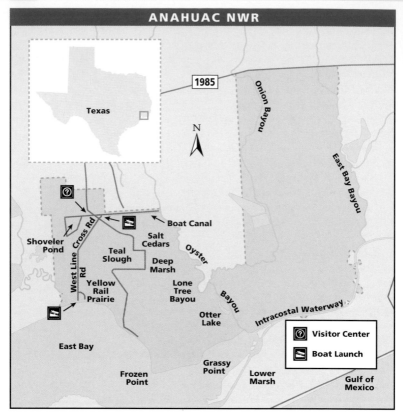

ANAHUAC NWR

1985

Texas

N

Boat Canal

Shoveler Pond

Salt Cedars

Teal Slough

West Line Cross Rd

Deep Marsh

Yellow Rail Prairie

Lone Tree Bayou

Oyster

Bayou

Otter Lake

Intracostal Waterway

East Bay

Frozen Point

Grassy Point

Lower Marsh

Gulf of Mexico

Onion Bayou

East Bay Bayou

Visitor Center

Boat Launch

processes and an active restoration program of native grasses, including big bluestem, little bluestem, switchgrass, Eastern grama grass, and longspike tridens.

Forests Dense linear woodlands dominated by hackberry border some of the many bayous snaking through the refuge. Vines creep up the trees, and an understory of scrub trees and bushes crowd the forest floor. Yaupon is festooned with honeysuckle; below, dense mats of decaying leaves and tree limbs are dotted with splashes of showy primrose.

Farmlands Rice farming on 600 to 1,000 acres of the refuge's 2,600 acres of farmland helps to feed visiting birds each year.

■ ANIMAL LIFE

Birds Between Oct. and March, visitors to Anahuac may find as many as 27 duck species, including green-winged teal, gadwall, shoveler, ruddy duck, and northern pintail. The bright orange bills of the common moorhen are easily distinguished. Clouds of snow geese, sometimes as many as 100,000 birds, feed on rice fields and moist soil management areas.

A number of birds reside here year-round, including the colorful northern cardinal, northern mockingbird, mottled duck, several varieties of egret and heron, the king rail, the sing-song eastern meadowlark, and the strutting boat-tailed grackle, a purple and black bird with shiny feathers and a fanned tail.

Warm-weather denizens include the wood stork, the rarely seen masked duck, the awkward-looking but lovely pinkish roseate spoonbill, and the snowy egrets with their spiked hairdo and comically colored yellow feet.

Of the 14 raptor species at Anahuac, the most often seen are red-tailed hawks, red-shouldered hawks, and northern harriers as they slowly sweep over the marshes. Bald eagles and peregrine falcons appear infrequently in fall and winter.

Diehard birders will thrill at the remote chance of spotting a yellow rail; these birds begin to arrive in Sept., reach peak concentrations from Dec. to April, and depart the refuge in May.

Yellow rail

Mammals Muskrat, nutria, and bobcat are some of the common refuge furbearers, but raccoon, opossum, skunk, and river otter are also present. Characteristics of the extirpated red wolf are sometimes noted in the coyotes seen roaming refuge roads and levees.

Reptiles and amphibians Anahuac is a popular place to observe alligators, found here in large numbers. The alligators here grow up to 12 feet long; if you spot one, be sure to keep your distance and make sure your dog is leashed at all times. Extreme heat or chilly winter days will limit the gators' activity, but they are visible year-round.

ACTIVITIES

■ **CAMPING:** The nearest camping is at Fort Anahuac Park in Anahuac.

■ **WILDLIFE OBSERVATION:** The refuge's most convenient and popular area for birdwatching is along the auto-tour route at Shoveler Pond, where you can observe waterfowl and wading birds, as well as the prominent population of American alligators. They like to sun themselves on marsh banks, where their comings and goings create muddy shelves. A raised viewing platform is found on the pond's west side.

Look for snow geese in rice fields and moist soil management areas near Shoveler Pond; also check along the refuge approach road, FM 1985, and within the East Bay Bayou Tract.

Still other birds flock along the shoreline of East Bay, such as the abundant laughing gull and Forster's tern (both here year-round) and an occasional herring gull.

Surveys have shown that the refuge's highest diversity of songbirds favors the narrow strip of woodlands bordering East Bay Bayou. A foot trail provides access. (See "Hikes and Walks," below.)

Other good birding spots include the beginning of the Shoveler Pond auto route. On the East Bay Rd. about two miles south of the refuge contact station, a stand of salt cedars is found. A side road leads into the trees; it is gated but open to people on foot. The salty prairies shelter other specific birds, including Le Conte's, seaside, sharp-tailed and Savannah sparrows, and sedge wrens. Occasionally, guided tours in April explore the Yellow Rail Prairie to search for the elusive yellow rail.

■ **PHOTOGRAPHY:** Late winter around Shoveler Pond is the best season for photographing gators. You'll need to stay at least 20 to 30 feet away from the alligators; a lens with a focal length of 300mm or larger is advised. The shady hackberry woodlands along East Bay Bayou provide an altogether different "look" for this refuge. Hackberry trees have rough, pimply bark and sandpaper-like leaves. Sunsets over East Bay can be magnificent.

■ **HIKES AND WALKS:** The Visitor Contact Station Trail crosses a meadow and passes some low trees to reach a few small ponds bordered by black willows. It is less than a 0.5-mile round-trip across flat terrain.

A hidden gem that many visitors overlook is the East Bay Bayou Trail, where light filters down in a misty softness through the thick canopy of branches overhead and breaks in the bower of trees arching over the bayou's dark waters. You may spot a great blue heron taking to the air with a hoarse cry or small songbirds like the bright cardinal flitting about in the treetops, offering fleeting glimpses of their colorful presence.

To get to this trail, drive 7.25 miles east from the refuge entrance road on FM 1985. After crossing the bayou on a bridge, turn right through an easily passed gate to park. (This gate is 0.75 miles east of the refuge's prominently marked East Unit Hunting Area gate; or 3.2 miles west of TX 124.) As you enter the parking lot, the trailhead is to your right. Proceed north a short distance to a levee, then west on the levee to reach the bayou. The trail follows the bayou for a mile, then circles back along a road through moist soil units and rice fields. A cutoff allows you to halve the distance traveled. There's a handicapped-accessible area at the far south end of the road.

HUNTING AND FISHING Hunting of **ducks, coots**, and **geese** is permitted in designated refuge areas from mid-Oct. to mid-Jan. Contact the refuge office for details.

Some of Texas's best wade fishing for **speckled trout, redfish**, and **southern flounder** is found on the refuge's East Galveston Bay shoreline at the end of West Line Road. Anglers may also fish from the shoreline, by canoe, or by rowboat at East Bay Bayou for **crappie, largemouth bass, gar, bowfin, channel catfish**, and **blue catfish**. There is a handicapped fishing access area at the south end of East Bay Bayou.

Fishing is allowed year-round. Occasionally there is a federally imposed limit on a specific species; be sure to check the refuge for current restrictions.

■ **SEASONAL EVENTS:** June (first Saturday): National Fishing Week Celebration, with fishing lessons and workshops on Galveston Bay marine ecology. September (second weekend): An area-wide event, Gatorfest!, held annually.

■ **PUBLICATIONS:** Friends of Anahuac newsletter, "Gator Tails"; brochure; bird list; hunting regulations.

Aransas NWR
Austwell, Texas

Aransas NWR, on the Gulf of Mexico

The wind is a constant presence at Aransas. Roaring or easing off the Gulf of Mexico, it slowly but perceptibly twists the tough oak trees into corkscrew shapes. Resident whooping cranes don't seem to mind the wind, however. Out on the immense mudflats and saltwater marshes, the world's last wild flock carries out its ancient courtship dance, bounding high into the air and loudly voicing its yearning for a prospective mate. Away from the bay the wind abates, and flowering shrubs shimmer with masses of small, bright songbirds. Javelinas root and snort in the undergrowth, while an alligator lazes about in the bright sunshine. At Aransas NWR, it's a good day for life in the wild.

HISTORY

Aransas is the second-oldest Texas federal refuge, established in 1937 to protect the vanishing wildlife and natural ecosystems of the Texas Bend coastal area. Its human history receded into prehistoric times, however, when it was occupied by the Karankawa Indians.

The Spanish passed by during their explorations of Texas and subsequent colonization of San Antonio and other inland sites in the 1700s, but they never settled in the immediate area. The Spanish did leave the refuge its name though, which derives from a Basque word, *aranzazu*, meaning "briars or thorny bushes".

The offshore barrier islands and shallow bays were also a popular refuge for pirates. Jean Lafitte is supposed to have disbanded his scurvy crew here after burying a fortune beneath a grouping of huge oaks; some say the very trees still sway in the wind at Big Tree Stand. Some historians believe Cabeza de Vaca began his seven-year wandering across the entire Southwest from this point.

Aransas NWR is located primarily on the Blackjack Peninsula; the 59,717-acre refuge is the primary unit visited there, where annual attendance tops

70,000. Altogether Aransas refuge encompasses 70,504 acres, including three subunits rarely seen by visitors: Myrtle Foester-Whitmire, Lamar, and Tatton.

GETTING THERE

The refuge is located 35 mi. northeast of Rockport. From TX 35 it can be reached from either the south (via FM 774) or the north (via FM 239). Either approach brings you to FM 2040, which you follow 7 mi. south to the refuge entrance.

■ **SEASON:** Year-round.

■ **HOURS:** Refuge open daily sunrise to sunset; Wildlife Interpretive Center open daily 8:30 a.m.–4:30 p.m.

■ **FEES:** Entrance fee $5 per car, $3 per hiker or biker.

■ **ADDRESS:** P.O. Box 100, Austwell, TX 77950-0100

■ **TELEPHONE:** 361/286-3559

■ **VISITOR CENTER:** The Wildlife Interpretive Center (WIC) has informative displays and a film, a nature bookstore, and restrooms. Bring food. No gasoline available.

TOURING ARANSAS

■ **BY AUTOMOBILE:** A 16-mile paved auto-tour road leads to a wonderful overviews of the refuge's many varied ecosystems and provides good opportunities for wildlife observation. The road is two-way for 5 miles (as far as the main observation tower); from there it continues in a one-way loop. Motorhomes are not recommended beyond the observation tower because of overhanging vegetation and sharp bends.

A 0.5-mile spur road runs off the auto route to Dagger Point. Bay Overlook, a turn-out 1.7 miles from the WIC, gives sweeping views of San Antonio Bay.

■ **BY FOOT:** Aransas has one of the most extensive foot-trail systems of all the southwestern refuges. Nine trails (some with branch loops) totaling more than 6 miles and a short boardwalk allow visitors to explore Aransas up close at an easy pace. Some trails have descriptive guides keyed to numbered posts (ask at the WIC). Some traverse flat terrain; others descend to beaches or climb the hills facing the bay.

Walking off-trail is not recommended because of the possible dangers posed by poison ivy, greenbriar, chiggers, ticks, and poisonous snakes.

■ **BY BICYCLE:** The auto-tour route is open to bicyclists. No off-road biking.

■ **BY CANOE, KAYAK, OR BOAT:** Launching boats is prohibited on Aransas, but commercial boat birding tours to view whooping cranes and other shore and wading birds are run Nov. 1 through Apr. 15 by a number of companies out of Rockport. Call the Chamber of Commerce (800/826-6441) for details.

WHAT TO SEE

■ **LANDSCAPE AND CLIMATE** Aransas, straddling the Blackjack Peninsula (named after the common blackjack oak), is surrounded on three sides by the sea. To the east is the vast San Antonio Bay; to the south, Mesquite Bay; and to the west, St. Charles Bay. Unlike its fellow Texan Gulf of Mexico refuges to the north and south, however, Aransas has some elevation as well, resulting in a greater variety of landscapes and habitats. Tidal marshes, flats, sand dunes, and pretty sand beaches front the bays, but rising at their backs are low hills (remnants of sand dunes) that shelter thick woodlands. Interspersed here and there are grasslands and prairie, freshwater ponds and lakes.

Almost constant breezes and occasional monster storms and hurricanes come off the bay, which work to literally reshape the area trees, sandy cliffs, and headlands.

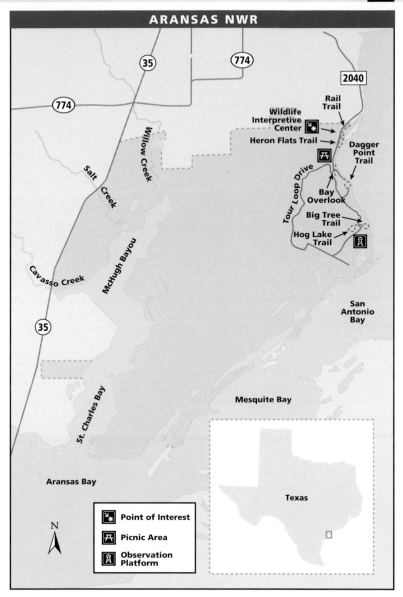

ARANSAS NWR

Rail Trail

Wildlife Interpretive Center

Heron Flats Trail →

Dagger Point Trail

Tour Loop Drive

Bay Overlook

Big Tree Trail

Hog Lake Trail →

Willow Creek

Salt Creek

McHugh Bayou

Cavasso Creek

San Antonio Bay

St. Charles Bay

Mesquite Bay

Aransas Bay

Texas

N

Point of Interest

Picnic Area

Observation Platform

Fall is warm, with days averaging 83-degree temperatures and nights mild; winter has mild days, with temperatures in the mid-60s, and cool nights; spring sees daytime highs averaging 78 degrees; and summer has daytime highs averaging a steamy 92 degrees and warm to hot nights. June, Aug., and Sept. receive the greatest rainfall. Not surprisingly, about 80 percent of the refuge's visitors come between Nov. and Apr.

■ PLANT LIFE

Wetlands There are several varieties of wetlands at Aransas. Saltwater wetlands are fringed by gulf cordgrass, glasswort, and saltwort. Brackish sloughs and marshes favor saltmarsh bulrush, marshhay cordgrass, and common reed, from which the Karankawa Indians fashioned arrow shafts. Cattail and sedges edge the inland freshwater ponds and lakes.

Grasslands Back from the sea's edge on raised ground are patches of grassland and coastal prairie dominated by bluestem meadows, which attract deer, bobcat, rodents, and certain raptors. Only a few feet from the bays, an elevation change of a couple of feet, combined with a sunny location, can create conditions favorable for cactus as well. Texas prickly pear grows alongside Spanish dagger, a yucca more commonly associated with deserts.

Forests A notable variety of trees and forest types are found here as well. Particularly prominent are the *mottes* or clusters of coastal live oak and redbay. Crush a sprig of the latter and smell its rich odor, reminiscent of bay leaf. Another common tree is mesquite, found throughout much of Texas. Tenaciously bordering the salt marshes is the hardy groundsel.

On ridges composed of crushed oyster shells, sand, and some soil, you will find gnarled clumps of hackberry; the smooth-barked Texas persimmon; and lime prickly ash, with its citrus-smelling leaves. Beneath these trees is a thick understory of tanglewood (look for its tiny greenish-yellow flowers in early Feb.), pearl milkweed vine, and the dark green shrub called Texas torchwood. Lantana, a bushy shrub covered with delicate orange blossoms in Feb.; mustang grape, with its choking arm-thick vines; and a great variety of wildflowers, including Turk's cap—a favorite of hummingbirds—also favor these shell ridges. Altogether, Aransas boasts more than 163 species of wildflowers.

■ ANIMAL LIFE

Birds Every season has its birding attractions and rewards at Aransas. The superstar of American birding, the whooping crane, winters here. The birds begin arriving in mid-Oct. from their warm-weather residence in Canada, climb to peak numbers between Nov. and Apr., and are generally gone by late April. In 1999, 183 whoopers overwintered here.

Although whoopers garner the lion's share of attention, they are hardly the only feathered friends present. In fact, Aransas at one time or another has had the second-highest species count in the national wildlife refuge system: 392 to date. Prominent among these are the large number of migrant neotropical songbirds passing through in spring and again in the fall, including tanagers, hummingbirds, flycatchers, thrushes, vireos, and 44 varieties of warblers and allied species. Some species remain to nest in summer, including plentiful painted buntings-arguably the most spectacularly colored member of North America's bird kingdom.

Shorebirds and wading birds

Whooping crane

pass through in spring and Aug., and many species remain to nest, including nine species of heron and egret. Osprey, Mississippi kite, northern harrier, broad-winged hawk, and Cooper's hawk are some of the raptors you are most likely to spot.

Waterfowl congregate at Aransas in large numbers in fall, particularly mottled duck, blue-winged teal, northern pintail, American wigeon, and Canada goose. In all, 37 species of geese and duck have turned up here in the past.

Mammals Aransas mammals range in size from the tiny least shrew, weighing no more than one-quarter of an ounce, to white-tailed deer, weighing more than 100 pounds. Fox squirrels scamper up live oaks looking for their favorite food, acorns. Mexican free-tailed bats are a common migrant winging through the evening skies in spring and fall. The javelina is a hoglike animal with a peppery gray coat and a whitish-gray collar; it is most commonly found in groups of 4 to 12. In the bays, dolphin arch from the water in play, while bobcats silently pad along the game trail.

Reptiles and amphibians The ranges of many reptiles and amphibians overlap at Aransas, producing a wide variety including 13 toads and frogs and 45 kinds of lizards and snakes. Most evident are alligators. Some cover themselves in a whitish mud, assuming an albino look. Blanchard's cricket frog produces a call that sounds like the clicking of pebbles. Basking on logs over ponds are the ever-watchful red-eared turtles, which plop into the water at the slightest hint of danger. Glass lizards have the ability to sever parts of their tails, leaving befuddled predators holding little other than a small piece of their anatomy. These snakelike creatures with long brown stripes can be seen sunning themselves along the roads.

Aransas is home to five poisonous snakes. Most often seen is the western

AMERICA'S TALLEST BIRD The whooping crane, brilliant white with a red cap and black facial feathers, may be the preeminent symbol of mankind's efforts to stem the loss of endangered species. It's certainly an admirable candidate for survival. America's tallest bird, standing close to 5 feet high and with a wingspan of 7 feet or more, the whooping crane once populated the continent, but by the winter of 1941–42, only 15 or so still roamed the wilds.

Today a flock (183 birds in 1999) spends its winters at the Aransas NWR on the Texas Gulf Coast and its summers at Wood Buffalo Park in the Canadian Northwest Territory, completing a migratory journey twice annually of 2,500 miles.

This is the only self-sustaining population left in the wild; efforts to establish a second flock flying a corridor from Grays Lake NWR, Idaho, to Bosque del Apache NWR, New Mexico, appear to have failed, and a program to set up a nonmigratory flock at Kissammee NWR, Florida, has yet to prove viable.

Whoopers mate for life and may live up to 25 years in the wild. Wetlands support their primary food sources, including crabs, crayfish, frogs, and large insects. In the uplands they feed on small grains, acorns, and berries. At night they roost, standing, in shallow water where they are safe from bobcats and coyotes. Females nest on small islands of bulrushes, cattails, and sedges and typically begin laying eggs when they are four or five years old, normally rearing one chick successfully each year.

cottonmouth. When alarmed, the serpent will open its mouth widely, exposing its white interior. Older cottonmouths are usually solid brown-black on their backs. Texas coral snakes are highly poisonous but spend most of their time below the surface. The old saying "Red and yellow is a venomous fellow" refers to the coral snake's distinctive ring pattern.

Five species of endangered sea turtles—the green, hawksbill, Atlantic ridley, loggerhead, and leatherback—occasionally ply the waters of various bays around Aransas.

ACTIVITIES

■ **CAMPING:** The closest public camping is near Rockport at Goose Island State Recreational Area. Aransas does have a shady picnic area.

■ **SWIMMING:** Swimming is prohibited at Aransas.

■ **WILDLIFE OBSERVA-TION:** A 40-foot-high concrete observation tower poking above the treetops is the favorite viewpoint for spotting Aransas' famous whooping cranes. The cranes are often far off in the marshes, however, and can be difficult to distinguish from the background without powerful binoculars or a spotting scope. Whooping cranes are sometimes seen at much closer quarters from the blind on Heron Flats Trail. (For boat tours to view whoopers, see "Touring" above.)

Javelina

In general, Heron Flats Trail and the Rail Trail serve up the best birding on the refuge, but the marine environment—including beaches and open water—includes many other flyers as well, including brown and white pelicans year-round; 28 species of sandpipers, phalaropes and allies; and 20 varieties of gulls, terns, and skimmers.

For spotting mammals, drive the auto route slowly or walk some of the lesser-used trails. You may see a herd of white-tailed deer stand frozen in a clearing or the flash of a bobcat across a road. You might note a raccoon calmly ambling along, or a mother javelina and her baby out rooting up the forest floor.

Alligator watching is a favorite activity at Aransas. Some large specimens can often be found right by the Visitor Center in Thomas Slough or in the pond along Heron Flats Trail. Sometimes they'll lie beneath the boardwalk at Jones Lake, tempting one to reach out and touch something. If you value your hand or arm, don't! Alligators may appear pokey, but they can move with amazing speed.

■ **PHOTOGRAPHY:** Aransas offers many fine opportunities for photography. The hiking trails lead through lovely forests filled with massive sculpted trees and wildflowers galore. The boardwalk near the observation tower ends at a handsome beach where great tree limbs lie buried in the sand, shorebirds scamper to the photographer's frustration (hold still!), and pelicans patrol the outer waters.

Spend some time on foot or driving near the picnic area to shoot javelina (they like this area). Alligators are sitting ducks if you have a long lens, and the light off the bays at sunrise and sunset can be magnificent.

■ **HIKES AND WALKS:** Rail Trail (0.3 mile) ambles easily along next to Thomas Slough, a long narrow pond filled with reeds and bordered by tall trees. The trail starts between the Wildlife Interpretive Center (WIC) and the refuge entrance gate.

Heron Flats Trail (1.4 miles) loops through several distinct habitats, first skirting Thomas Slough and then crossing over a boardwalk to an observation platform. It then runs alongside several brackish ponds favored by alligators and climbs over a series of low, heavily forested oyster shell ridges. This is a pretty, easygoing, and popular walk. The trailhead is 0.6 miles from the WIC along the auto-tour route, and it links to the Rail Trail. A numbered trail guide provides an excellent introduction to the path's flora and fauna.

Dagger Point Trail (0.9 miles) offers another outstanding walk. One branch climbs to the top of tall, thickly forested sand dunes, where views of San Antonio Bay and beaches can be seen between the foliage. The trail eventually descends to a beach at the point, where an interpretive panel describes how the headland is being washed away by wave and wind action. Remnants of an old home, now protruding from the beach, give credence to this story. The turnoff to the trailhead is 3.2 miles from the WIC.

Jones Lake Trail is a short paved trail to a wooden observation platform overlooking a freshwater lake. Its parking lot is 4.5 miles from the WIC.

Big Tree Trail (0.7 miles) leads walkers into a cool forest of massive, ancient live oaks-some more than 450 years old. This flat route also reaches a quiet beach. The trailhead is situated almost opposite the Jones Lake parking area.

Hog Lake Trail (0.9 miles) follows the edge of an ephemeral lake (sometimes dry) that can provide good waterfowl observation. The trailhead is about 5 miles from the WIC on the one-way portion of the auto route.

Near the observation tower a short boardwalk crosses a salt marsh to a beach; two short birding trails are located along the auto route; and a universally accessible trail begins at the WIC and passes through a butterfly garden to an alligator viewing area.

HUNTING AND FISHING There are very limited seasons on the Aransas refuge. Week-long firearm and bow hunting of **whitetail deer** is allowed in Nov. and Oct., respectively, on certain parts of Aransas. Contact the refuge for details. Fishing is not allowed on refuge waters, but walk-in access for wade fishing on the bays is granted from April 15 to Oct. 15. Species most commonly sought by anglers include **drum, redfish, spotted seatrout,** and **flounder**.

■ **SEASONAL EVENTS:** The refuge conducts one special event each month, from Nov. to May, including guided van tours, guided hiking tours, and birding and flora workshops.

■ **PUBLICATIONS:** Brochure; bird, mammal, wildflower, amphibian and reptile species lists; trail guide. *A Birders Guide to Aransas National Wildlife Refuge.* Barry Jones, Southwest Natural and Heritage Conservation Association, 1992, $9.95. *Aransas: A Naturalist's Guide.* Wane & Martha McAlister, U. of Texas, 1995, $19.95.

Attwater Prairie Chicken NWR
Eagle Lake, Texas

Attwater's prairie chicken

It's springtime on a fine patch of tallgrass prairie. Emerging new grass is rippled by a gentle breeze. Blankets of wildflowers color the plains in bold blues and scarlet reds. A black and white loggerhead shrike darts past, crying out *queedle queedle*. Nearby, bison stomp the ground with impatient hooves, and the air resounds with the booming mating call of the endangered Attwater's prairie chicken, one of America's rarest birds.

HISTORY

Attwater Prairie Chicken NWR (called "Attwater" here), visited by about 7,000 people each year, was established in 1972 around a core 3,500 acres purchased by the World Wildlife Fund in the mid-1960s. Today its acreage has more than doubled, to 8,790. Visitors should note that much of the refuge is closed to the public to protect the few remaining prairie chickens.

GETTING THERE

Attwater belongs to south-central Texas, about 50 mi. west of Houston. From Sealy, on I-10, head south on TX 36 just over 1 mi. and turn southwest (right) onto FM 3013. Proceed 10 mi. to the refuge entrance road (right). From Eagle Lake, head northeast on FM 3013 for 6.5 mi. to the refuge entrance road (left). The Visitor Center is 2 mi. down the road at its end.

■ **SEASON:** Open year-round.

■ **HOURS:** Daily sunrise to sunset. Visitor Center open weekdays, 7:30 a.m.–4 p.m.

■ **FEES:** Free entry.

■ **ADDRESS:** P.O. Box 519, Eagle Lake, TX 77434

■ **TELEPHONE:** 409/234-3021

■ **VISITOR CENTER:** More than 100 mounted birds, a video on the Attwater's prairie chicken, plus wildflower and tallgrass displays and guides. Toilets not available on weekends or after hours.

TOURING ATTWATER PRAIRIE CHICKEN

■ **BY AUTOMOBILE:** A 5-mile auto-tour loop crosses native prairie and wetlands, providing outstanding wildlife viewing opportunities. The unimproved road is occasionally closed during rainy weather.

■ **BY FOOT:** Two hiking trails-1.5-mile Pipit Trail and 2-mile Sycamore Trail-offer options for exploration on foot. You may also walk the auto-tour route. Off-trail walking is not encouraged because of the presence of poisonous snakes.

WHAT TO SEE

■ **LANDSCAPE AND CLIMATE** Situated in the heart of the upper Texas coastal tallgrass prairie, Attwater is one of the best examples left of this ecosystem, which once covered millions of acres.

The land—at an elevation of around 200 feet—is generally flat, marked with pothole depression wetlands and sandy knolls. A few small creeks drain toward the San Bernard River, along the refuge's east border.

Rainfall averages 40 inches a year. Winter day highs average 70 degrees, while summer highs are typically 95 degrees. Only one or two hard frosts set in each winter. Spring is a popular time to visit Attwater, both for the pleasant climate and the blooming wildflowers.

■ PLANT LIFE

Grasslands Attwater's grasslands are its most prominent feature. Because little of its terrain was ever plowed or converted to croplands, in spring after a wet winter these virgin grasslands explode in a riot of colorful wildflowers, attracting bees and butterflies.

First up are scarlet Indian paintbrush, with their fat-tipped 4- to 8-inch flowering stalks, and Texas bluebonnets, the state flower. Other wildflowers follow, such as phlox (tiny violet-blue flowers, foot-long stems), butterfly milkweed, and coreopsis. The latter resembles a sunflower, standing on stalks four to five feet tall when mature. Peak blooming occurs from March to early summer, but several of the refuge's 250 species of flowering plants remain in bloom until late fall's first frost.

Most noteworthy among the grasses here are Indian grass, little bluestem, big bluestem, and switchgrass. When fully mature, switchgrass has a 3/8-inch-wide blade and stands 4 to 5 feet, its fine seeds waving overhead.

Refuge staff work diligently to maintain this outstanding example of a prairie ecosystem. Nature's prescription for healthy grasslands calls for an occasional burst of fire to remove dead grass (duff) on the surface while simultaneously controlling invasive brush (see "Fire Ecology" sidebar, below). The burned grasses and wildflowers quickly regenerate from their vast root systems. About 2,000 acres of refuge prairie undergo carefully prescribed burns each winter. Refuge staff are also revegetating former farm fields with seeds gathered from virgin grasslands. The conversion process takes several years.

Also on the prairie is McCartney's rose, another exotic. While showy (standing in clumps up to 10 feet tall, with white flowers blooming in May and June), it is actually an interloper. Introduced from India in the late 1800s, this rose has taken over large swaths of grasslands, forming dense thickets that hide many of the predators feeding on the endangered Attwater's prairie chicken.

ATTWATER PRAIRIE CHICKEN NWR

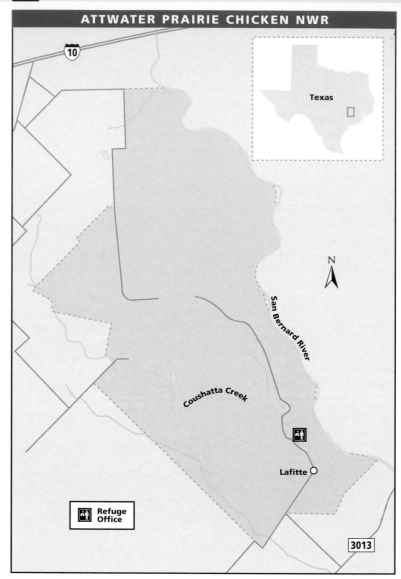

Wetlands Fringing the San Bernard River, Coushatta Creek, and potholes collecting surface runoff are a variety of emergent plants, including cattail, spider lily, and sedges. Clumps of beautiful American lotus float on the water's surface, mainly in the artificially created marshes and some ponds.

Forests Small woodlands containing live oak and sycamore border the San Bernard River. Also present is the Chinese tallow, another exotic.

■ ANIMAL LIFE

Birds The refuge takes its name from the endangered Attwater's prairie chicken. A century ago, up to a million of these large, ground-dwelling, grouselike birds lived on 6 million acres of coastal prairie, from Corpus Christi, Texas, to Bayou Teche, Louisiana. Hunting, overgrazing, agriculture, and urban growth led to a precipitous decline in the bird population and its habitat, and by 1996 only 42 birds could be found. Today some 18 birds reside on the refuge. With intensive oversight and reintroduction of chicks hatched in off-site breeding facilities, these birds are returning to their *leks* on this refuge and two other nearby sites.

A lek, or booming ground, is an area used typically year after year for the bird's courting activity. Males gather here each morning and evening from Feb. through mid-May. Holding their tails erect, they inflate air sacks on their neck, emitting a *whur-ru-rrr* sound while stomping their feet. The females largely ignore these displays, but mating does follow. Your chances of actually seeing such activity is unlikely, however. Sightings are unusual, for several reasons: the small population of birds; their secretive nature and ability to blend in with the native grasses; and the fact that large portions of the refuge are closed to visitors to protect the birds.

The refuge does, however, support another 265 or so bird species, providing good birding opportunities. In winter, four species of geese (Ross's, snow, Canada, white-fronted) abound in the refuge's marshlands, along with 21 species of duck that migrate along the Central Flyway. Listen for the squealing, slurred whistling call of both the fulvous (tawny-colored) and black-bellied (rusty with dark belly and bright coral bill) whistling ducks. Also in winter look for sandhill cranes, Sprague's pipit, and several kinds of sparrows.

On wetland edges, particularly in low-water periods, you'll find shorebirds and wading species by the thousands, including least, pectoral, and stilt sandpiper, common snipe, Wilson's phalarope, yellowlegs, and Hudsonian godwit. A regular visitor in summer and fall is the wood stork, a four-foot-tall wading bird with a white body and a black head, tail, and largely black wings.

During the summer months, overall birdlife declines, but prominent are the scissor-tailed flycatchers and dickcissels on the grasslands. In the marshes great

FIRE ECOLOGY: AN ANCIENT TOOL REDISCOVERED Fire is an integral aspect of the natural life cycles of grasslands and marshes, a process that we have come to understand only in the past 15 years or so.

In marshes, periodic fires consume excess organic matter that might otherwise fill in the wetlands and slowly transform them into solid ground or impenetrable thickets of little use to wildlife.

On grasslands, fire plays a critical role in stemming the invasion of brush, trees, and other flora. Without fire, grasslands can be slowly but inexorably taken over by woody plants, branch by shady branch.

Not only does fire have an important role in keeping marsh and grassland ecosystems in healthy stasis, but it simultaneously delivers important nutrients to the soil while doing little to harm to either typical marsh flora or prairie grasses, which simply resprout from their roots.

For decades, however, it was the national policy to suppress wildfires. Today almost all the refuges in the Southwest practice some form of fire management, using it as a tool to maintain or improve natural habitat, from the thick marshes of McFaddin NWR in far southeastern Texas and the tamarisk thickets of Bosque del Apache NWR, to the rich grasslands of Buenos Aires in Arizona and the moist-soil units at Ruby Valley NWR in Nevada. So if you see large burned areas on a refuge, don't fret! Come back in three months to see how the natural plant life is rising, phoenix-like and green as ever, out of the blackened earth.

blue herons do their elegant, freeze-frame stalking, while roseate spoonbills sweep the water with their wide bills. Look for anhingas perched on branches, with their wings spread wide to dry.

Raptors here include white-tailed hawks, crested caracaras, and vultures patrolling over the prairies, and Cooper's and sharp-shinned hawks darting through the woodlands.

Mammals While few in number, buffalo, or bison, are probably the most prominent of Attwater's 50 mammal species. The 6-foot-tall, 1-ton shaggy-coated critters once darkened the prairie as far as the eye could see, playing an important role in grassland ecology as feeders and soil cutters. Attwater's small (40 or so) herd was transplanted from breeding stock elsewhere and can be seen lying in the tall grassy meadows. White-tailed deer are also found on the grasslands, while nutria ply marsh waters. Nighttime prowlers include nine-banded armadillo, coyote, bobcat, opossum, and skunk.

Reptiles and amphibians Because of Attwater's uniquely varied habitats, alligators have found their own living space on a refuge where bison roam. A handful of American alligators live in intermittent ponds, natural depressions, and swampy creek areas. Spiny softshell turtles, along with bullfrogs and upland chorus frogs, live in the refuge ponds and wetlands. Keep an eye peeled for three venomous snakes: Texas coral, western cottonmouth, and southern copperhead.

ACTIVITIES

■ **CAMPING:** There is no camping on the refuge. But you may enjoy picnic tables at Visitor Center. Stephen F. Austin State Park (409-885-3613) is 25 miles away, near San Felipe, and has camping facilities.

■ **SWIMMING:** There is no place to swim on the refuge.

■ **WILDLIFE OBSERVATION:** The auto-tour loop is an obvious place to begin wildlife viewing. One stretch near the loop's south end offers a duck's-eye view of waterfowl as they dabble for emergent plants and bottom-dwelling crustaceans and insects. The best chance of seeing bison is along the auto-tour route, but it's not a given because they often lie down in the tall grass.

Also be sure to spend some time walking on the trails here; they provide excellent opportunities for isolated wildlife viewing in both prairie and woodland habitats. The tallgrass prairies shelter northern bobwhite quail, Eastern and Western meadowlarks, killdeer, mountain plover in spring, loggerhead shrikes, and many kinds of sparrows.

The woodlands support many red-bellied and downy woodpeckers year-round, as well as many types of migratory songbirds in fall and spring, including painted bunting (one of the continent's most spectacularly colored birds, with a red breast and rump, violet-blue head, and lime-green back), plus northern cardinal, blue grosbeaks, and some 28 visiting or resident warbler species.

> **HUNTING AND FISHING** Hunting and fishing are not allowed on the refuge.

■ **SEASONAL EVENTS:** The annual Attwater's Prairie Chicken Festival is held late March or early April.

■ **PUBLICATIONS:** Brochure, bird list.

Brazoria NWR
Angleton, Texas

Boardwalk, Brazoria NWR

Here is a terrain that's more water than land, a place never far from the restless lapping and stirring of salt and fresh water. Dense interlocking marshes rise almost imperceptibly to low prairies, while vast flocks of ducks wheel in the sky and splash down on the water for the night—one of thousands of migratory waterfowl that make this Gulf Coast refuge home for the winter.

HISTORY

Brazoria NWR was established in 1966, its name derived from the root word *brazos*, Spanish for "arms." The refuge is designated as an internationally significant shorebird site by the Western Hemisphere Shorebird Reserve Network, and a popular environmental science program for local schoolchildren has existed here for several years. The Big Slough Public Use Area was first opened in the late 1980s but only recently became available full-time; it offers a raised boardwalk and trail that winds over and along the edges of a major slough, one of the best places on the refuge to view wildlife. Some 19,000 people visit annually.

GETTING THERE

Located in south Brazoria County, 12 mi. southeast of Angleton. From the intersection of TX 35 and FM 523 in Angleton, head south on FM 523 9.5 mi. to County Rd. 227. Turn east (left) and proceed 1.7 mi. to the refuge entrance road on your right.

■ **SEASON:** Year-round; intermittent access June to Aug.

■ **HOURS:** Open Sept. 1 to May 31 daily 8 a.m.–4 p.m.; intermittent access June to Aug., when the refuge may be open only during the week and the first weekend of every month.

■ **FEES:** Free entry.

■ **ADDRESS:** 1212 N. Velasco, Suite 200, Angleton, TX 77515

■ **TELEPHONE:** 409/849-6062

■ **VISITOR CENTER:** There is no Visitor Center, but a visitor welcome pavilion at the head of the Big Slough Auto Route has restrooms, literature, interpretive panels. Bring drinking water.

TOURING BRAZORIA

■ **BY AUTOMOBILE:** The gravel Big Slough Auto Route runs 7.5 miles through the Big Slough Public Use Area, the heart of Brazoria NWR, wrapping around Olney and Teal ponds, and accessing Big Slough and Rogers Pond. The 3-mile entrance road from County Rd. 227 (which passes through private lands) also can provide wildlife viewing. County Rd. 227 cuts through some of the refuge's best bluestem prairie terrain.

■ **BY FOOT:** Brazoria provides several footpaths in different settings, leading to a wide variety of habitat experiences. All manner of pathways are available, from a boardwalk to an abandoned railroad right-of-way to woodland and bayou trails. None of the walks is especially long, and all are on relatively flat terrain. Wandering off-trail here is not advised, however, because alligators and poisonous snakes reside in the taller grasses.

■ **BY BICYCLE:** The gravel auto-tour route is open to biking.

■ **BY CANOE, KAYAK, OR BOAT:** Boats are permitted on Nicks, Salt, and Lost lakes. Two boat ramps: one, on the west bank of Bastrop Bayou, just off County Rd. 227; another, off County Rd. 257 on the refuge's southwestern boundary.

WHAT TO SEE

■ **LANDSCAPE AND CLIMATE** Brazoria has a complex mix of landforms and features, but its fresh and salt marshes, mudflats, and saltwater lakes connected by large sloughs, bayous, and two intermittent freshwater streams are its dominant characteristics. Abutting the Gulf of Mexico, Brazoria is largely aqueous. The Gulf Intracoastal Waterway cuts across its southern edge, further complicating its fresh- and salt-water flows. Because the Waterway is deeper than surrounding bodies of water, it creates a deep-water conduit for salt water. Water levels are controlled in many marshes through a system of dikes and irrigation ditches. More than 5,000 acres of now-rare coastal bluestem prairie provide a sharp contrast to these wetlands. Here and there patches of slightly higher ground support low-growing trees.

Armadillo

With its seaside location, Brazoria's climate is temperate and quite wet, averaging 50 inches of rain a year; winter days average 41 to 55 degrees, and summer days 84 to 91 degrees.

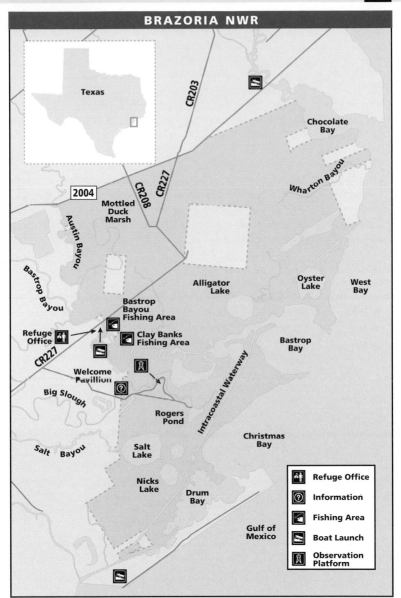

■ PLANT LIFE

Wetlands Cordgrass is one of the refuge's most common wetlands plants. The three species of cordgrass—intertidal water smooth cordgrass, marshhay cordgrass, and Gulf cordgrass—are all salt-tolerant and greenish in color but grow to different heights. Smooth cordgrass is Brazoria's predominant salt marsh wetlands plant. Brackish marshes are primarily composed of marshhay cordgrass and distichlis grass. Slightly fresher marshes are characterized by Olney bulrush; cattail, California bulrush, and sedges favor freshwater marshes.

Grasslands Brazoria also shows off a thriving example of original Texas coastal bluestem prairie dominated by little bluestem, bushy bluestem, and switch grass.

Various wildflowers, including the scarlet-colored Texas Indian paintbrush and evening primrose, bloom from late Feb. through Sept. The best area for viewing this ecosystem is along County Rd. 227 east of Bastrop Bayou.

Another of Brazoria's many biotic communities is prairie that is subject to periodic saltwater flooding. Look for the 3- to 4-foot-high baccharus bush—an invasive wood shrub kept to manageable levels through summer burning programs—and gulf cordgrass on the salt-water prairie flanking the access road.

Forests Although it's a stretch to call the small clumps of trees in Brazoria "forests," there are some limited woodlands of hackberry, ash, yaupon, and the exotic Chinese tallow on patches of slightly higher ground. Chinese tallow can grow to 30 feet and is a tenacious invasive; in five years it can completely blanket an area. Herbicides and summer burnings are used to keep its growth in check. Toothache, a small thorny shrub, is so named because it was found that chewing on its bark made the mouth numb. The exotic salt cedar is found in Brazoria as well, but because it is not as invasive as it is elsewhere in the Southwest, refuge managers have left it standing for passerines and nesting birds.

■ ANIMAL LIFE

Birds Brazoria's varied ecosystems support a great diversity of birds: More than 300 species have been recorded here to date. Most prominent are the two dozen types of duck (20,000 to 30,000 individuals) and large flocks of snow geese, in combination with smaller bodies of Canada geese and white-fronted geese (totaling 30,000 to 50,000 members). Waterfowl generally begin arriving in late Oct.; by mid-April most have left except the mottled duck, which nests in deep cordgrass.

Wading and shorebirds also gather at Brazoria in extraordinary numbers; up to 32 species are common. Mid-April is typically peak season, but they are usually present between mid-March and mid-May and again in lesser concentrations from July through Sept., when some 15 species nest here. Herons, ibis, gulls, terns (including more than 100 least terns in recent years), snipe, avocets, sandpipers, and stilts are common, but there is also a chance you can spot yellow rails, roseate spoonbills, reddish egrets, whitefaced ibis, double-crested cormorants, American

Double-crested cormorant

MESQUITE The three varieties of mesquite growing in the Southwest produce one of the region's more important natural foods, long-prized by both Native tribes and a wide variety of wildlife. The trees' 2- to 7-inch-long seed pods are rich in sugar, minerals, and fiber and can be eaten green or dried.

Honey mesquite, growing as a large shrub or with a multibranching trunk no more than 20 feet high, are widely found throughout the Chihuahuan and Mojave deserts and east to the Texas plains and coastal prairies. Velvet mesquite, the tallest variety, reaches 40 feet or so on a single spreading trunk and grows prolifically in the Sonoran Desert. Screwbean (*tornillo* in Spanish) mesquite, named for its pods' corkscrew shape, is found less commonly throughout the Southwest and northern Mexico.

Once relegated to large woodlands flanking rivers and arroyos, cattle have spread mesquite seeds far and wide. Ranchers consider it a nuisance plant because it displaces grasslands and can grow in thick, almost impenetrable armed tangles. Its durable wood, however, is actually quite versatile, in earlier times serving as fuel, wagon wheels, and a furniture and construction material. Today it's best known as an excellent barbecuing and grilling wood, burning hot but cleanly while imparting a subtle flavor.

bitterns, wood storks, and common gallinules. If you're really fortunate, you may even see a black rail. Dowitchers, dunlins, lesser yellowlegs, and semipalmated and western sandpipers probe the mudflats for worms, shrimp, and other crustaceans.

The limited woodlands also attract large numbers of migratory songbirds in spring and fall, particularly a great range of warblers and wrens. Some stay on to nest, including orioles and many eastern meadowlarks. If your birding list lacks sparrows, you've come to the right place. Thirteen sparrow species winter at Brazoria, including Le Conte's sparrow, seaside sparrow, and the lark sparrow.

Not surprisingly, this healthy ecosystem also supports a large number of raptors. Most common are red-tailed hawk, kestrel, and northern harrier, but you also stand a good chance of spotting a caracara, Mexico's national bird.

Mammals One of the more common and easily seen critters at Brazoria is the peaceful, armor-plated armadillo. Found throughout the refuge, they are most often spotted along roadsides. You may also catch a fleeting glimpse of a coyote or bobcat, but more likely you'll spot signs of raccoon and otter.

Reptiles and amphibians The American alligator is a common resident of Brazoria's marshes and sloughs. Take care when walking on remote paths or roadways near water—although the alligators will most likely sense your coming long before you see them splash into the water. Gators emit loud grunts during mating season in late spring. Water moccasins and Western diamondback rattlesnakes like the deep grasses—not your best choice for a walk!

ACTIVITIES

■ **WILDLIFE OBSERVATION:** Teal Pond is a popular early-morning and late-evening stop for large numbers of geese, who come here to eat gravel, which aids their digestion. This same spot is also renowned for hawk, harrier, kestrel, and white-tailed kite sightings. A universally accessible observation platform at Teal Pond offers viewing scopes and interpretive panels.

Rogers Pond, at the auto-tour's turnaround point, is a great place to observe

wading birds, shorebirds, or waterfowl, depending on water levels
and seasons. Middle Bayou Trail
leads to views of birds that favor
grasslands and prairies, including
bobwhite quail, sandhill cranes,
and four species of dove. Prime
grounds to scout for gators include
the banks of Big Slough near Cox
Lake because it is one of the
refuge's last bodies of water to dry
up in a drought. Mottled Duck
Marsh, off CR 208 on the refuge's
northern edge, rewards visitors on
the lookout for waterfowl and
shorebirds.

■ **PHOTOGRAPHY:** The boardwalk over Big Slough provides a
close encounter with a lovely
marsh crowded with spiky cattails
and bulrush. For satisfying photos
of wildflowers, visit the bluestem
prairie along County Rd. 227.

■ **HIKES AND WALKS:** The
Big Slough Boardwalk and Trail
winds over and along the edges of a
major slough on a raised board-

HUNTING AND FISHING Waterfowl
hunting for **ducks**, **geese**, and **coots**
is permitted on Christmas Point
Hunting Area (southeast of the Intracostal Waterway on 4,000 acres)
reached by boat access only, and on
Middle Bayou (1,500 acres), reached
by both walk-in and boat access. The
season runs from late Oct. through
mid-Jan. For details, contact the
refuge.

Fishing is allowed year-round.
The refuge has a handicapped fishing area at Bastrop Bayou. To reach
the designated area, cross over the
bridge and circle under it. Bank fishing for **redfish**, **spotted seatrout**,
black drum, **sheepshead**, and **flounder** is allowed at the Clay Banks,
which are accessible via a gravel road
running south from Bastrop fishing
pier, and at the salt lake area. Boat
fishing is permitted on Salt, Nicks,
and Cox lakes.

walk. The trail winds through low forests of yaupon trees and small clearings to
an observation platform. Benches provide opportunities to rest and quietly
observe wildlife. Loop trails branch and rejoin this primary trail, allowing for isolated observation of passerines perching in the trees and bushes. The main loop
is 0.6 mile long; other loops run 0.1, 0.25, and 0.5 mile. Start at the visitor welcome
pavilion.

Middle Bayou Trail follows 2 miles along an abandoned railroad right-of-way
parallel to County Rd. 227 on the east side of Bastrop Bayou (trailhead at Bastrop
Bayou fishing pier). Don't miss this trail for a stroll overlooking grasslands.

Visitors can also walk on shorter foot paths forking off the Big Slough Auto
Route, including Alligator Trail.

■ **SEASONAL EVENTS:** Mid-April: Friends of the Brazoria Wildlife Refuges
host Migration Celebration (speakers, seminars, trade show, field trips, and other
activities at Brazoria and San Bernard NWRs; 800/725-1106). Dec.: The
Audubon/Freeport Christmas (bird) Count is a popular gathering.

■ **PUBLICATIONS:** A Friends of Brazoria newsletter, "Wingbeats";
brochure, bird list.

Buffalo Lake NWR
Umbarger, Texas

Shortgrass prairie

Buffalo Lake was once a stomping ground of the great buffalo herds that roamed the southern Plains. These days, the bison are largely gone, but the visitors who come to Buffalo Lake NWR see an array of birds and wildflowers and an outstanding short-grass prairie. Situated about 30 miles southwest of Amarillo, the refuge lies on the largely flat High Plains of the Texas Panhandle at an elevation of 3,550 feet. Buffalo Lake is set in a steep-walled canyon flanked by rock outcroppings and ledges carved by Tierra Blanca Creek—today largely dewatered.

HISTORY

Following the Dust-bowl disaster of the early 1930s, the U.S. Soil Conservation Service acquired the 7,664-acre Buffalo Lake tract in 1937. In 1958 it came under control of the U.S. Fish & Wildlife Service. Some 5,000 to 8,000 people visit the refuge annually.

GETTING THERE

Head west from Canyon, TX on US 60 for 10 mi. to Umbarger, turn south (left) on Farm Rd. 168, and proceed 1.5 mi. south to the entrance gate.
■ **SEASON:** Open year-round.
■ **HOURS:** Refuge open 8 a.m. to 8 p.m. daily, Apr. 1 to Sept. 30, and 8 a.m. to 6 p.m. Oct. 1 to Mar. 31. Refuge office open 8 a.m. to 4:30 p.m. weekdays.
■ **FEES:** $2 per day per vehicle.
■ **ADDRESS:** P.O. Box 179, Umbarger, TX 79091
■ **TELEPHONE:** 806/499-3382

TOURING BUFFALO LAKE

■ **BY AUTOMOBILE:** A 5-mile auto-tour route with interpretive natural-history panels runs from the refuge headquarters south through grasslands,

Canada geese in flight

woods, a dry playa, and farm fields to an observation deck and photo blind over-looking Stewart Marsh.

■ **BY FOOT:** Two foot trails provide good opportunities for exploring the Buffalo Lake refuge on foot. Cottonwood Canyon Birding Trail (0.5 mile round-trip) begins off the road to the picnic area. The trailhead for Prairie Dog Town Interpretive Trail (0.25 mile) is located along FM 168 about 2 miles south of the intersection with FM 1714.

■ **BY BICYCLE:** Biking is allowed only on the auto-tour route.

WHAT TO SEE

■ **LANDSCAPE AND CLIMATE** The refuge's namesake, Buffalo Lake, once trapped behind an artificially created dam, is now gone, obliterated by drought and the draining of the nation's largest aquifer—the Oglala—by more than 80 feet in just 25 years.

Average annual precipitation is about 19.5 inches, most of that coming in intense summer thunderstorms that may also spawn tornadoes. July and Aug. daytime highs can top 105 degrees, while Dec. and Jan. nights can drop close to the zero mark; spring often brings strong winds. Visitors should come prepared for variable weather.

■ **PLANT LIFE**

Wetlands A 300-acre area of wetlands sealed off behind Stewart Dike is all that remains of Buffalo Lake. Here vegetation is dominated by cattail, smart weed, Texas bulrush, and Texas spangletop.

Grasslands The predominant landscape of Buffalo Lake National Wildlife Refuge, which covers 4,373 acres, is shortgrass prairie, characterized by blue grama and buffalo grass. One 175-acre plot is of such superior quality that it was declared a National Natural Landmark in 1975. Spring and summer find a profusion of wildflowers blooming in the grasslands, such as scarlet globe mallow, false garlic, and purple prairie coneflower. In drier areas, look for hedgehog and prickly pear cactus.

Forests About 70 acres of the refuge are forested with plains cottonwood and elm trees, and another 278 acres are covered by mixed woodlands and brushlands.
Farmlands The 2,600-acre bed of dry Buffalo Lake is used today for farm fields growing wheat, milo, and hay, and there are plots dominated by invaders like Russian tumbleweed. Refuge managers control 40 acres as moist-soil units, where native emergent wildlife foods, including millet, are grown.

■ **ANIMAL LIFE**
Birds The refuge's impressive native short-grass prairie attracts a number of birds, including grasshopper sparrow, Cassin's sparrow, lark sparrow, lark bunting, mountain plover, and peregrine falcon. Ring-necked pheasant, northern bobwhite quail, and wild turkey are also common. Prominent members of the raptor clan include ferruginous hawk, kestrels, and bald eagles, which arrive during winter. Summer finds as many as 150 turkey vultures roosting in dead trees between the picnic and camping grounds.

Sitting beneath the Central Flyway, Buffalo Lake also attracts migratory songbirds, and, while the huge numbers of cranes and waterfowl are no longer present, the wetlands do draw flocks of ducks (mallards, green-winged teal, northern pintail, and shovelers) and the shade tree warblers, yellow-billed cuckoos, flycatchers, tanagers, and orioles. Roughly 274 birds are listed as common or semiregular residents or visitors here.
Mammals A thriving colony of black-tailed prairie dogs takes full advantage of Buffalo Lake's healthy native grasslands. An unusual feature is the overlapping of ranges of both mule deer and white-tailed deer. Other frequently seen residents include coyote and cottontail and jack rabbits.
Reptiles and amphibians Wetlands support the plains leopard frog and snapping turtle, while the dry uplands are home to the horned lizard and both Western diamondback and prairie rattlesnakes.

ACTIVITIES
■ **CAMPING:** Camp sites (fuel stoves only) with tables, toilets, and water are available on a first-come basis.
■ **WILDLIFE OBSERVATION:** The best place to look for songbirds at Buffalo Lake is in the riparian forests along the Cottonwood Canyon Birding Trail; the best times are fall and spring. Waterfowl congregate on the moist soil units just above Stewart Dike and can be watched from the observation deck at the end of the auto-tour route. In spring look for rare mountain plover in the short grass around prairie dog towns, which also attract burrowing owls.
■ **PUBLICATIONS:** Bird list.

Hagerman NWR
Sherman, Texas

Lakeside, Hagerman NWR

On the southern Great Plains, the vast Lake Texoma forms part of the flooded Red River Valley. Fishing in this artificially created body of water is the refuge's star attraction, but Hagerman NWR offers much more. Rimming the lake are marshes and wetlands, flourishing forests of hardwood trees, and immense prairies that dip and rise in waves of shining grass. In summer, thunderheads tower overhead, a wind kicks up, whipping the lake's surface to froth. Anglers, birds, and animals alike hunker down in the marshes to wait out the blow.

HISTORY

Hagerman NWR was established in 1946 following the completion of Denison Dam on the Red River in 1945. The artificial but immense Lake Texoma (behind the dam) required the evacuation of a town called Hagerman, named after a prominent official of the Missouri, Kansas, and Texas Railroad that once ran through the region.

Oil was discovered here in 1951, and many operating oil rigs still dot the landscape, their rhythmic thumping adding incongruous sounds to those of wind and wildlife. It's a glaring example of what refuge management considers to be "incompatible uses" of refuge lands.

Hagerman, covering 11,320 acres, is a popular place, receiving nearly 200,000 visitors a year—most of them anglers.

GETTING THERE

You will find Hagerman on Lake Texoma, northwest of Sherman in north-central Texas near the Oklahoma line, 75 mi. north of Dallas. Head west out of Sherman on US 82 and turn north (right) onto FR 1417. A mile north of the airport turnoff, turn west (left) onto Refuge Rd. and follow it 6 mi. to the Visitor Center. If approaching from the west—Gainesville and I-35—head east on US 82 through Sadler. At 4 mi. east of Sadler, turn north (left) onto Southmayd Rd. and make a series of 90-degree turns onto Judge Elliot Rd. (right) and Bennett Ln. (left), leading onto the refuge property.

■ **SEASON:** Open year-round.
■ **HOURS:** The refuge is open dawn to dusk. Visitor Center open weekdays 7:30 –4 p.m.; open occasionally on weekends Oct. to April
■ **FEES:** Free entry.
■ **ADDRESS:** 6465 Refuge Rd., Sherman, TX 75092-5817
■ **TELEPHONE:** 903/786-2826

TOURING HAGERMAN

■ **BY AUTOMOBILE:** A 3-mile self-guided gravel auto-tour route proceeds through the refuge's heart, ending at Crow Hill—overlooking Lake Texoma, wild prairies, and farm fields. It begins at the kiosk near the Visitor Center.

■ **BY FOOT:** Crow Hill Trail (1-mile loop) cuts through a patch of native prairie and woodlands. The trailhead is at the end of the auto-tour route, south of the Visitor Center. Meadow Pond Trail (2.5 miles, one-way) is a vehicle-restricted road, accessing more isolated woodland and marsh areas. You will find the trailhead about 2.5 miles from the Visitor Center, along the auto route. It is closed periodically in fall and winter for hunting. You can also walk various service roads, subject to closures for hunting. Inquire at the Visitor Center.

■ **BY BICYCLE:** Mountain biking is permitted on all the roads open to the public and along a former railroad right of way.

■ **BY CANOE, KAYAK, OR BOAT:** Boating is allowed April to Sept. Boats may be launched only at designated sites (see map). Boats are not allowed on any of the refuge ponds. No skiing or jet-skiing is allowed.

WHAT TO SEE

■ **LANDSCAPE AND CLIMATE** Hagerman NWR lies at the southern end of the Big Mineral Arm of Lake Texoma, on the Red River between Texas and Oklahoma. Some 3,000 acres of marshes and wetlands limn the water, flanked by 8,000 acres of largely flat, open uplands of the southern Great Plains. Woodlands, native tallgrass prairie, recovering prairie, and some farm fields patch these uplands.

Hagerman experiences wide temperature swings: from summer highs commonly exceeding 90 degrees to winter lows well below freezing. Precipitation averages 35 to 40 inches a year, with damp spring and fall seasons, and dry winters and summers.

■ **PLANT LIFE**
Wetlands Hagerman's extensive shoreline fronting Lake Texoma and many creeks draining into the lake provide footing for vast tracts of cattail, bulrush, and pickerel weed. On the

Bluestem prairie grass

HAGERMAN NWR

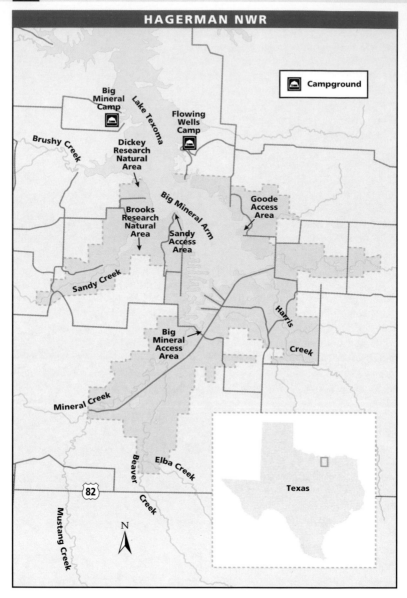

lake water's surface float large clumps of American lotus, a large lily with a 6- to 8-inch flower. Its seed pod grows as large as 4 inches, producing a seed that was ground into flour by Native American people in the past.

Grasslands The predominant upland native tallgrass prairie here favors Indian grass, switch grass, and big bluestem. Growing as tall as 6 feet, bluestem is also known as "turkey foot"-a reference to the shape of its seed heads. Hagerman also has dazzling wildflower blooms. Late winter to early summer brings on brilliant red Indian paintbrush and galardia. In spring look for coneflowers. Summer finds an abundance of pink penstemon, a variety of sunflowers, yellow neptunia, mimosa, and larkspur.

Forests Growing on both the uplands and occasionally closer to the water are woodlands of cedar elm, blackjack oak, post oak, and red oak. In general, the western half of the refuge is more heavily timbered. Here you'll find elms, eastern red cedar, pecan, hickory, willow, oaks, hackberry, cottonwood, and at the water's edge Osage-orange, green ash, and buttonbush.

Farmlands Some 600 acres of land are farmed at Hagerman. Milo and corn-fields provide high-energy foods for birds during the coldest winter months, while green browse (wheat, rye, and small grains) is a staple for geese. The refuge also manages various moist-soil units where such wild foodstuffs as millet, sedges, and smartweed are raised for waterfowl.

■ ANIMAL LIFE

Birds Geese are prolific at Hagerman refuge, arriving in late fall from breeding grounds northward along the Central Flyway. From late Oct. through March, 7,500 or more congregate here, primarily snow and Canada geese, supplemented with lesser numbers of greater white-fronted and Ross's geese.

During the southern migration in fall, dabbling ducks such as mallard, pintail, and teal land here as well, along with diving ducks such as redhead, ringneck, and scaup. Many spend the winter, forming large "rafts" on Lake Texoma, while others fuel up and continue flying south.

When water levels drop in Lake Texoma (for summer and fall irrigation releases), mud flats and shallows are exposed, drawing large numbers of shore-birds and wading species. Late July and Aug. often finds clouds of various phalaropes, semipalmated and Western sandpipers, plying the water's edge searching for their next bite-just a few of the 28 species of this clan found at Hagerman. July is also peak time for wading birds, but many are present through-out the warmer months, and some—including great blue heron and cattle egret—are present year-round.

Other notable warm-weather residents that arrive in large numbers are scis-sor-tailed flycatchers. These pearly gray birds with pinkish sides and wing linings are easily distinguished by their extremely long, divided tails. Flights of American white pelicans in April and Sept. can be a striking sight—as many as 50,000 birds funnel through the refuge like a prairie blizzard.

The prairie uplands shelter other species, including 17 kinds of sparrows, such

Lesser scaups

as white-throated, white-crowned, Harris', fox, and Lincoln's, almost all setting down in spring, fall, and winter, although numerous dickcissels are found on fenceposts in summer. Other prairie residents include northern bobwhite, quail, and greater roadrunner.

Spring and fall migrations bring more than 20 species of warbler to Hagerman, including black and white, Kentucky warblers, common yellowthroat, and yellow-breasted chat.

Crisscrossing the sky are Mississippi kites and sharp-shinned, broad-winged, Cooper's, and rough-legged hawks. The kites, with whitish heads, are graceful flyers with pointed wings. From below they display a light gray body and wings and a black tail. Nesting raptors

Ross's geese

include red-tailed, red-shouldered, and broad-winged hawks and Mississippi kite.

All told, 316 bird species have been recorded here to date, although 43 of these are classified as "accidentals."

Mammals A high-profile mammal here is the white-tailed deer, most often noted in farm fields along the auto route. Hagerman is a good place to spot coyotes and cottontail rabbits. By the water's edge, scan mud patches for the tracks of raccoon, which are abundant. Opossums, although mainly a nocturnal animal, are common at Hagerman, and another largely nocturnal browser, often seen in daylight poking about in leaf litter for grubs and insects, is the nine-banded armadillo. Gnawed trees, bank dens, lodges, and slides attest to the presence of beaver, but, because they are most active at night, they are not commonly noted. Of the refuge's two squirrel species, the fox squirrel is the one most often observed. Seldom seen are gray fox and bobcat and, even more rarely, cougar. You are likely to find cattle grazing on the refuge. Today they fill the ecological niche once inhabited by buffalo.

Reptiles and amphibians The refuge contains several varieties of poisonous snakes, so beware! Broadband copperheads prefer the leaf-littered forest floors, while western cottonmouths are found in and near the marshes. Timber rattlers, rarely seen, are on the Texas state endangered species list. The extensive wetlands support 18 varieties of toads and frogs, including the gray tree frog and *bufo speciosus*, the Texas toad.

ACTIVITIES

■ **CAMPING:** There is no camping on the refuge, but there are several picnic areas with fire-pits. Eisenhower State Park, 9 miles northeast of refuge, has camping, and there are many other options nearby.

■ **SWIMMING:** Swimming is not allowed in Lake Texoma from the refuge; the water is shallow and full of stumps.

■ **WILDLIFE OBSERVATION:** Sandy Pt. at the north end of Sandy Rd. on the refuge's west side offers excellent viewing of bald eagles fishing over Lake Texoma from late Oct. through March. Here, too, you'll find large numbers of mallard, golden eye, common merganser, horned grebe, Canada goose, and Franklin's gull. The woods in the refuge's northwest corner near Sandy Creek and Brushy Creek, and in the Big Mineral Access Area, shelter occasional pileated woodpeckers and white-breasted nuthatch. Nuthatches are small, stubby birds that always move down a tree headfirst when feeding on insects in the bark.

Give Mineral Marsh a look for its variety of waterbirds, including white pelicans. Diving birds, including cormorants and redhead ducks, seem to favor Steedman Marsh. Elm Pond, with its dead *bois d'Arc* snags, has colonies of nesting great blue herons and great egrets.

■ **PHOTOGRAPHY:** The auto tour route provides exceptionally close approaches to geese, if you remain in your vehicle. Scenic overview shots are easy from the high point of the Crow Hill Trail. But position yourself down low to fill your lens with waving grasses of the prairies. A strong telephoto lens will provide excellent results of various waterfowl on Lake Texoma.

■ **HIKES AND WALKS:** Crow Hill Trail first passes through a forest of cedar elm often harboring perching neotropical songbirds. Beyond the woodlands the trail breaks out onto tallgrass prairie. Meadow Pond Trail skirts the edge of thick forests of oak and pecan, passing some ponds often used by waterfowl, waders, and shorebirds. This path is far less commonly traveled than Crow Hill Trail.

■ **SEASONAL EVENTS:** Free birding tours are provided by volunteers twice weekly on winter mornings. June, first Sat.: Kid's Fishing Derby, no license required.

■ **PUBLICATIONS:** Brochure, auto route guide, bird list.

HAGERMAN HUNTING AND FISHING SEASONS

Hunting (Seasons may vary)	Jan	Feb	Mar	Apr	May	Jun	Jul	Aug	Sep	Oct	Nov	Dec
dove									■			
quail			■									
squirrel			■						■			
rabbit		■	■						■			
feral hogs										■	■	
white-tailed deer										■	■	

Limited hunting of **dove** is allowed in Sept. only, **quail** in Feb. to mid-March. **Squirrel** and **rabbit** are in season in Sept. and Feb. **Feral hogs** and **deer** may be hunted in Sept. and/or Oct., with bows only. Make inquiries at refuge for exact dates.

Fishing is allowed in Lake Texoma year-round in accordance with state regulations for **striped and black bass, crappie, bream,** and **channel cat.** Fishing in refuge ponds is allowed only from April to September; fishing from bridges is prohibited at all times. Check with the refuge for any current restrictions.

Laguna Atascosa NWR
Rio Hondo, Texas

Cactus in bloom, beachside, Laguna Atascosa NWR

Laguna Atascosa NWR is one of the nation's richest biological pools, with diverse flora and fauna, including many Mexican and Meso-American species living at their northern limits. It contains the largest contiguous protected area of natural habitat left in the Lower Rio Grande Valley. Within the refuge, the air carries a salty scent. Along the sandy beaches a storm is churned up in the immense Laguna Madre bay. A coal-black grooved bill ani calls from the edge of a stunted deciduous forest, while an aplomado falcon flutters over the waving grasses of a coastal meadow. Back in the thorn forests rests the rarest of America's felines: a reddish-gray jaguarundi, a species that found its way to this sanctuary.

HISTORY

On a natural travel corridor parallel to the Gulf Coast, Spanish and Mexican armies and individuals crossed through this area frequently. The first to arrive was Alvarez de Pineda, who sailed up the Rio Grande in 1519. The refuge's name, Laguna Atascosa (muddied lagoon) comes from its large, shallow lagoon, the bottom of which gets stirred up in high winds.

The refuge was created in 1946, when an aerial World War II gunnery range was transferred over to the U.S. Fish & Wildlife Service. Other tracts were subsequently purchased, bringing its total size to 45,187 acres. In 1999, opportunities to acquire significant new tracts encompassing 172,000 acres adjoining the present refuge were under active pursuit. Field biologists estimate that only 5 percent of the original habitat of the Lower Rio Grande Valley remains intact today, thus the importance of this refuge.

The refuge is a favored stop for serious birders worldwide and for thousands of "snowbirds" (northern people who winter in south Texas), pushing its annual visitorship over 200,000.

GETTING THERE

Laguna Atascosa NWR lies close to the Mexican border, sitting north of Brownsville and east of Harlingen in extreme south Texas. From Brownsville, take Farm Rd. 1847 (Parades Line Rd.) north through Los Fresnos and proceed 10 mi. farther to Farm Rd. 106. Turn east (right) and continue 3 mi. to the T-intersection with Buena Vista Rd. Turn north (left) and go 3 mi. to the Visitor Center.

From Harlingen take Farm Rd. 106 north to Rio Hondo, and then east 14 mi. to its T-intersection with Buena Vista Rd. Turn north (left) and proceed 3 mi. to the Visitor Center.

■ **SEASON:** Open year-round.

■ **HOURS:** Tour roads open daily, sunrise to sunset. Visitor Center open Oct.–April, daily 10 a.m.–4 p.m.; May weekends only, 10 a.m.–4 p.m.; summer months, open sporadically.

■ **FEES:** Entrance fee $2 per vehicle.

■ **ADDRESS:** P.O. Box 450, Rio Hondo, TX 78583

■ **TELEPHONE:** 956/748-3607

TOURING LAGUNA ATASCOSA

■ **BY AUTOMOBILE:** Two all-weather roads are suitable for auto touring. Bayside Dr. winds 15 miles past thorn forest, coastal prairies, bayside beaches, and freshwater ponds. Lakeside Dr. runs 1.5 miles from the Visitor Center to the refuge's namesake lake, Laguna Atascosa, crossing over a large slough. No restrooms or drinking water along auto routes.

■ **BY FOOT:** Six dedicated foot trails wander into various refuge areas. The shortest one, Kiskadee Trail, begins right behind the Visitor Center, as does the Mesquite Trail. Other trails are best reached by car. Paisano Trail is an improved-surface trail; some portions follow an old paved road, and these parts are handicapped accessible. In addition, there are several dirt service roads that can be walked. Inquire at the Visitor Center for details. Off-trail and off-road foot travel is forbidden.

■ **BY BICYCLE:** The two refuge auto-tour routes and some service roads can be biked. Inquire first before biking on service roads.

■ **BY CANOE, KAYAK, OR BOAT:** A boat launch is located within the refuge at Adolph Thomae County Park, a 53-acre park cooperatively managed by the Cameron County Parks system. This is where the refuge's boating, fishing, and camping takes place.

WHAT TO SEE

■ **LANDSCAPE AND CLIMATE** The flat, broad ancient floodplain of the Rio Grande forms a fertile mosaic of land, freshwater lakes and ponds, and coastline fronting the Gulf of Mexico's vast Laguna Madre. Great storms may sweep in suddenly over the refuge off its large bays, driving the seas up and over the extensive mudflats and sand beaches, salt and brackish marshes, and the lowlands. Away from the shore, higher lands are densely forested with wind-stunted trees; drylands, with thick thorn forests.

Other prominent features include Laguna Atascosa—a substantial, if shallow, landlocked water body covering 3,000 acres—and the smaller, brackish Pelican Lake. Laguna Atascosa's eastern boundary is the mean high tide mark of Laguna Madre, the huge saltwater bay running north, clear to Corpus Cristi, formed by the mainland and the offshore barrier island, Padre.

A large slough and a series of *resacas* (oxbow ponds) run from southwest to northeast across the refuge's south end. This is one of the many flood channels of the once-wandering Rio Grande; today it fills with water draining off slightly higher grounds. Water levels in many of the refuge water bodies are regulated by a man-made system of dikes and conveyance ways, or natural waterways.

The refuge's seaside location provides it with dependable rainfall, averaging 24 inches a year. Winters are mild, with temperatures normally in the 60s and 70s. Northern cold fronts do push through, but snow is extremely rare. Summer temperatures are harsh, often over 100 degrees with high humidity.

■ **PLANT LIFE** The south Texas landscape is a unique blending of temperate, subtropical, coastal, and desert habitats, producing an amazingly diverse range of flora—more than 450 species.

Wetlands Wetlands are found along the lengthy coastline of the Laguna Madre and around interior sloughs, ponds, and Laguna Atascosa. The freshwater wetlands favor cattail, bulrush, and sedges, while the brackish coastal marshes favor wigeon grass, smooth cordgrass, and the submerged shoal grass and turtle grass.

Grasslands Only a few feet above sea level are Laguna Atascosa's vast coastal prairie grasslands, which dominate the refuge. Most common near the bays are the sharp-ended gulf cordgrass and salt flat grass. Further inland, on upland savannalike grasslands, you will find giant sacaton, three-awn, and sandy dropseed. Hereabouts are large areas entirely colonized by exotic grasses, including the prolific bufflegrass, originally from Africa, which compete with native species for nutrients.

Arid lands Up in the refuge's higher points, untouched by storm surges, are true desert lands. Here, robust clumps of beavertail and prickly pear cactus, the low-growing "horse crippler" cactus, and tall Spanish dagger yucca thrive among various low grasses and seasonal wildflowers. Interspersed with this desert terrain are 8,000 acres of so-called thorn forests, or simply brush. These tangled thickets stand 6 feet high and are a mix of immature trees and bushes, including spiny hackberry, lote bush, colima, allthorn, and elbow bush.

Forests In addition to the thorn forest (see above), the refuge has stands of more densely foliated trees. Casting their cooling shade are sugar hackberry, Texas ebony, honey mesquite, and *huisache*. Many of these species can be found in the woods behind the Visitor Center.

Coastal Pockets of beaches and dunes on the long Laguna Madre coastline support their own distinctive plant communities. Gulf cordgrass grows extensively in the saltwater marshes, while salt wort and railroad vine thrive on the dunes. You'll have to arrive early to catch the beach morning glories.

■ **ANIMAL LIFE**

Birds With its overlapping ecosystems and location on both the Central and Mississippi flyways, south Texas has the greatest diversity of birds found in the United States. Laguna Atascosa has recorded 405 species to date—the highest number of any federal refuge—and another 31 species have been spotted in surrounding Cameron County.

Most common are the many varieties of duck. At the height of their winter residence, more than 250,000 may be present, including huge rafts of redheads. The black-bellied whistling duck and mottled duck are two of the more uncommon ducks found here. The former is gooselike, with a rusty body, black belly, and bright coral-red bill. It ranges from south Texas to north Argentina and is most commonly

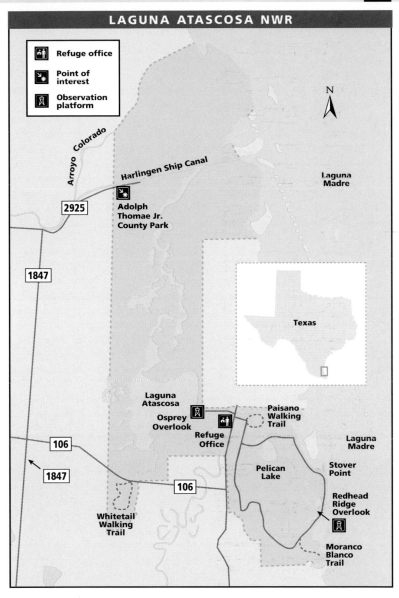

LAGUNA ATASCOSA NWR

- Refuge office
- Point of interest
- Observation platform

Arroyo Colorado

Harlingen Ship Canal

Laguna Madre

2925

Adolph Thomae Jr. County Park

1847

N

Texas

Laguna Atascosa

Osprey Overlook

Refuge Office

Paisano Walking Trail

Laguna Madre

106

Pelican Lake

Stover Point

1847

106

Redhead Ridge Overlook

Whitetail Walking Trail

Moranco Blanco Trail

seen here in spring and summer (although sightings are made year-round). The latter, which is darker than a female mallard, ranges along the Gulf Coast from Florida to Tamualipas, Mexico. At Atascosa it is only uncommon in winter.

Another outstanding bird population is the refuge's wood warblers. An astounding 43 species have been spotted here. But only two nest locally—the yellow-breasted chat and the common yellowthroat—so time a visit for the spring or fall migrations to see the greatest variety. The trees near the Visitor Center are a good place to look for these and other perching songbirds.

If you're on a quest for sparrows, Atascosa is a superb destination. To date, 29 species have been noted, including Botteri's sparrow, found only in small areas of southern Arizona and south Texas. Almost identical to Cassin's sparrow, it is best distinguished by its voice: a constant tinkling and pitting, sometimes carrying into a trill on the same pitch.

The refuge's prolific wildlife supports a large population of raptors—22 species in all, including kites, eagles, and hawks. Osprey are most abundant and are seen in all seasons but spring. Harris hawks nest on the refuge and are also common. White-tailed hawks also nest here, but are seen infrequently. The most uncommon bird of prey is the northern aplomado falcon (see sidebar, below).

Most Atascosa visitors are drawn to its lakes and ponds, so the wealth of its coastal wildlife often goes overlooked. Don't forget that the wild beaches, headlands, and dunes along the Laguna Madre shoreline support 30 species of sandpipers and phalaropes, including greater and lesser yellowlegs, willet, long-billed curlew, dunlin, long-billed dowitcher, and least sandpiper (all common or abundant). They are joined by assemblies of raucous laughing gulls, ring-billed gulls, and Caspian and gull-billed terns.

The dry uplands and thorn forests shelter yet other birds, including a south Texas specialty, the white-tipped dove. Along roads, forest edges, and agricultural lands, keep an eye peeled for the grove-billed ani, another local species that ranges southward across Mexico. This coal-black, 13-inch-long bird has a long, loose-jointed tail and a prominent puffinlike bill with parallel grooves.

Refuge forests are home to species reaching their northern limit in the Rio Grande Valley, including the striking great kiskadee and the lovely green jay.

Still other birds restricted in range in the United States include the pauraque, a member of the nightjar family, Couch's (tropical) kingbird, the Chihahuan raven, and the bronzed cowbird. These birds are more commonly found in Mexico and Central America.

Mammals Among the more common mammals are the javelina, which live in the dry uplands and thorn forests. These thick tangles of plants (often barbed) also shelter the endangered ocelot—a spotted three-foot-long leopard-like cat—and the even rarer, furtive jaguarundi. The Rio Grande Valley is the last refuge for this small long-bodied feline (slightly larger than a housecat); its habitat in Mexico and the

NORTHERN APLOMADO FALCON
While the peregrine falcon gets more attention, the dramatically colored northern aplomado falcon is in even graver danger of extinction. The peregrine once ranged across Texas coastal shrublands and open grasslands of New Mexico, Arizona, and northern Mexico, but sightings of this bird in the Southwest had become a rarity by the 1940s.

This is one handsome raptor—with its arresting striped head (black moustache, white throat, gray cap, and buff stripe behind the eye), its black cummerbund, buff chest, black and white banded tail, steel gray back, and blue-gray wings. Smaller than the prairie falcon or the peregrine, the aplomado in flight resembles a kestrel as it hunts birds, small mammals, reptiles, and insects.

Like the peregrine, the aplomado seems to be on the rebound. In 1993 a handful of adults captured in southern Mexico were released at Laguna Atascosa NWR. Some 39 were released at other Texas sites in 1996, and future releases are planned for New Mexico and Arizona. With luck and careful management, this aerial icon of the Southwest may someday again commonly grace southwestern skies.

United States is almost entirely gone. In Laguna Madre schools of bottlenose dolphin frolic. Scan the fields for brown and white long-tailed weasels, ferocious hunters that often climb trees to nab their prey.

Reptiles and amphibians The most prominent reptile is the American alligator, whose numbers rise and fall according to the availability of fresh water in the refuge's sloughs and ponds. During droughts the alligators bury themselves in the mud of a lake or river bottom in order to stay moist and cool. If the drought is severe, they will either migrate or die. But western diamondback, the horned lizard, Texas spiny lizard, spotted whiptail, and Texas tortoise are also Atascosa residents.

Ocelot with radio collar, Laguna Atascosa NWR

ACTIVITIES

■ **CAMPING:** Camping is permitted within Adolph Thomae County Park (956-748-2044) in the refuge's northern end but not elsewhere on the refuge.

■ **WILDLIFE OBSERVATION:** Different areas of the refuge attract different species. On the floor of the dry thorn forests look for the Texas tortoise out for a stroll on a spring, summer, or fall day. Look, too, for the bright and beautiful green jay and the drab chachalaca. You may hear the snorting of javelinas in the forest, but you won't likely see them. In even drier desert terrain you'll spot birds such as a scootin' roadrunner chasing down a lizard or a pretty verdin perched on a branch. A cactus wren makes its harsh cry as it flutters out of its thorny nest.

Down by the old *resaca*, gators gather to socialize, and whistling ducks proclaim, "We know you're there." A particularly good spot to view the large reptiles is Alligator Pond, 0.25 mile south of Osprey Overlook, at the end of Lakeside Dr.

On the beaches and mudflats of Laguna Madre, you might see a gathering of roseate spoonbills clacking their fat bills. Huffy herons next door pay them no mind, while the egrets just stare at them. This is a good place to observe osprey. The large white-and-black raptors fish over open water, often setting down on beaches to consume their catch.

From late fall to late winter, Osprey Overlook provides a good observation point to see the huge duck population. Bring powerful binoculars or a spotting scope. The ponds flanking Redhead Ridge Overlook, on Bayside Dr., are also favored by ducks. A pull-off just past the overlook actually offers a closer view of one pond. Pelican Lake, also on Bayside Dr., is another good spot to look for waterfowl, wading birds, and shorebirds. Aplomado falcons are most often seen along the final third of Bayside Dr.

Different seasons bring different species as well. Fall migration usually peaks in Nov. Spring migration may start as early as March, but usually peaks in April or early May. However, the temperate climate encourages some birds to remain here year-round, including wading birds, shorebirds, and songbirds. Volunteers and rangers lead guided birding tours on weekends Nov. through April.

■ **PHOTOGRAPHY:** The Visitor Center bird feeding station, with a blind, provides excellent opportunities for photographing green jays, woodpeckers, other birds, and eastern cottontail rabbits. Feeders are stocked early every morning. A wide variety of landscape pictures are possible on this refuge, from the verdant edges of the *resacas* and ponds, to dry thorn forests, desert patches, and coastal beaches and marshes. From Feb. through March the creamy white blossoms of flowering yucca are a signature shot at Laguna Atascosa.

HUNTING AND FISHING White-tailed deer and **feral pigs** may be hunted, but only with a special permit—contact the refuge for details. Bow hunting is allowed in early Dec., firearms in late Dec. Fishing is prohibited, except at the Adolph Thomae County Park. You may fish there year-round, from the banks or from a boat (convenient boat launches are available). Commonly found species include **red** and **black drum**, **speckled seatrout**, and **sheepshead**.

■ **HIKES AND WALKS:** Six dedicated foot trails wander into various refuge areas. The shortest one, Kiskadee Trail, starts right behind the Visitor Center, as does the Mesquite Trail. Other trails are best reached by car. Paisano Trail is paved, making it a good choice in wet weather. In addition, there are several dirt service roads that can be walked. Inquire at the Visitor Center for details. Off-trail and off-road foot travel is forbidden.

Kiskadee Trail runs in a short loop (.1 mile) through low forest around a shallow pond, offering surprisingly good birding. The trail begins behind the Visitor Center.

Mesquite Trail (same trailhead) runs 1.5 miles in a figure-eight through open savannas and low forests, passing two small ponds that hold water in wet years. Signs of deer and coyote are often evident on the trail.

Paisano Trail, an old gunnery range route, runs in a 1-mile paved loop through thorn forest and drylands dotted with yucca and various cactus. Find the trailhead at the beginning of Bayside Dr., where it makes a 90-degree turn to the south.

Lakeside Trail parallels the shoreline of Laguna Atascosa in a 1.5-mile loop through thorn forests. Wildflowers are plentiful, especially in March and April. The trailhead is at Osprey Overlook.

Moranco Blanco trail crosses coastal marshes, passes some small ponds, and then strikes through a thorn forest to emerge on the Laguna Madre beach. This linear primitive route runs just over 3 miles (round-trip). Locate the trailhead just past Redhead Ridge Overlook on Bayside Drive's southern edge.

Whitetail Trail makes a 2-mile loop through thick thorn brush on the refuge's uplands. Trailhead: south side of FM 106, just inside the refuge's west boundary.

Just a bit further east on FM 106 is a service road that can be walked. It runs north less than 1 mile to the southern edge of the lagoon, Laguna Atascosa.

■ **SEASONAL EVENTS:** November: The regional Rio Grande Valley Birding Festival (956/423-5440).

■ **PUBLICATIONS:** At the refuge, ask for their brochure and bird list. Also helpful, given the number of species here, is *Field Guide to the Birds of Texas,* by Peterson and Chalif, Houghton Mifflin, 1963.

Lower Rio Grande Valley NWR

Lower Rio Grande Valley, Texas

Green kingfisher

This refuge dazzles visitors with its variety of landscapes and plethora of flora and fauna. Indeed, the lower Rio Grande Valley of south Texas is one of the nation's richest areas in terms of biotic diversity, with hundreds of plants and many animals and birds found nowhere else in North America. Habitats range from Gulf of Mexico coastal estuaries to inland tidal pools, from the green floodplains of the Rio Grande River to massive salt lakes, from upland desert and scrubland to gently undulating grassland prairies.

HISTORY

The Rio Grande region has a long human history, extending back to prehistoric people who were drawn to its dependable waters and abundant food sources. The Spanish explorer Alonso Alvarez de Pineda first sailed up the mouth of the Rio Grande River in 1519, naming it the Rio de las Palmas (River of Palms). Permanent Hispanic settlement occurred much later (1748) than that, however, because the area was controlled by various native tribes that fiercely defended it.

La Sal de Rey and La Sal Vieja, northeast of McAllen, are large natural salt lakes. These lakes were the only sources of valuable salt for northeastern Mexico, Texas, and Louisiana in Spanish colonial times, and, as such, were one of few places noted on Spanish maps of the territory between Monterrey, Mexico, and San Antonio. A Civil War battle was fought for their control. All of La Sal de Rey and part of La Sal Vieja are now within Lower Rio Grande (LRGV) refuge.

A portion of Palmito Ranch, site of the final land battle of the Civil War (May 12 to 13, 1865, 34 days *after* Robert E. Lee surrendered at Appomattox), also forms part of the refuge. A bronze information plaque on TX 4 (western border of Boca Chica Tract) marks the battle's general vicinity.

LOWER RIO GRANDE VALLEY NWR

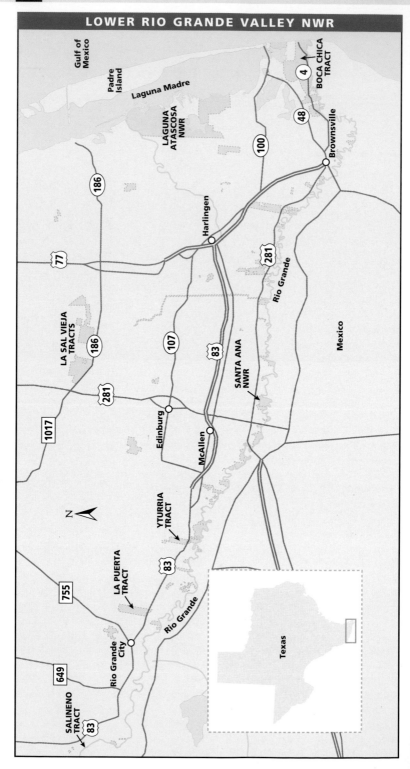

In the 20th century, "the Valley," as it is called, was transformed into a vast agricultural region, growing citrus fruits and many vegetable varieties. Today, increased trade with Mexico has led to a regional population boom. Land clearing for farming, water diversion, urban expansion, and other processes have meant the loss or major alteration of more than 95 percent of the Valley's original habitat-thus, the critical need for this new refuge.

Lower Rio Grande Valley NWR, established in 1979, consists of noncontiguous tracts totalling 90,000 acres in the Rio Grande Valley running for 290 miles in the southernmost tip of Texas. Portions of seven open tracts were opened to public use in 1999; but land acquisition is ongoing, and the refuge will eventually encompass 132,500 acres.

GETTING THERE

Boca Chica Tract rests on either side of TX 4, beginning 15 mi. southeast of Brownsville. La Sal Vieja and Sal de Rey tracts are just off TX 186. West of McAllen you will find Yturria and La Puerta tracts, just off US 83, while Salineno Tract is still farther west. For more specific directions to the seven tracts open to the public, see Touring below or contact the refuge office.

■ **SEASON:** Year-round.

■ **HOURS:** All tracts are open daily from sunrise to sunset; refuge office is staffed weekdays 8 a.m–5 p.m.

■ **FEES:** Free entry.

■ **ADDRESS:** Rte. 2, Box 202A, Alamo, TX 78516. Refuge office is on the nearby Santa Ana NWR.

■ **TELEPHONE:** 956/787-3079, ext. 100

■ **VISITOR CENTER:** No visitor facilities (as of late 1999), but the nearby Santa Ana NWR Visitor Center serves LRGV visitors.

TOURING LOWER RIO GRANDE VALLEY

■ **BY AUTOMOBILE:** No formal auto-tour routes exist on any of the tracts, most of which can only be entered on foot. However, TX 4 bisects the Boca Chica Tract, and several rough, unpaved side roads branch off it (you will want a 4-wheel-drive vehicle). One such road runs north through the Loma Preserve to the Brownsville Shipping Channel; another goes south past a large resaca, or oxbow lake, to the banks of the Rio Grande. TX 4 dead-ends on a beach on the Gulf of Mexico, and you can drive along the beach itself (but only with a 4-wheel-drive).

TX 186 travels east-west along the southern edge of the large La Sal de Rey Tract, while Brushline Rd. (off TX 186) runs between the Schaleben Tract and La Sal de Rey Tract, providing good wildlife viewing opportunities.

■ **BY FOOT:** Because the refuge has only recently opened to public visitation, no formal hiking trails exist as yet, but all have dirt roads open to people on foot (duck under the auto gates). The beach on the Gulf of Mexico on the Boca Chica Tract also makes a good walk.

■ **BY BICYCLE:** Biking is not allowed.

WHAT TO SEE

■ **LANDSCAPE AND CLIMATE** The lower Rio Grande Valley is not really a valley but a largely flat and fertile deltic plain built up over eons by sediment carried toward the Gulf by the river.

The refuge begins at the edge of the sea on sandy barrier islands, where waves boom off a wind-whipped Gulf of Mexico. Behind the beaches lie huge mud flats that fill and drain according to tide and wind. The flats are dotted with low clay hills (*lomas*) formed by wind-blown clay particles deposited during droughts. When the climate turns wetter, plant life returns to the lomas, which helps protect them against further wind erosion.

Move farther inland, up the Rio Grande River Valley, and you see the land slowly rising, dominated by prairie grasslands and shrub "thorn" forests. In the La Puerta Tract area, low hills are bisected by arroyos dropping to the Rio Grande.

Rainfall varies widely over the refuge: 27 inches annually on the coast, but on the western edge of the refuge only 17 inches on average per year. Temperatures range from coastal highs of about 93 (lows of 50); on the western tracts highs average nearly 100 and lows around 43. Fall to early spring is the most pleasant period.

■ **PLANT LIFE** Subtropic, temperate, coastal, and desert influences converge in the lower Rio Grande Valley, creating ideal conditions for species diversity. The refuge, in fact, protects 11 different habitat types and an amazing 1,100 plant species. Based on relative density of occurrence within the refuge (least to most), the plant communities include Chihuahuan thorn forest, Sabal palm forest, coastal brushland potholes, upland thornscrub, upper valley flood forest, *barretal* (native citrus), mid-valley riparian woodlands, clay-loma tidal flats, *ramaderos* (brush strips running along arroyos), mid-delta thorn forests, and wooded potholes and basins.

Groove-billed ani

■ **ANIMAL LIFE**
Birds More than 400 bird species are expected to be documented on the refuge, placing it at the forefront of diversity in the nation. On the coast, seabirds play on the sea breezes, and wading birds periodically invade the mud flats to feed on millions of fiddler crabs. Scores of raptors perch on telephone poles and fence posts or patrol overhead, while migratory songbirds flit about the luxurious growth of the lomas.

The interior grasslands and prairies support many other families of birds. On a late February afternoon you might see a white-tailed hawk, a loggerhead shrike, a Texas ladder-backed woodpecker, or a peregrine falcon. On a recent visit, a Couch's kingbird settled on a telephone wire, and, as it swooped out of a low forest, a screech owl terrified a mouse with its call. Around the salty waters of La Sal de Rey you may see snow geese, sandhill cranes, snowy plovers, and common ground doves gathering. In the thorn forests look for curved-billed thrasher, green-tailed towhee, olive sparrow, pyrrhuloxia, and speedy roadrunner. Scanning the ground from above are red-tailed hawk and caracara.

Down near the Rio Grande, in the small remnant patches of riparian woodland, still other types of birds gather. Here you may spot the beautiful green jay, or the brown jay—both species found nowhere else in the nation—a verdin, or a golden-fronted woodpecker.

Mammals Although its habitat is fragmented, LRGV refuge protects a fantastic range of mammals, some pushed here to the brink of extinction—such as the jaguarundi, an extremely rare feline, and the ocelot, another rare small cat. They are joined by abundant javelina, bobcat, white-tailed deer, coyote, and plentiful rodents. On La Sal de Rey is an exotic mammal of the antelope family called nilgai, originally imported from India by a private rancher.

Reptiles and amphibians LRGV supports a high diversity of reptiles and amphibians. Giant toads inhabit the resacas, while the lomas are home to Texas tortoises that dig into the soft sands to hibernate in winter. Western diamondback rattlesnakes slip and slide from the seacoast to the refuge's western boundary. Also present are beautiful indigo snakes, horned lizards, and, on the western tracts, very large reticulated collared lizards, often seen sunning themselves.

ACTIVITIES

■ **SWIMMING:** Visitors may enjoy swimming in the Gulf of Mexico on the Boca Chica Tract, where the beach is actually state property and open to the public.

■ **WILDLIFE OBSERVATION:** The easiest place for visitors to view a variety of wildlife is on the Boca Chica Tract. A February birding walk can turn up Harris hawks, white-tailed kites (also known as the black-shouldered kite), northern harriers, long billed curlews, ospreys, Mexican crows, and ravens. The large resaca (oxbow lake) south of the highway is home In winter to black-crowned and yellow-crowned night herons. Nearby, look for the sandy mounds of thousands of blue crabs living on flats under trees they've stripped of all low vegetation. The waters of the Rio Grande may show floating spoonbills, tricolored herons, and ducks. Boca Chica beach is habitat for sanderlings and willets, among other water-edge species and seabirds.

Elsewhere on the refuge, Yturria Tract has a 1.2-mile walkable road north from US 83 to a windmill where a water tank attracts lots of wildlife, including bobcat. The large salt lake on La Sal de Rey Tract is an excellent spot to see waterfowl, wading birds, and other wildlife in winter. On the lake's east edge a seeping artesian well is popular with javelina and the exotic nilgai. To reach the salt lake, walk along a dirt road under the powerline at 90 degrees to Brushline Rd. (off TX 186).

> **HUNTING AND FISHING** Fishing with state license and salt-water stamp is allowed on Boca Chica Tract—contact the refuge for details on how to obtain these permits. You will find **black** and **red drum, spotted trout, flounder, golden croaker, sheepshead,** and **gray snapper**. Hunting is currently not allowed, but it may be in the near future. Contact the refuge to see if any policies have been changed.

Another gated road on La Sal de Rey Tract (at the historical marker on TX 186) brings you to a seasonal small pond with some nesting boxes around it. Here, an abandoned home and barn attract occasional barn owls.

■ **PUBLICATIONS:** Information flyers on public tracts.

McFaddin and Texas Point NWRs

Sabine Pass, Texas

Seaside, McFaddin NWR

A sea of raspy cordgrass ripples and bends in the wind blowing off the Gulf of Mexico, carrying with it the sharp cry of gulls and the sodden breath of salt. A leaden sky portends rain in a land where earth and sky merge into one watery realm.

HISTORY

Occupation of these vast marshlands extends back many thousands of years, evidenced by Paleo-Indian hunting relics recovered at the McFaddin Beach cultural site. Later, Cajun trappers harvested muskrat, nutria, and mink. In the early 1900s William McFaddin, a Scottish immigrant, controlled a parcel of land along the Texas Gulf Coast at the site of the present McFaddin refuge. The 57,000-acre McFaddin NWR was launched in 1980 and the 8,900-acre Texas Point NWR in 1979. Texas Point NWR includes its namesake Texas Point, the state's southeasternmost spit of land, which projects into the Gulf of Mexico. Today some 43,000 people, mainly local hunters and anglers, visit the two refuges annually.

GETTING THERE

McFaddin NWR is west of the small town of Sabine Pass, which is south of Port Arthur. From Sabine Pass head west on TX 87 for 12 mi. past Sea Rim State Park; turn north (right) onto Clam Lake Rd. Texas Point NWR is also reached via TX 87; a walk-in path begins 2 mi. west of Sabine Pass on the south side of TX 87. FR 3322, running south from Sabine Pass, provides boat access for Texas Point.
■ **SEASON:** Open year-round.
■ **HOURS:** McFaddin NWR: Clam Lake Rd. is open to Ten Mile Cut Bridge daily 6 a.m. to a half hour before sunset. Beyond this bridge, access is restricted week-

days from 7:30 a.m.–3 p.m. Closed all holidays. Texas Point NWR: open daily, daylight hours.

■ **FEES:** Free entry.

■ **ADDRESS:** Both refuges: P.O. Box 609, Sabine Pass, TX 77655.

■ **TELEPHONE:** 409/971-2909

■ **VISITOR CENTER:** The Visitor Contact Station has no interpretive facilities but does have people who can answer questions and provide useful information.

TOURING McFADDIN AND TEXAS POINT

■ **BY AUTOMOBILE:** The predominance of marshlands limits access by car, particularly at Texas Point, where there are no interior roads. McFaddin National Wildlife Refuge contains 10 miles of interior gravel roads open to the public. There is no designated auto-tour route, but for a good overview of the landscape, take Clam Lake Rd. from TX 87 north past the refuge headquarters to the Intracoastal Waterway, then west parallel to the waterway, and then backtrack. Oil-field industrial roads also cross the refuge; they are signed and closed to the public. TX 87 extends westward from Clam Lake Rd. along the Gulf but is officially closed and not maintained.

At Texas Point, FR 3322 runs along the eastern boundary, and TX 87 is adjacent to its northern boundary.

■ **BY FOOT:** A watchable wildlife trail follows a levee 0.2 mile across a wetland. It begins just behind the refuge headquarters. You can walk McFaddin's public roads and its beach along the Gulf Coast, but there are no dedicated hiking trails.

Texas Point includes one marshy cattle trail that runs almost 2 miles south from TX 87. The trailhead, which is 2 miles from Sabine Pass on the south side of TX 87, can become quite boggy during warm, wet seasons, bringing out the refuge's 60 or so species of mosquitoes.

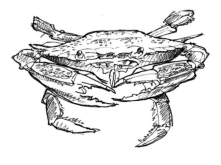

■ **BY BICYCLE:** Biking is permitted on McFaddin's public roads.

Blue crab

■ **BY CANOE, KAYAK, OR BOAT:** Clam Lake is the refuge's largest body of water. Shallow water boats are favored modes of water travel in the lake; air boats with less than 10 hp motors are also allowed. McFaddin refuge has seven launch ramps; boat access ditches, primarily used by hunters, provide entry to remote sections of the refuge.

WHAT TO SEE

■ **LANDSCAPE AND CLIMATE** This far-southeastern corner of Texas is dominated by the Upper Texas Coastal Plain, a broad, predominantly flat landmass that barely rises above the sea. Beneath the marshes and open waters lie enormous oil and gas fields; the horizon is often punctuated with tall oil rigs. Long, low forested ridges called *cheniers* snake across the landscape. These remnant beach ridges of sand, silt, and shell fragments, no more than 10 feet high, provide important habitat for many songbirds and other wildlife.

The Intracoastal Waterway, a man-made shipping channel, cuts across McFaddin, creating additional management difficulties for this complex system of marshes, ponds, lakes, and ditches.

Because of onshore winds, temperatures rarely exceed 100 degrees in summer, and winters are mild with occasional frosts.

■ **PLANT LIFE** McFaddin's tidal marshes range from salty to freshwater and blends of both. Here you'll find pondweed and widgeon grass beneath the water; California bulrush, Olney 3-square (a favored food of snow geese), and leafy 3-square growing out of the water; and stands of tall phragmites cane.

The land at Texas Point slopes slightly from north to south and is more heavily influenced by the tides than is McFaddin. Cordgrasses that tolerate high salinity are prevalent. Look for smooth cordgrass, a coarse grass growing to a height of 4 feet; marshy cordgrass, which grows to a height of 2 feet or so; and the low-growing seashore salt grass.

Roughly 2 percent of each refuge consists of forested *cheniers* covered with dense stands of hackberry, laurel oak, and live oak, as well as the invasive Chinese tallow. Shrubs, vines, and brambles create a dense understory in these woodlands.

■ **ANIMAL LIFE**
Birds Significant populations of Central Flyway waterfowl overwinter at these refuges, including up to 70,000 snow geese at McFaddin and 100,000 ducks on the two refuges combined, as well as spectacular numbers of wading birds, marsh birds, and shorebirds. Even during a short visit in February, you could view red-winged blackbirds, many great egrets, king rails, kingfishers, osprey, great blue herons, double-crested cormorants, killdeer, spotted sandpiper, loggerhead shrikes, black-necked stilts, and green and blue-winged teal. Patrolling the skies overhead are osprey, black-shouldered kite, kestrel, and turkey vultures.

Spring and fall bring numerous and diverse migratory songbirds, with different species observed day to day, including warblers, orioles, tanagers, thrushes, and vireos. The refuge also shelters year-round nesting populations of mottled duck, whose range is restricted to Gulf Coastal marshes.

Brown pelicans

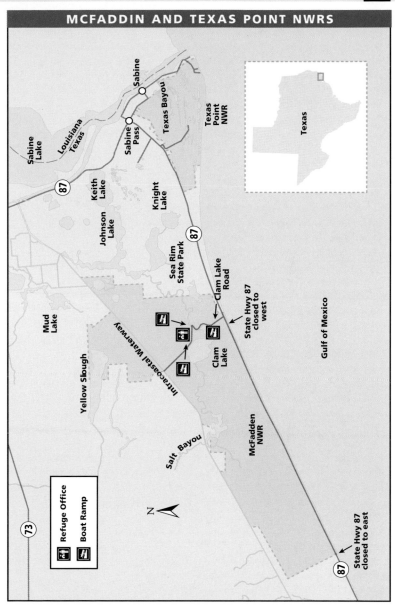

MCFADDIN AND TEXAS POINT NWRS

(Map labels: Sabine, Texas Bayou, Texas Point NWR, Sabine Pass, Sabine Lake, Louisiana/Texas, Keith Lake, Knight Lake, Johnson Lake, 87, Sea Rim State Park, 87, Clam Lake Road, State Hwy 87 closed to west, Mud Lake, Intracoastal Waterway, Clam Lake, Gulf of Mexico, Yellow Slough, Salt Bayou, McFadden NWR, Texas, State Hwy 87 closed to east, 87, 73, N, Refuge Office, Boat Ramp)

Visitors can spot threatened and endangered birds—such as least tern, brown pelican, piping plover, bald eagle, and peregrine falcon—among the 289 bird species identified in the area.

Mammals The marshy character of this region does not make for ideal habitat for major mammals, but occasionally at dusk you may be able to spot nutria, muskrat, skunk, opossum, armadillo, and raccoon along roadsides. In the early mornings, look for mink, river otter, and bobcat. Most elusive are the large, darkly colored coyotes, descendants of hybrid crosses with red wolves, now extinct on the Texas coastal plains.

Reptiles The once-endangered American alligator is thriving here today. About 1,500 gators, some as large as 12 feet and 350 pounds., reside at McFaddin. Visitors often see them napping on sunny banks along roadways and marsh edges. Observe from a safe distance!

Fish The salt marsh ecosystem is one of the world's most productive biological communities, and the waters of McFaddin and Texas Point are important habitat for significant populations of red drum, blue catfish, and flounder.

Invertebrates It's quite common to find folks fishing for blue crabs from the bridge at Ten Mile Cut at McFaddin. The delicious, 9-inch bottom feeder is caught in traps and pulled to the surface. Fiddler crabs also frequent these waters .

ACTIVITIES

■ **CAMPING:** Primitive camping is allowed on the McFaddin Beach, but most campers head to the adjoining Sea Rim State Park (information, 409/971-2559; reservations, 512/389-8900), which has an interpretive marsh boardwalk and Visitor Center.

■ **SWIMMING:** Not recommended in ponds because of alligators and "nutria itch" parasite. It's fine, though, to swim in the Gulf along McFaddin Beach. Shoes are advised.

■ **WILDLIFE OBSERVATION:** With lakes, ponds, freshwater and brackish marshes, and upland patches of forest, McFaddin provides prime grounds for observing birdlife. Without a boat, birding at Texas Point is limited to the cow trail walk in or drive south on FR 3322 from Sabine. Water-loving birds increase their numbers in winter, but some waterfowl species, including mottled duck, reside here year-round.

Spring migrations, peaking in early April, are spectacular. As birds cross the Gulf of Mexico, they occasionally encounter northern headwinds and arrive on the Texas coast utterly exhausted, descending into the first woodlands they find. The Sabine Woods, between Sabine Pass and the parking pullout on TX 87 for Texas Point, is famed for its spring migrations.

At McFaddin, birders can approach a fenced nesting area for least terns on a spur road off the main auto route.

Be sure to spend some time padding along the sands of McFaddin Beach. Here you'll find royal terns, willet, ring-billed gulls, and plovers.

■ **PUBLICATIONS:** Brochure covering both refuges.

HUNTING AND FISHING
You may hunt **ducks**, **coots**, and **geese** from late Oct. through mid-Jan. The season officially lasts 74 days—call the refuge for exact dates. Fishing is allowed throughout the year. Anglers often catch **red drum, flounder, alligator gar**, and **blue catfish**, as well as **blue crabs**.

Muleshoe NWR
Muleshoe, Texas

Greater sandhill cranes

Alternately wet and bone dry, shivering cold and beastly hot, the Texas panhandle is a challenge to both wildlife and people. But rewards are big for those who venture out to Muleshoe NWR. Here visitors are outnumbered by birds drawn to the grass prairies and salt playa lakes.

HISTORY

The oldest national wildlife refuge in Texas, Muleshoe was a pioneer in 1935, but it's small by Texas standards: only 5,809 acres, most of it upland prairie. There's water, too, a fact that helps explain the outstanding attraction at Muleshoe—its wintering lesser sandhill cranes. Human visitors average around 9,000 a year.

GETTING THERE

Muleshoe NWR rests on the southwestern edge of the Texas panhandle, southwest of Amarillo. From the town of Muleshoe, head south on TX 214 for 20 mi.; at the refuge sign, turn west (right) and proceed 2.25 mi. to refuge office.
■ **SEASON:** Open year-round.
■ **HOURS:** Except for the refuge campground, public use is allowed on the refuge during daylight hours only. Office is open weekdays 8 a.m.–4:30 p.m.
■ **FEES:** Free entry.
■ **ADDRESS:** P.O. Box 549, Muleshoe, TX 79347
■ **TELEPHONE:** 806/946-3341
■ **VISITOR CENTER:** The refuge office, when open, has a few interpretive displays and an emergency phone. The Visitor Center lobby is always open.

TOURING MULESHOE

■ **BY AUTOMOBILE:** There are 5 miles of caliche (limestone) roads running to the refuge's three saline lakes. TX 214 also crosses the refuge.

■ **BY FOOT:** Muleshoe's 1-mile nature trail with interpretive panels begins at the campground. A dirt trail (0.125 mile) climbs to the top of a hill that overlooks Lower Paul's Lake. Visitors may also walk the refuge's dirt roads.

■ **BY BICYCLE:** Bikes are allowed on Muleshoe's unpaved roads and in the fire lanes.

WHAT TO SEE

■ **LANDSCAPE AND CLIMATE** Set on the High Plains of West Texas, not far from the New Mexico border, Muleshoe NWR is a place of undulating native grass prairies, broken by two caliche rimrock outcroppings. The refuge contains three shallow saline playa lakes—White Lake, Paul's Lake, and Goose Lake—each averaging 200 acres. These large depressions have no outlets and gather rain and occasional snowmelt. A permanent spring feeding Upper Paul's Lake occasionally spills over into Lower Paul's. Upper Paul's is the only lake on the refuge that normally holds water year-round.

The temperatures vary wildly here, from more than 105 degrees in summer to an occasional below-zero winter night. Nov. and Dec. days average highs of 66 and 55 degrees respectively, while lows average 56 and 24 degrees. Most of the annual average precipitation of 16 inches falls in summer thunderstorms. Visitors should come prepared for extremes.

■ **PLANT LIFE**
Grasslands Native grama grasses (growing up to a foot high), short grasses (like blue grama), and buffalo grasses are the dominant vegetation of the upland

Prairie falcons

prairie. A thousand acres of alkali sacaton grows on the highly limed earth near the lakes, helping to protect and stabilize the soil against wind erosion.

■ ANIMAL LIFE

Birds Muleshoe's sandhill cranes normally begin arriving near the end of Sept. and reach peak concentrations between Dec. and mid-Feb. An all-time-high crane count came in 1981 with 250,000 present! Recent droughts and changes in the types and size of crops grown on nearby farmland have led to major declines in the refuge's sandhill population, and only 16,000 were counted here in the winter of 1999.

When enough water is present, waterfowl visitation is also impressive. Pintail, green-winged teal, American wigeon, and mallard are most common; ruddy duck, blue-winged teal, canvasback, redhead, lesser scaup, ring-necked, and bufflehead occur in lesser numbers. The ducks begin arriving in Aug. and are most numerous at the end of the year.

Water levels also influence the presence of wading and shore birds, including bitterns, herons, and egrets, long-billed curlews, stilt sandpipers, black terns, and ring-billed gulls.

The most common of the refuge's 16 species of kites, eagles, hawks, and falcons are Swainson's, northern harrier, ferruginous, and red-tailed hawks. There are also American kestrels. Each of these species favor Muleshoe year-round, except the Swainson's. If you're lucky, you'll catch sight of a prairie falcon or even a peregrine falcon. Turkey vultures, masters of float, drift idly on summer and fall thermals, rocking their wings occasionally to adjust their steady glide. Golden eagles swoop by in fall or winter; in Jan. or Feb. an occasional bald eagle is sighted. Great horned owls use the refuge year-round.

Mammals Prairie dog towns occupy quite a spread here, covering 360 acres. Dirt hillocks protect the prairie dogs' underground homes: These mounded burrows help keep water from running down into the holes. Coyote, cottontail and jackrabbits are common as well. Harder to spot are bobcat, deer, badger, skunk, and porcupine, but all live on Muleshoe refuge.

Reptiles and amphibians Be careful to watch for prairie rattlesnakes; they often take up residence, compatibly, in prairie dog tunnels. The rattlers hibernate in winter but are otherwise most active in early morning or late evening, spending the days carefully hidden in the shade under logs and rocks.

ACTIVITIES

■ **CAMPING:** A campground with firepits and tables is situated 0.125 mile from the Visitor Center.

■ **WILDLIFE OBSERVATION:** The small woods near the campground provide much-needed refuge for perching songbirds. During times of drought, Upper Paul's Lake is generally the last body of water to dry up, which makes it a good place to view waterfowl and wading and shorebirds. Each of the other lakes has an access road (drivable) and a parking area overlooking the water, affording good wildlife observation under the right conditions.

To watch prairie dog antics, stop near the headquarters at the observation turnout on the tour road; from there you'll look out on some draws, or shallow gullies, housing a sizable "doggie" town.

Red fox are occasionally seen on the refuge entrance road in midsummer.

■ **PUBLICATIONS:** Brochure, bird list.

San Bernard NWR
Angelton, Texas

Snow geese rising off coastal marsh, San Bernard NWR

San Bernard is a haven for migratory birds. During the mild Gulf winter, as many as 100,000 geese travel along the Central Flyway to congregate in the refuge's salt marshes. In springtime, great numbers of migratory songbirds, shorebirds, and waders find the refuge a welcome resting place on their long journey northward.

HISTORY

San Bernard NWR, named for a local river, was created in 1968 and covers 27,414 acres. It is comanaged by nearby Brazoria NWR and shares many of Brazoria's characteristics. Some 23,000 people visit annually.

GETTING THERE

Located 12 mi. southwest of Lake Jackson in southern Brazoria and Matagorda counties. Head west out of Lake Jackson on FM 2004 for 7 mi. At Jones Creek, FM 2004 turns into FM 2611. Proceed on FM 2611 for 4 mi., then turn south (left) onto FM 2918 for 1 mi. to County Rd. 306. Turn west (right) and pass the refuge field office to reach the entrance road.

■ **SEASON:** Year-round.

■ **HOURS:** Grounds open daily sunrise to dusk; office weekdays 8 a.m.–5 p.m.

■ **FEES:** Free entry.

■ **ADDRESS:** Rt. 1, Box 1335, Brazoria, TX 77422.

■ **TELEPHONE:** Main office (Brazoria NWR) 409/849-6062; field office 409-964-3639.

■ **VISITOR CENTER:** No Visitor Center. Restroom and emergency phone at the refuge field office. Bring drinking water and food.

TOURING SAN BERNARD

■ **BY AUTOMOBILE:** A 3-mile auto route circles Moccasin Pond, and other refuge roads provide additional wildlife viewing opportunities.

■ **BY FOOT:** Three hiking trails to explore: Scissor Tail Trail (0.8 mile), Cowtrap Trail (1.5 miles), and Cockleburr Slough/Bobcat Woods Trail (about 1 mile with side loops, including a handicapped-accessible boardwalk). Visitors are also free to walk the refuge public roads.

■ **BY BICYCLE:** Bicyclists are welcome on all refuge roads open to public vehicles.

■ **BY CANOE, KAYAK, OR BOAT:** A boat ramp at the refuge's southeast corner (end of FM 2918 and County Rd. 317) provides boating access to the Cedar Lakes area. Canoes, kayaks, and motorboats are also allowed on Cedar Lake Creek.

WHAT TO SEE

■ **LANDSCAPE AND CLIMATE** Elevations at the San Bernard refuge run from 3 feet below sea level to 9 feet above, on the "upland" prairies. Bordering the Gulf, the refuge has mild winters, with daytime temperatures averaging 41 to 55 degrees; in summer, the range is 84 to 91 degrees; in a particularly rainy year, 50 inches may fall.

Nearby is a satellite refuge, the 5,000-acre Big Boggy NWR, which is comanaged by San Bernard. Public access is limited to hunters during waterfowl-hunting season and special birding tours in fall and spring.

■ **PLANT LIFE**

Wetlands Marsh hay cordgrass and salt grass are far and away the dominant plants of San Bernard's extensive salt marshes. Clumps of cattail and California bulrush grow around the freshwater ponds and marshes, providing food and nesting materials for birds. Willows at Moccasin Pond provide good cover for many bird families, including perching birds and such songbirds as jays, blackbirds, finches, warblers, and sparrows.

Grasslands San Bernard has some limited grasslands featuring bluestem grass and baccharis bush at the higher elevations and gulf cordgrass and marsh hay cordgrass on the salt prairies.

Snow goose

Forests Beautiful shady woodlands of live oak, yaupon, and hackberry—some draped with Spanish moss—can best be seen along the Bobcat Woods Trail. Below the trees lie striking green palmetto fans, poison ivy, wild onions, wild iris, red salvia, and white spider lilies.

■ ANIMAL LIFE

Birds Migratory bird "fallouts" sometimes occur here in April and May. A fallout occurs when songbirds flying north over the Gulf of Mexico run into headwinds and descend, exhausted, en masse upon the first woodlands they encounter. Even without this phenomenon, one can see dozens of species here in a visit of only a few hours as the birds refresh themselves for their continued northward migrations. Particularly plentiful are warblers.

During Jan. and Feb., huge flocks of geese—primarily snow geese—arrive, along with smaller numbers of Canada and white-fronted geese. Joining their fellow waterfowl are many species of duck, including pintail, cinnamon teal, gadwall, wigeon, and mottled. You may also see the strikingly colored purple gallinule.

The refuge prairies attract doves, hawks, owls, vultures, and kites. Over at the colonial waterbird rookery in the Cedar Lakes area, more than 7,000 pairs of laughing gulls, royal terns, black skimmers, tricolored herons (brownish-red, white, and blue), cattle egrets, and great blue herons nest in the summer.

Mammals Feral hogs, raccoons, coyotes, and nutria use the prairie, woodlands, and marshes for food and shelter. The feral hogs and nutria are invasive species that are harmful to native animals. In the soft soil along Cockleburr Slough, signs of deer, river otter, bobcat, and armadillo can often be found.

> **HUNTING AND FISHING**
> **Waterfowl hunting** is permitted in specific areas during fall and winter. Contact the refuge for details. **Fishing** and **crabbing** are allowed on the Cedar Lakes, Cow Trap Lakes, and Cedar Lake Creek.

Reptiles and amphibians Moccasin Pond is aptly named—keep an eye out for the deadly water moccasin at San Bernard. Small numbers of alligators also swim in the refuge waters.

Fish and invertebrates Cow Trap Lake system is one of the most pristine marshes of the Texas coast, providing a valuable nursery for spotted sea trout, redfish, black drum, sheephead, and flounder, as well as blue crab, several species of shrimp, and colonial oysters.

ACTIVITIES

■ **WILDLIFE OBSERVATION:** The easiest viewing opportunities are afforded on the Moccasin Pond auto route; the foot trails can reward with wildlife spottings as well. Cow Trap, for instance, heads across a huge marsh and prairie dotted with small potholes. In Feb. the air is filled with the plaintive honking of thousands of snow geese, an impressive sight for hikers crossing this sea of grass.

■ **SEASONAL EVENTS:** April (mid-month): Regional Migration Celebration.

■ **PUBLICATIONS:** Brochure, bird list.

Santa Ana NWR
Alamo, Texas

Zebra butterfly and gallardia, Santa Ana NWR

The ground is so dry it cracks open, but the hardy stands of *retama*, *huisache*, and mesquite are filled with flashes of color as green jays, altamira orioles, and chachalacas flit about. The dense shade and humidity edging a pond are welcome relief to humans and animals alike; pondside is a good spot to watch red-eared slider turtles sunning on logs, black-bellied whistling ducks paddling in the distant marshes, and a hook-billed kite working the forest edge. A remnant pocket containing a great number of endangered plants and animals, Santa Ana NWR feels ancient, and yet ever renewed by its profusion of life forms.

HISTORY

Established in 1943, Santa Ana NWR spans 2,088 acres. Its name derives from a 15-square-mile Mexican land grant issued in 1834 to Benigno Leal, a rancher. The grant is said to have been traded at one point for a fiddle and a new suit. The ranch cemetery, enclosed by a hand-hewn 100-year-old ebony fence, is just off the auto-tour route. The marked and unmarked graves are occasionally adorned with fresh flowers, signaling family ties to those buried here.

This southernmost corner of Texas is popular with snowbirds—not feathered friends, but retirees from cold northern states and Canada who flock to the Lower Rio Grande Valley every winter. They boost annual visitation at Santa Ana to over 165,000.

GETTING THERE

Located southeast of McAllen or northwest of Brownsville. From Alamo on US 83, go 7.5 mi. south on FM 907 to US 281; turn east (left) and proceed 0.25 mi. to the refuge entrance.

■ **SEASON:** Year-round.

■ **HOURS:** Refuge open daily sunrise to sunset. Visitor Center open Nov.-May, daily, 9 a.m.–4:30 p.m. (Except Christmas and New Year's Day); June–Oct., Tues.–Sat., 8:30 a.m.–4 p.m.

■ **FEES:** Free entry at this time.

■ **ADDRESS:** Rte. 2, Box 202A, Alamo, TX 78516

■ **TELEPHONE:** 956/787-3079, ext. 100

■ **VISITOR CENTER:** The refuge has an excellent Visitor Center, with displays, photographs, video room, public-use computer birding database, borrowable binoculars, bookstore-gift shop, restrooms, and pay phone.

TOURING SANTA ANA

■ **BY AUTOMOBILE OR TRAM** A 7-mile paved auto-tour route rolls through the refuge, providing easy access to most of its outstanding features and good wildlife viewing opportunities. The route is open to private vehicles 9 a.m.-4 p.m., Tues. and Wed., year-round. The route is closed, however, to private vehicles from Thurs.-Mon. year-round. From the Fri. after Thanksgiving to May 1, on Thurs.-Mon., commercial, naturalist-guided open-air tram tours are operated. Tours depart the Visitor Center four times daily and run about 75 minutes. Adult fare: $3, children 12 and under: $1.

■ **BY FOOT** An extensive system of foot trails and service roads measuring 12 miles spans the refuge, including a handicapped-accessible trail. The trails are well-marked, open daily sunrise to sunset, and provide excellent wildlife viewing. Visitors may also walk the levee tops, pond dikes, and the auto-tour route.

■ **BY BICYCLE** Biking is allowed on the auto-tour route from sunrise to sunset on Tues.-Weds., from the Fri. after Thanksgiving to May 1, and daily the rest of the year.

WHAT TO SEE

■ **LANDSCAPE AND CLIMATE** Santa Ana NWR lies in the Lower Rio Grande Valley ("the Valley"), which flanks the Rio Grande upstream for 290 miles from the river's terminus at the Gulf of Mexico. The fabled rio runs along the refuge's southern border; just across the surprisingly narrow river lies Mexico. Prior to damming, the Rio Grande periodically jumped its banks to meander over a wide floodplain, leaving behind water-filled channels and oxbow lakes, locally called *resacas,* fringed with marshes. Growing between these resacas were thick hardwood forests broken by grassy openings.

The confluence of several landscapes has created an area that is a biologic test tube, a haven for an astonishing 450 (or more) species of plants and 380(or more) animals now found on the refuge. The Valley is connected to the larger subtropical Tamaulipan geographic region extending far

Palm trees along a slough, Santa Ana NWR

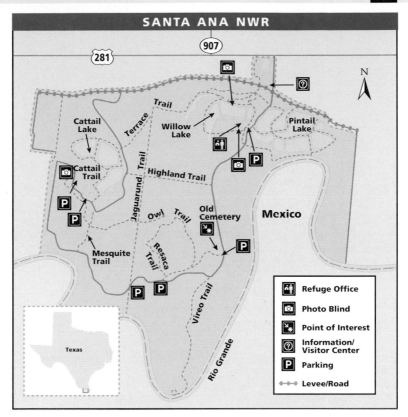

southward into Mexico, the Texas Gulf Coastal plains to the east, and the Chihuahuan Desert to the northwest.

Since the 1920s, however, ranching, farming, water diversion, urban growth, and other activities have consumed or significantly altered more than 95 percent of the Valley's original ecosystems. Santa Ana is the largest remaining example of original habitat located directly along the Rio Grande itself. It protects some 120 acres of reseca wetlands, 60 acres of river-edge flood forest, and almost 2,000 acres of bottomland and upland forests.

The handful of resacas are maintained through judicious use of a manmade irrigation system. Other than the channel cut by the Rio Grande, the terrain is basically flat.

Rainfall is highly erratic in the Lower Rio Grande Valley, both seasonally and annually. The late 1990s saw a prolonged drought throughout the area, but typically 20 inches of rain fall each year. Daytime highs average about 50 degrees in winter and 95 degrees in summer. Winter and late spring are the preferred visiting periods.

■ PLANT LIFE
Wetlands Typical freshwater marsh flora—cattails, sedges, and arrowhead—fringe Santa Ana's rescacas and its man-made ponds.
Forests While the water of the resacas and ponds is a key element in Santa Ana's flourishing wildlife, its forests are its most remarkable characteristic, covering 93 percent of the refuge and harboring many of its diverse plant species.

Green jay

In drier upland sections many of the trees are studded with thorns, giving rise to the name "thorn forest." Common members of the prickly set are *retama* (also called Jerusalem thorn), with its lime-green branches, and *huisache*, whose yellow puffball flowers begin blooming as early as January. Poking above the tree canopy are black-trunked honey mesquites.

Below the canopy are tall clumps of prickly pear cactus, with orange, red, or yellow flowers blooming in spring. (The sticks and forest detritus often piled around their bases are the armored homes of southern plains woodrats.)

But not all the woods are armed. In the slightly wetter bottomlands, cedar elm is a common resident. Arching over the resacas are tall Rio Grande ash, and scattered here and there are sugar hackberry, Texas ebony (whose wood is 20 times denser than oak), and western soapberry. Its brown seeds contain lye, used by settlers to make soap. These thick tree canopies create open, cooler understories suitable for wildflowers. Around the old headquarters site on the auto route, look for the shrimp plant, an introduced exotic beloved by hummers, and the scarlet flowers of the giant turkscap, a native flower also popular with hummers.

Along the refuge's four miles of Rio Grande riverfront—hard to get to and not commonly seen by visitors—is a narrow margin of about 60 acres of seasonally flooded habitat. Dominant trees here include Rio Grande ash, willow, and sugar hackberry.

Many tall trees wear drapings of Spanish moss. While appearing parasitic, this exotic-looking moss draws moisture directly from the air, doing little to harm its host. Look too for the round clumps of another moss type, called, appropriately, ball moss.

■ ANIMAL LIFE

Birds Santa Ana is a holy grail of birding. Its overlapping habitats and status as the last, relatively large intact natural habitat of the entire Lower Rio Grande Valley provide for a tremendous diversity of birdlife. Many species reach the northern limit of their range in the area, yet are easily observed here, including the groove-billed ani, the dapper-looking green jay, the drab and chatty plain chacalaca, and the Altamira orioles (like a hooded oriole but considerably larger). In all, 397 species have been recorded here to date, placing it at the forefront of the entire national refuge system.

The resacas, ponds, lakes, and river draw large numbers of waterfowl, 31 species, in fact! There are south Texas specialties like the fulvous whistling duck (here year-round, though uncommon in spring) and the masked duck (rare), as well as other unusual water birds like the least grebe. Many waterfowl are present from late fall through early spring.

At Santa Ana you can spot also a good cross section of raptors—24 in all. A rare sight for U.S. birders is the hook-billed kite, in its northernmost range here, nesting year-round. Look for its prominently hooked beak. Another local specialty is the gray hawk, also here year-round but less common. More often seen are the Harris hawk, Cooper's hawk, and red-shouldered hawk. The refuge's population of three kingfisher species is noteworthy: the common belted and the uncommon (for the United States) ringed and green.

The many varieties of flowering plants are a magnet for hummingbirds. Among the nine species is another regional specialty, the buff-bellied hummer, a rather large green bird with a red bill, found on the refuge year-round. Also present at any season are ruby-throats, black-chinned, and rufous varieties.

Not surprisingly, the flourishing forests attract lots of woodpeckers. Most impressive and abundant of the three main species is the golden-fronted woodpecker, with its patches of contrasting yellow and red. Spring and fall bring migratory wading birds; some stay to nest in summer, including least bitterns and green herons.

Migratory and some resident neotropical songbirds make music here, ranging from 35 warbler species (including golden-winged, magnolia, palm, northern parula, and yellow-brested chat) to the great kiskadee—limited in the United States to this area. Abundant and resident year-round, you can't miss its incessant calls and brilliant yellow breast and head stripes of black, white, and yellow. The kiskadee is one of 25 species of flycatcher and allies who feed off the prolific flying insects of this refuge.

Mammals The tangled thorn forest of Santa Ana is one of the few places left in the nation (and Mexico) where three feline species still prowl together—the bobcat, the ocelot, and the extremely rare jaguarundi. Each need large contiguous land bases in order to survive.

Nine-banded armadillos dig in the earth for grubs, and seen scampering up trees are fox squirrels. Also present are coyote and several bat species.

Reptiles and amphibians Twenty or so species of snakes live at Santa Ana, including the blue indigo, a rare endemic (but not yet officially endangered) bluish-black creature. Coral snakes are among the poisonous varieties, but live most of their lives hidden away.

Invertebrates Half of all North America's butterfly varieties have been seen fluttering through Santa Ana, an astounding 285 species—the highest number in any federal refuge. The lovely wings of the malachite span a dazzling 5 inches.

ACTIVITIES

■ **CAMPING:** No camping is allowed on the refuge. Camping facilities are available 35 miles away in Bentsen State Park (956/585-1107). Picnicking is allowed only within visitor vehicles.

■ **WILDLIFE OBSERVATION:** The best period for birdwatching runs from Nov. through April. If you arrive early in the morning, you will spot your first birds at the refuge feeding station. Chachalacas and green jays, competing for "noisiest refuge resident," flock to the seed spread here, along with squirrels and other birds.

Willow and Pintail lakes are kept inundated from the fall through the spring and so are favored by waterfowl and other wildlife. The easternmost pond at Pintail Lake is a bit off the beaten path but a good place to see waterbirds that are sensitive to observation pressure.

The levy provides a good, and often overlooked, vantage point for birding, because its height puts one at eye level with the tops of the surrounding trees. Cattail Lake is a shallow water body; in certain conditions it can be a favorite place for waterfowl or wading birds.

A flower garden in front of the visitor center attracts numerous butterflies, floating jewels. The trails (see below) offer many unique viewing opportunities. A trip on the tram tour is also highly recommended. The speakers are true naturalists and point out many sights you might otherwise overlook. The tour loop also takes in areas you probably won't visit on foot.

The use of calling devices to attract wildlife is forbidden.

■ **HIKES AND WALKS:** Three primary trails wend about Santa Ana. "A" Trail (0.5 mile) is paved, handicapped accessible, and popular. It leads to Willow Lake, where cedar elms and Rio Grande ash cast cooling shade over the water's edge. A wooden platform with benches provides a great place to sit silently and wait for the birds to come to you. The woodlands along the way to the lake provide views of chachalacas and green jays.

> **HUNTING AND FISHING** No hunting or fishing is allowed on the refuge.

"B" Trail (1.6 miles) wanders amid four distinct plant and animal communities. Its first leg cuts through a dry thorn forest with cactus wren nesting in prickly pear clusters. It then dives into denser, greener forests drapped with Spanish moss, crosses a resaca, and eventually winds along a shore of Willow Lake and back into the thorn forest.

"C" Trail (2 miles) passes Willow Lake, cuts past the old refuge headquarters (only great trees and flower gardens noted for good birding remain), and passes over the auto-tour route and south of Pintail Lake to the north bank of the Rio Grande.

In addition, there are many miles of trails that see infrequent visitor use, including the Owl, Resaca, Terrace, and Highland trails. Inquire at the Visitor Center about these remote paths.

■ **PHOTOGRAPHY:** There are several photo blinds for close-up shots of birds. The largest and best sits on the north edge of Willow Lake on the "A" Trail. Another is near the old refuge headquarters area, and a third is positioned just off the auto route west of Cattail Lake. For a chance to get a bird photo without an expensive camera, stake out the feeding station at the Visitor Center. Wildflower season also makes for lovely pictures.

■ **SEASONAL EVENTS:** The refuge conducts free talks, and guided birding and naturalist tours daily from Nov. through March.

■ **PUBLICATIONS:** Brochure, bird list.

Appendix

NONVISITABLE NATIONAL WILDLIFE REFUGES

Below is a list of other National Wildlife Refuges in the Southwest states. These refuges are not open to the public.

Leslie Canyon NWR
c/o San Bernardino NWR
P.O. Box 3509
Douglas, AZ 85608
520/364-2104

Amargosa Pupfish Station
c/o Ash Meadows NWR
HCR 70, Box 610-Z
Amargosa Valley, NV 89020
775/372-5435

Anaho Island NWR
c/o Stillwater NWR
P.O. Box 1236
Fallon, NV 89407-1236
702/423-5128

Moapa Valley NWR
c/o Desert Complex
1500 North Decatur Blvd.
Las Vegas, NV 89108-1218
702/646 3401

San Andres NWR
P.O. Box 756
Las Cruces, NM 88004
505/382-5047

Trinity River NWR
P. O. Box 10015
Liberty, TX 77575
409/336-9786

FEDERAL RECREATION FEES

Some—but not all—NWRs and other federal outdoor recreation areas require payment of entrance or use fees (the latter for facilities such as boat ramps). There are several congressionally authorized entrance fee passes:

■ **ANNUAL PASSES**

Golden Eagle Passport Valid for most national parks, monuments, historic sites, recreation areas and national wildlife refuges. Admits the passport signee and any accompanying passengers in a private vehicle. Good for 12-months. Purchase at any federal area where an entrance fee is charged. The 1999 fee for this pass was $50.00

Federal Duck Stamp Authorized in 1934 as a federal permit to hunt waterfowl and as a source of revenue to purchase wetlands, the Duck Stamp now also serves as an annual entrance pass to NWRs. Admits holder and accompanying passengers in a private vehicle. Good from July 1 for one year. Valid for *entrance* fees only. Purchase at post offices and many NWRs or from Federal Duck Stamp Office, 800/782-6724, or at Wal-Mart, Kmart or other sporting good stores.

■ **LIFETIME PASSES**

Golden Access Passport Lifetime entrance pass—for persons who are blind or permanently disabled—to most national parks and NWRs. Admits signee and any accompany passengers in a private vehicle. Provides 50% discount on federal use fees charged for facilities and services such as camping, or boating. Must be obtained in person at a federal recreation area charging a fee. Obtain by showing proof of medically determined permanent disability or eligibility for receiving benefits under federal law.

Golden Age Passport Lifetime entrance pass—for persons 62 years of age or older—to national parks and NWRs. Admits signee and any accompanying passengers in a private vehicle. Provides 50% discount on federal use fees charged for facilities and services such as camping, or boating. Must be obtained in person at a federal recreation area charging a fee. One-time $10.00 processing charge. Available only to U.S. citizens or permanent residents.

For more information, contact your local federal recreation area for a copy of the *Federal Recreation Passport Program* brochure.

VOLUNTEER ACTIVITIES

Each year, 30,000 Americans volunteer their time and talents to help the U.S. Fish & Wildlife Service conserve the nation's precious wildlife and their habitats. Volunteers conduct Fish & Wildlife population surveys, lead public tours and other recreational programs, protect endangered species, restore habitat, and run environmental education programs.

The NWR volunteer program is as diverse as are the refuges themselves. There is no "typical" Fish & Wildlife Service volunteer. The different ages, backgrounds, and experiences volunteers bring with them is one of the greatest strengths of the program. Refuge managers also work with their neighbors, conservation groups, colleges and universities, and business organizations.

A growing number of people are taking pride in the stewardship of local national wildlife refuges by organizing non-profit organizations to support individual refuges. These refuge community partner groups, which numbered about 200 in 2,000, have been so helpful that the Fish & Wildlife Service, National Audubon Society, National Wildlife Refuge Association, and National Fish & Wildlife Foundation now carry out a national program called the "Refuge System Friends Initiative" to coordinate and strengthen existing partnerships, to jump start new ones, and to organize other efforts promoting community involvement in activities associated with the National Wildlife Refuge System.

For more information on how to get involved, visit the Fish & Wildlife Service Homepage at http://refuges.fws.gov; or contact one of the Volunteer Coordinator offices listed on the U.S. Fish & Wildlife General Information list of addresses below or the U. S. Fish & Wildlife Service, Division of Refuges, Attn: Volunteer Coordinator, 4401 North Fairfax Drive, Arlington, VA 22203; 703/358-2303.

U.S. FISH & WILDLIFE GENERAL INFORMATION

Below is a list of addresses to contact for more inforamation concerning the National Wildlife Refuge System.

U.S. Fish & Wildlife Service Division of Refuges
4401 North Fairfax Dr., Room 670
Arlington, Virginia 22203
703/358-1744
Web site: fws.refuges.gov

F & W Service Publications:
800/344-WILD

U.S. Fish & Wildlife Service Pacific Region
911 NE 11th Ave.
Eastside Federal Complex
Portland, OR 97232-4181
External Affairs Office: 503/231-6120
Volunteer Coordinator: 503/231-2077
The Pacific Region office oversees the refuges in California, Hawaii, Idaho, Nevada, Oregon, and Washington.

U.S. Fish & Wildlife Service Southwest Region
500 Gold Ave., SW
P.O. Box 1306
Albuquerque, NM 87103
External Affairs Office: 505/248-6285
Volunteer Coordinator: 505/248-6635
The Southwest Region office oversees the refuges in Arizona, New Mexico, Oklahoma, and Texas.

U.S. Fish & Wildlife Service Great Lakes-Big Rivers Region
1 Federal Dr.
Federal Building
Fort Snelling, MN 55111-4056
External Affairs Office: 612/713-5310
Volunteer Coordinator: 612/713-5444
The Great Lakes-Big Rivers Region office oversees the refuges in Iowa, Illinois, Indiana, Michigan, Minnesota, Missouri, Ohio, and Wisconsin.

U.S. Fish & Wildlife Service Southeast Region
1875 Century Center Blvd.
Atlanta, GA 30345
External Affairs Office: 404/679-7288
Volunteer Coordinator: 404/679-7178
The Southeast Region office oversees the refuges in Alabama, Arkansas, Florida, Georgia, Kentucky, Lousiana, Mississippi, North Carolina, South Carolina, Tennessee, and Puerto Rico.

U.S. Fish & Wildlife Service Northeast Region
300 Westgate Center Dr.
Hadley, MA 01035-9589
External Affairs Office: 413/253-8325
Volunteer Coordinator: 413/253-8303
The Northeast Region office oversees the refuges in Connecticut, Delaware, Massachusetts, Maine, New Hampshire, New Jersey, New York, Pennsylvania, Rhode Island, Vermont, Virginia, West Virginia.

U.S. Fish & Wildlife Service Mountain-Prairie Region
P.O. Box 25486
Denver Federal Center
P. O. Box 25486
Denver, CO 80225
External Affairs Office: 303/236-7905
Volunteer Coordinator: 303/236-8145, x 614
The Mountain-Prairie Region office oversees the refuges in Colorado, Kansas, Montana, Nebraska, North Dakota, South Dakota, Utah, and Wyoming.

U.S. Fish & Wildlife Service Alaska Region
1011 East Tudor Rd.
Anchorage, AK 99503
External Affairs Office: 907/786-3309
Volunteer Coordinator: 907/786-3391

NATIONAL AUDUBON SOCIETY WILDLIFE SANCTUARIES

National Audubon Society's 100 sanctuaries comprise 150,000 acres and include a wide range of habitats. Audubon managers and scientists use the sanctuaries for rigorous field research and for testing wildlife management strategies. The following is a list of 24 sanctuaries open to the public. Sanctuaries open by appointment only are marked with an asterisk.

EDWARD M. BRIGHAM III ALKALI LAKE SANCTUARY*

c/o North Dakota State Office
118 Broadway, Suite 502
Fargo, ND 58102
701/298-3373

FRANCIS BEIDLER FOREST SANCTUARY

336 Sanctuary Rd.
Harleyville, SC 29448
843/462-2160

BORESTONE MOUNTAIN SANCTUARY

P.O. Box 524
118 Union Square
Dover-Foxcroft, ME 04426
207/564-7946

CLYDE E. BUCKLEY SANCTUARY

1305 Germany Rd.
Frankfort, KY 40601
606/873-5711

BUTTERCUP WILDLIFE SANCTUARY*

c/o New York State Office
200 Trillium Lane
Albany, NY 12203
518/869-9731

CONSTITUTION MARSH SANCTUARY

P.O. Box 174
Cold Spring, NY, 10516
914/265-2601

CORKSCREW SWAMP SANCTUARY

375 Sanctuary Rd. West
Naples, FL 34120
941/348-9151

FLORIDA COASTAL ISLANDS SANCTUARY*

410 Ware Blvd., Suite 702
Tampa, FL 33619
813/623-6826

EDWARD L. & CHARLES E. GILLMOR SANCTUARY*

3868 Marsha Dr.
West Valley City, UT 84120
801/966-0464

KISSIMMEE PRAIRIE SANCTUARY*

100 Riverwoods Circle
Lorida, FL 33857
941/467-8497

MAINE COASTAL ISLANDS SANCTUARIES*

Summer (June–Aug.):
12 Audubon Rd.
Bremen, ME 04551
207/529-5828

MILES WILDLIFE SANCTUARY*

99 West Cornwall Rd.
Sharon, CT 06069
860/364-0048

NORTH CAROLINA COASTAL ISLANDS SANCTUARY*
720 Market St.
Wilmington, NC 28401-4647
910/762-9534

NORTHERN CALIFORNIA SANCTUARIES*
c/o California State Office
555 Audubon Place
Sacramento, CA 95825
916/481-5440

PINE ISLAND SANCTUARY*
P.O. Box 174
Poplar Branch, NC 27965
919/453-2838

RAINEY WILDLIFE SANCTUARY*
10149 Richard Rd.
Abbeville, LA 70510-9216
318/898-5969 (Beeper: leave message)

RESEARCH RANCH SANCTUARY*
HC1, Box 44
Elgin, AZ 85611
520/455-5522

RHEINSTROM HILL WILDLIFE SANCTUARY*
P.O. Box 1
Craryville, NY 12521
518/325-5203

THEODORE ROOSEVELT SANCTUARY
134 Cove Rd.
Oyster Bay, NY 11771
516/922-3200

LILLIAN ANNETTE ROWE SANCTUARY
44450 Elm Island Rd.
Gibbon, NE 68840
308/468-5282

SABAL PALM GROVE SANCTUARY
P.O. Box 5052
Brownsville, TX 78523
956/541-8034

SILVER BLUFF SANCTUARY*
4542 Silver Bluff Rd.
Jackson, SC 29831
803/827-0781

STARR RANCH SANCTUARY*
100 Bell Canyon Rd.
Trabuco Canyon, CA 92678
949/858-0309

TEXAS COASTAL ISLANDS SANCTUARIES
c/o Texas State Office
2525 Wallingwood, Suite 301
Austin, TX 78746
512/306-0225

BIBLIOGRAPHY AND RESOURCES

Birds

Peterson, Roger Tory and Edward L. Chalif. *A Field Guide to Mexican Birds*, Boston: Peterson Field Guides/Houghton Mifflin Co., 1973.

Peterson, Roger Tory. *A Field Guide to Texas Birds and Adjacent States*, Boston: Peterson Field Guides/Houghton Mifflin Co.

Peterson, Roger Tory. *A Field Guide to Western Birds*, Boston: Peterson Field Guides/Houghton Mifflin Co., 1990.

Cultural History

Guderjan, Thomas and Carol Canty. *The Indian Texans*, San Antonio: University of Texas/Institute of Texas Cultures, 1989.

Natural History & Wildlife Field Guides

Carr, John. *Arizona Wildlife Viewing Guide*, Helena/Billings, Mont.: Falcon Press, 1992.

Cockrum, E. Lendell & Yar Petryszyn. *Mammals of the Southwestern United States and Northwestern Mexico*, Tucson: Treasure Chest Publications, 1992.

Desert Trees, Tucson: Arizona Native Plant Society, 1990.

Easy Field Guide to Common Trees of Arizona, Phoenix: Primer Publications, 1985.

Fischer, Pierre C. *70 Common Cacti of the Southwest*, Tucson: Southwest Monuments and Parks Association, 1989.

MacCarter, Jane S. *New Mexico Wildlife Viewing Guide*, Helena/Billings, Mont.: Falcon Press, 1994.

Manning, Reg. *What Kinda Cactus Izzat?*, Phoenix: Reganson Cartoon Books, 1941/1969.

Nelson, Richard and Sharon. *Easy Field Guide to Southwestern Snakes*, Phoenix: Primer Publications, 1996.

Page, Jake. *The Southwest: Smithsonian Guides to Natural America*, Washington, D.C.: Smithsonian Books, 1995.

Tweit, Susan J. *The Great Southwest Nature Factbook*, Seattle: Alaska Northwest Books, 1992.

Wall, Dennis. *Western National Wildlife Refuges*, Santa Fe: Museum of New Mexico Press, 1996.

Regional and state guides

Castleman, Deke. *Nevada Traveler's Handbook*, Chico, Calif.: Moon Publications, 1998.

Cummings, Joe. *Texas Traveler's Handbook*, Chico, Calif.: Moon Publications, 1998.

Gibson, Daniel. *American Southwest*, Santa Fe: John Muir Publications, 1998.

Gibson, Daniel. *New Mexico Travel Smart*, Santa Fe: John Muir Publications, 1999.

Weir, Bill and Robert Blake. *Arizona Traveler's Handbook*, Chico, Calif.: Moon Publications, 1996.

GLOSSARY

Accidental A bird species seen only rarely in a certain region and whose normal territory is elsewhere. *See also* occasional.

Acre-foot The amount of water required to cover one acre one foot deep.

Alkali sink An alkaline habitat at the bottom of a basin where there is moisture under the surface.

Alluvial Clay, sand, silt, pebbles and rocks deposited by running water. River floodplains have alluvial deposits, sometimes called alluvial fans, where a stream exits from mountains onto flatland.

Aquifer Underground layer of porous water-bearing sand, rock, or gravel.

Arroyo A wash or gully with near-vertical dirt sides that fills with water only occasionally, normally after heavy rains.

Arthropod Invertebrates, including insects, crustaceans, arachnids, and myriapods, with a semitransparent exoskeleton (hard outer structure) and a segmented body, with jointed appendages in articulated pairs.

Barrier island Coastal island produced by wave action and made of sand. Over time the island shifts and changes shape. Barrier islands protect the mainland from storms, tides, and winds.

Basking The habit of certain creatures such as turtles, snakes, or alligators of exposing themselves to the pleasant warmth of the sun by resting on logs, rocks, or other relatively dry areas.

Biome A major ecological community such as a marsh or a forest.

Blowout A hollow formed by wind erosion in a preexisting sand dune, often due to vegetation loss.

Bosque The spanish word for thicket or woods.

Bottomland Low-elevation alluvial area, close by a river.

Breachway A gap in a barrier beach or island, forming a connection between sea and lagoon.

Cambium In woody plants, a sheath of cells between external bark and internal wood that generates parallel rows of cells to make new tissue, either as secondary growth or cork.

Canopy The highest layer of the forest, consisting of the crowns of the trees.

Climax In a stable ecological community, the plants and animals that will successfully continue to live there.

Colonial birds Birds that live in relatively stable colonies, used annually for breeding and nesting.

Coniferous Trees that are needle-leaved or scale-leaved; mostly evergreen and cone-bearing, such as pines, spruces, and firs. *See also* deciduous.

Cordgrass Grasses found in marshy areas, capable of growing in brackish waters. Varieties include salt-marsh cordgrass, hay, spike grass, and glasswort.

Crust The outer layer of the Earth, between 15 to 40 miles thick.

DDT An insecticide (C14H9Cl5), toxic to animals and human beings whether ingested or absorbed through skin; particularly devastating to certain bird populations, DDT was generally banned in the U.S. in 1972.

Deciduous Plants that shed or lose their foliage at the conclusion of the growing season, as in "deciduous trees," such as hardwoods (maple, beech, oak, etc.). *See also* coniferous.

Delta A triangular alluvial deposit at a river's mouth or at the mouth of a tidal inlet. *See also* alluvial.

Dominant The species most characteristic of a plant or animal community, usually influencing the types and numbers of other species in the same community.

Ecological niche   An organism's function, status, or occupied area in its ecological community.

Ecosystem   A mostly self-contained community consisting of an environment and the animals and plants that live there.

Emergent plants   Plants adapted to living in shallow water or in saturated soils such as marshes or wetlands.

Endemic species   Species that evolved in a certain place and live naturally nowhere else. *See also* indigenous species.

Ephemeral plant life   Plant life that flowers for very brief periods.

Ephemeral water bodies   Lakes and ponds that fill and empty or dry up, streams or rivers that flow intermittently.

Epiphyte   A type of plant (often found in swamps) that lives on a tree instead of on the soil. Epiphytes are not parasitic; they collect their own water and minerals and perform photosynthesis.

Esker   An extended gravel ridge left by a river or stream that runs beneath a decaying glacier.

Estuary   The lower part of a river where freshwater meets tidal salt water. Usually characterized by abundant animal and plant life.

Evergreen   A tree, shrub, or other plant whose leaves remain green all year.

Exotic   A plant or animal not native to the territory.

Extirpation   The elimination of a species by unnatural causes, such as overhunting or fishing.

Fall line   A line between the piedmont and the coastal plain below which rivers flow through relatively flat terrain. Large rivers are navigable from the ocean to the fall line.

Fledge   To raise birds until they have their feathers and are able to fly.

Floodplain   A low-lying, flat area along a river where flooding is common.

Flyway   A migratory route, providing food and shelter, followed by large numbers of birds.

Forb   Any herb that is not in the grass family; forbs are commonly found in fields, prairies, or meadows.

Frond   A fern leaf, a compound palm leaf, or a leaflike thallus (where leaf and stem are continuous), as with seaweed and lichen.

Front Ranges   The easternmost ranges (and their southern extensions) of the Rocky Mountains.

Glacial outwash   Sediment dropped by rivers or streams as they flow away from melting glaciers.

Glacial till   An unsorted mix of clay, sand, and rock transported and left by glacial action.

Gneiss   A common and rather erosion-resistant metamorphic rock originating from shale, characterized by alternating dark and light bands.

Grassy bald   A summit area devoid of trees due to shallow or absent soil overlying bedrock (ledge).

Greentree reservoir   An area that is seasonally flooded by opening dikes. Oaks, hickories, and other water-tolerant trees drop nuts (mast) into the water. Migratory birds and other wildlife feed on the mast during winter.

Hammock   A fertile spot of high ground in a wetland that supports the growth of hardwood trees.

Hardwoods   Flowering trees such as oaks, hickories, maples, and others, as opposed to softwoods and coniferous trees such as pines and hemlocks.

Heronry   Nesting and breeding site for herons.

Herptiles   The class of animals including reptiles and amphibians.

High Plains   The southern and westernmost fringes of the Great Plains abutting the Front Ranges of the Rocky Mountains.

Holdfast   The attachment, in lieu of roots, that enables seaweed to grip a substrate such as a rock.

Hot spot   An opening in the earth's interior from which molten rock erupts, eventually forming a volcano.

Humus   Decomposed leaves and other organic material found, for instance, on the forest floor.

Impoundment   A manmade body of water controlled by dikes or levees.

Indigenous species   Species that arrived unaided by humans but that may also live in other locations.

Inholding   Private land surrounded by federal or state lands such as a wildlife refuge.

Intermountain West   Area of the Southwest between Front Ranges of the Rocky Mountains and the Sierra Nevada mountains.

Intertidal zone   The beach or shoreline area located between low- and high-tide lines.

Introduced species   Species brought to a location by humans, intentionally or accidentally; also called nonnative or alien species. *See also* exotic.

Lek   Grounds where prairie chickens assemble for courtship.

Lichen   A ground-hugging plant, usually found on rocks, produced by an association between an alga, which manufactures food, and a fungus, which provides support.

Loess   Deep, fertile, and loamy soil deposited by wind, the deepest deposits reaching 200 feet.

Magma   Underground molten rock.

Management area   A section of land within a federal wildlife preserve or forest where specific wildlife management practices are implemented and studied.

Marsh   A low-elevation transitional area between water (the sea) and land, dominated by grasses in soft, wet soils.

Mast   A general word for nuts, acorns, and other food for wildlife produced by trees in the fall.

Meander   A winding stream, river, or path.

Mesa   Flat-topped landforms with steeply sloping sides, larger than buttes but smaller than plateaus. From "Table" in Spanish.

Meso-America   Landmass of Mexico and Central America.

Midden   An accumulation of organic material near a village or dwelling; also called a shell mound.

Migrant   An animal that moves from one habitat to another, as opposed to resident species that live permanently in the same habitat.

Mitigation   The act of creating or enlarging refuges or awarding them water rights to replace wildlife habitat lost because of the damming or channelization of rivers or the building of roads.

Moist-soil unit   A wet area that sprouts annual plants, which attract waterfowl. Naturally produced by river flooding, moist-soil units are artificially created through controlled watering.

Moraine   A formation of rock and soil debris transported and dropped by a glacier.

Neotropical   New-world tropics, generally referring to central and northern South America, as in *neotropical* birds.

Nesting species   Birds that take up permanent residence in a habitat.

Occasional   A bird species seen only occasionally in a certain region and whose normal territory is elsewhere.

Old field   A field that was once cultivated for crops but has been left to grow back into forest.

Old-growth forest   A forest characterized by large trees and a stable ecosystem. Old-growth forests are similar to precolonial forests.

Oxbow   A curved section of water, once a bend in a river that was severed from the river when the river changed course. An oxbow lake is formed by the changing course of a river as it meanders through its floodplain.

Passerine   A bird in the Passeriformes order, primarily composed of perching birds and songbirds.

Peat   An accumulation of sphagnum moss and other organic material in wetland areas, known as peat bogs.

Petroglyph   Carving or inscription on a rock.

Pictograph   Pictures painted on rock by indigenous people.

Pit and mound topography   Terrain characteristic of damp hemlock woods where shallow-rooted fallen trees create pits (former locations of trees) and mounds (upended root balls).

Plant community   Plants and animals that interact in a similar environment within a region.

Playa(s)/playa lakes   Flat-bottomed lands of the Intermountain West or High Plains that occasionally fill with shallow, ephemeral water bodies; from "beach" in Spanish.

Pluvial   A rainy, wet period over a centuries-long time frame.

Prairie   An expansive, undulating or flat grassland, usually without trees, generally on the plains of mid-continent North America. In the southeast, prairie refers to wet grasslands with standing water much of the year.

Prescribed burn   A fire that is intentionally set to reduce the buildup of dry organic matter in a forest or grassland to prevent catastrophic fires later on or to assist plant species whose seeds need intense heat to open.

Proclamation area   An area of open water beside or around a coastal refuge where waterfowl are protected from hunting.

Rain shadow   An area sheltered from heavy rainfall by mountains that, at their higher altitudes, have drawn much of the rain from the atmosphere.

Raptor   A bird of prey with a sharp curved beak and hooked talons. Raptors include hawks, eagles, owls, falcons, and ospreys.

Rhizome   A horizontal plant stem, often thick with reserved food material, from which grow shoots above and roots below.

Riparian   The bank and associated plant-life zone of any water body, including tidewaters.

Riverine   Living or located on the banks of a river.

Rookery   A nesting place for a colony of birds or other animals (seals, penguins, others).

Salt marsh   An expanse of tall grass, usually cordgrass and sedges, located in sheltered places such as the land side of coastal barrier islands or along river mouths and deltas at the sea.

Salt pan   A shallow pool of saline water formed by tidal action that usually provides abundant food for plovers, sandpipers, and other wading birds.

Scat   Animal fecal droppings.

Scrub   A dry area of sandy or otherwise poor soil that supports species adapted to such conditions, such as sand myrtle and prickly pear cactus, or dwarf forms of other species, such as oaks and palmettos.

Sea stack   A small, steep-sided rock island lying off the coast.

Second-growth forest   Trees in a forest that grow naturally after the original stand is cut or burned. *See also* old growth.

Seeps   Small springs that may dry up periodically.

Shrub-steppe   Desertlike lands dominated by sagebrush, tumbleweed and other dry-weather-adapted plants.

Sinkhole   A hole formed in surface rock by the action of water welling up from below.

Slough   A backwater or creek in a marshy area.

Southern Plains   The portion of the Great Plains covering eastern New Mexico and sections of Texas and Kansas.

Successional   Referring to a series of different plants that establish themselves by territories, from water's edge to drier ground. Also, the series of differing plants that reestablish themselves over time after a fire or the retreat of a glacier.

Sump   A pit or reservoir used as a drain or receptacle for liquids.

Swale   A low-lying, wet area of land.

Swamp   A spongy wetland supporting trees and shrubs (as opposed to a marsh, which is characterized by grasses). Swamps provide habitat for birds, turtles, alligators, and bears and serve as refuges for species extirpated elsewhere. *See also* extirpated.

Test   The hard, round exoskeleton of a sea urchin.

Tuber   A short underground stem with buds from which new shoots grow.

Understory   Plants growing under the canopy of a forest. *See also* canopy.

Vascular plant   A fern or another seed-bearing plant with a series of channels for conveying nutrients.

Vernal pool   Shallow ponds that fill with spring (vernal) rains or snowmelt and dry up as summer approaches; temporary homes to certain amphibians.

Wader   A long-legged bird, such as a crane or stork, usually found feeding in shallow water.

Wetland   A low, moist area, often marsh or swamp, especially when regarded as the natural habitat of wildlife.

Wilderness Area   An area of land (within a national forest, national park, or a national wildlife refuge) protected under the 1964 Federal Wilderness Act. Logging, construction, and use of mechanized vehicles or tools are prohibited here, and habitats are left in their pristine states. Designated Wilderness is the highest form of federal land protection.

Wrack line   Plant, animal, and unnatural debris left on the upper beach by a receding tide.

Xeric   A drying up; i.e., prolonged (centuries-long) drying of a climate and landscape.

INDEX

ACKNOWLEDGMENTS

This book is dedicated to Joanna Hurley, who was my refuge while this was written.

A book of this scope involves the help of many people. Some of those I'd like to single out include the following.

Thanks to Texas refuge personnel: Dave Blankenship, outstanding wildlife biologist of the Lower Rio Grande Valley refuge; Byran Winton of Santa Ana; Nancy Brown and Larry Ditto of Santa Ana/Lower Rio Grande Valley; Kimberly Halpin of Aransas; Tom Schnider of Brazoria/San Bernard; Martin Brockman of Brazoria; Michele Hannon of Anahuac; and Dan Drinker of Texas Point.

Thanks to Nevada refuge personnel: David St. George of Ash Meadows; Marti Collins of Desert; Kevin Sloan of Pahranagat; Kim Hanson of Ruby Lake.

Thanks also to Arizona refuge personnel: Wayne Shifflet of Buenos Aires; Don Tiller of Cabeza Prieta; Renee Robichard of Imperial, Ray Varney of Kofa; Dr. Kathleen Blair of Bill Williams; and Matt Connolly of Havasu.

New Mexico refuge personnel providing help included Cheryl Carnegie of Bosque del Apache; Marta Curti of Sevilleta; Jerry French of Maxwell; and Joe Rodriquez and Philip Garcia of Las Vegas.

I'd also like to thank places that provided lodging: Desert Inn Resort, Las Vegas, Nevada; in Arizona, The Boulders, Carefree; Casa Bella B&B, Arivaca; La Tierra Linda, Tucson; The Coronado, Yuma; in Texas, Holiday Inn, Port Arthur; Victorian Condo Hotel, Galveston; Microhotel, McAllen; Red Roof Inn, Brownsville.

Finally, I'd like to thank my children, Travis and Isabel, who put up with me during this massive project and accompanied me to several Arizona refuges.

—Daniel Gibson

ABOUT THE AUTHOR

Daniel Gibson wrote a natural-history guidebook, *The American Southwest*, has contributed to numerous magazines covering the region, and is a columnist for the *Santa Fe Reporter*.

PHOTOGRAPHY CREDITS

We would like to thank the U. S. Fish & Wildlife Service for permission to publish photos from their collection, as well as the other contributing photographers for their wonderful imagery. The pages on which the photos appear are listed after each contributor.

f-stop fitzgerald: p. 132

Daniel Gibson: pp. ii-iii, 5, 16, 21, 23, ?8 4?, 66, 73, 81, 86, 90, 93, 103, 108, 114, 122, 149, 176, 184, 188

John & Karen Hollingsworth: pp. 4, 6, 14, 26, 32, 35, 39, 45, 50, 57, 64, 76, 88, 113, 127, 130, 155, 158, 164, 171, 187

Gary Kramer: pp. xii, 7, 8, 27, 31, 43, 46, 52, 55, 61, 63, 78, 84, 97, 98, 100, 106, 111, 125, 142, 152, 156, 161, 162, 174, 178, 190

U.S. Fish & Wildlife Service: pp. 25, 36, 37, 68, 70, 118, 120, 135, 137, 140, 144, 169, 181

NATIONAL AUDUBON SOCIETY
Mission Statement

The mission of National Audubon Society, founded in 1905, is to conserve and restore natural ecosystems, focusing on birds, other wildlife, and their habitats for the benefit of humanity and the earth's biological diversity.

One of the largest, most effective environmental organizations, Audubon has more than 560,000 members, numerous state offices and nature centers, and 500+ chapters in the United States and Latin America, plus a professional staff of scientists, lobbyists, lawyers, policy analysts, and educators. Through our nationwide sanctuary system we manage 150,000 acres of critical wildlife habitat and unique natural areas for birds, wild animals, and rare plant life.

Our award-winning Audubon magazine, published six times a year and sent to all members, carries outstanding articles and color photography on wildlife and nature, and presents in-depth reports on critical environmental issues, as well as conservation news and commentary. We also publish Field Notes, a journal reporting on seasonal bird sightings continent-wide, and Audubon Adventures, a bimonthly children's newsletter reaching 500,000 students. Through our ecology camps and workshops in Maine, Connecticut, and Wyoming, we offer professional development for educators and activists; through Audubon Expedition Institute in Belfast, Maine, we offer unique, traveling undergraduate and graduate degree programs in Environmental Education.

Our acclaimed World of Audubon television documentaries on TBS deal with a variety of environmental themes, and our children's series for the Disney Channel, Audubon's Animal Adventures, introduces family audiences to endangered wildlife species. Other Audubon film and television projects include conservation-oriented movies, electronic field trips, and educational videos. National Audubon Society also sponsors books and interactive programs on nature, plus travel programs to exotic places like Antarctica, Africa, Australia, Baja California, Galapagos Islands, Indonesia, and Patagonia.

For information about how you can become an Audubon member, subscribe to Audubon Adventures, or learn more about our camps and workshops, please write or call:

National Audubon Society
Membership Dept.
700 Broadway
New York, New York 10003
212/979-3000
http://www.audubon.org/audubon

JOIN THE NATIONAL AUDUBON SOCIETY—RISK FREE!

Please send me my first issue of AUDUBON magazine and enroll me as a temporary member of the National Audubon Society at the $20 introductory rate—$15 off the regular rate. If I wish to continue as a member, I'll pay your bill when it arrives. If not, I'll return it marked "cancel," owe nothing, and keep the first issue free.

____ Payment Enclosed   ____ Bill Me

Name _____

Street _____

City _____

State/zip _____

Please make checks payable to the National Audubon Society. Allow 4–6 weeks for delivery of magazine. $10 of dues is for AUDUBON magazine. Basic membership, dues are $35.

Mail to:

> NATIONAL AUDUBON SOCIETY
> Membership Data Center
> PO Box 52529
> Boulder, CO 80322-2529